from
NATIONALISATION
to
PRIVATISATION

—⟫●⟪—

MY LIFE ON BRITISH RAILWAYS

By

Jack A. Turner

A Jacett Publication

A Jacett Paperback

Copyright: Jack A. Turner

Cover design from a painting by Margaret Davies.

ISBN: 978-0-9576871-0-3

First impression 2013

Printed by Lion Press
19 Market Square
Sandy
Bedfordshire SG19 1EH
Tel: 01767 680368
sales@thelionpress.co.uk

Further copies can be obtained from:
Jacett Publications
2 Regency Court
Alexandra Road
Hemel Hempstead
Hertfordshire HP2 4AX
Tel: 01442 251540
info@jacettpublishing.co.uk
or our website: www.jacettpublishing.co.uk

From Nationalisation to Privatisation

FOREWORD

No less a person than P. G. Woodhouse wrote that the first duty a writer asked to provide a foreword to a book must be to explain what his qualifications are for so doing. Well, mine are simple. I loved the same railway world that Jack inhabited. I am of his generation, and of course we worked together during my time on the London Midland Region. We both did our national service in the 1950s in the RAF, returning in a seamless way to the 'Mother Railway'.

Most of Jack's experiences in this book go to reinforce the loyalty and love of railways that typified his generation. It also, in a gentle, unassuming and almost anonymous way, illustrates why the railway was as efficient as it was. He and colleagues like him were quietly putting right such problems that if allowed to develop would have caused massive disruptions to service.

Additionally there are interesting little anecdotes illustrating the way of life. It is truly a social history as well as one man's railway career.

Peter Rayner
(Former Regional Operating Manager, London Midland Region)

INTRODUCTION

I had long toyed with the idea of putting pen to paper, in order to record my long, interesting and varied railway career, so that it could be shared with others. This was a potential project that I had thought about doing for quite a number of years after I took early retirement from British Rail in March 1993, having served the railway industry for a total of some forty-six years. However, for one reason or another (and apart from writing odd articles for different railway publications), I had never actually got around to beginning my writing project.

That is, until a casual conversation with fellow railway enthusiast (and Locomotive Club of Great Britain (LCGB) house magazine editor) Murray Eckett revived the idea of the book which you now see before you. As a result of our conversation, Murray kindly offered to edit my writing efforts and also to assist in any other way that he could. This he has done, and I must place on record my sincere thanks for this, for without Murray's help and advice, the production of this book would never have happened. Thank you Murray.

I also want to record my thanks to Margaret Davies, for the illustration on the front cover of this book, which she has kindly painted for me. My thanks also go to Bill, Margaret's husband, a recently retired fellow railwayman and enthusiast, for his suggestions regarding its format and layout. I would also like to pass on my deep gratitude to Bryan Cross of the LCGB Bedford Branch for his considerable help in scanning and processing the illustrations found within the book.

I have tried to write this story in the actual order that particular events took place. However, in a number of chapters, for one reason or another, it has not been possible to relate the events described in their correct date order. Likewise, I would like to apologise to you, the reader, if on occasions I am not one hundred per cent accurate with my dates, especially as the happenings described took place some time ago, and my memory is not as good as it used to be.

I hope that you will enjoy reading this book as much as I enjoyed writing it.

Jack A. Turner

CONTENTS

Foreword by Peter Rayner i

Introduction iii

Chapter One: Early Days 1

Chapter Two: On the Footplate 9

Chapter Three: Aylesbury High Street Loco 17

Chapter Four: Aylesbury Town Loco 29

Chapter Five: Main Link Memories 39

Chapter Six: A Change of Career 53

Chapter Seven: Signalling Memories 63

Chapter Eight: From Wages Staff to Salaried Staff 75

Chapter Nine: My Days as a Relief Station Master 81

Chapter Ten: My Days as a Relief Station Master (Part Two) 99

Chapter Eleven: Pity the Poor RSM! 109

Chapter Twelve: Operating Engineering Section 117

Chapter Thirteen: Kensington Olympia 125

Chapter Fourteen: Kensington Olympia (Part Two) 131

Chapter Fifteen: Promotion to District Signalman's Inspector Willesden 139

Chapter Sixteen: Fires and Derailments 147

Chapter Seventeen: West London Line 153

Chapter Eighteen: Special Projects and Sporting Events 161

Chapter Nineteen: A Move to Euston 169

Chapter Twenty: Bombs and Bad Weather 175

Chapter Twenty-One: New Plans and Projects 181

Chapter Twenty-Two: New Upgrades 189

Chapter Twenty-Three: Watford and Beyond .201

Chapter Twenty-Four: Retirement Beckons 207

Chapter Twenty-Five: Now and Then 213

Appendicies 219

Picture 1 A rare 1954 view at Aylesbury Town, with former GWR 1473 arriving on an auto-train working from Princes Risborough. The author's first home at Penn Road backed onto the railway premises on the right of this picture. Therefore, this would have been a familiar scene to the author during the first five years of his life (Author).

Picture 2 Park Street level crossing, Aylesbury. As a youth, the author traversed this crossing twice-daily, on his way to and from school (the late Geoff Williams).

CHAPTER ONE

EARLY DAYS

I do not know whether it was the location of my birthplace, Southcourt Council Estate in Aylesbury, Buckinghamshire, which had any bearing on my lifelong passion for all things railway.

Southcourt is situated within the parish of Aylesbury which, at the time of my birth and for many years afterwards, had two railway lines within its boundaries, namely the Great Western Railway (GWR) cross-country route to Princes Risborough and the former Great Central Railway (GCR) main line link between Manchester and London Marylebone, which was operated jointly with the Metropolitan Railway between Quainton Road and Harrow. In addition, on the far side of Aylesbury, was situated the branch line to Cheddington, which had earlier gained a notable place in railway history as the first line of its type in the world when it was opened in June 1839. What is certainly true is that the sights and sounds of these local lines were very much part of my formative years, living where I did.

I was born on March 15th 1932 at 62 Penn Road, Southcourt, which, as mentioned previously, was a suburb of Aylesbury. For the first five years of my life, I lived with my mother and father in this dwelling, which backed onto the junction of where the Princes Risborough and Marylebone lines joined, at the south end of Aylesbury Town station. When I was born, I was christened Jack Allardice Turner, my middle name being given to me by my mother, who had previously worked for a family who had lived on the East Coast of Scotland, which is where the name Allardice originally comes from. Apart from the railway, other industries in Aylesbury included the nearby ink works, which belonged to a company known as Hazell, Watson and Vineys. When I was five years old, my parents decided to move from Penn Road to a new residence at 20 Park Street, still in Aylesbury, but on the opposite side of town to the original house. In another railway coincidence, a working level crossing was situated a mere one hundred yards from our new house – the line using this was the branch to Cheddington.

I began my compulsory schooling at the age of five in 1937, attending Queens Park Infants School (which was three-quarters of a mile from my home), starting at the Easter Term of that year. Three years later, at the age of eight, I moved up into the Boys School. However, by this time, the Second World War had started, and it was having an enormous effect on the local education system.

Pupil numbers were swollen by the arrival of evacuees, class sizes becoming as large as forty or fifty children. Added to this was a teacher shortage, with younger men being called up into the armed forces, and a combination of retired and trainee teachers having to take their place. The school week was re-organised to try and head off these problems. On many occasions, I found myself attending lessons on only two full days and three half days per week. For a period of a few months, my schooling took place at a hall situated in nearby Oxford Road, before returning to Queens Park. One teacher that I do remember from this time was Mr Percy Jones. He was the school's headmaster, a nice person and a singer in a choir based at St John's Church, Aylesbury where, as a coincidence, I was an alter server. Outside of school, I became a Wolf Cub. During the Second World War, people were encouraged to take part in various saving schemes, contributing towards the massive effort required to finance the ongoing struggle. The Wolf Cub patrol of which I was a part carried out many fund raising schemes during this time. One of my most treasured possessions is a 'thank you' letter that I received from Mrs Clementine Churchill, wife of Britain's wartime PM, acknowledging my help with these activities.

By the time I was thirteen, my father had been called up for military service in the Army. Around this time, I faced another change in my schooling when I moved to Berkhamsted for a period of some six months. The reason for this was that, unfortunately, an aunt of mine had become seriously ill. My mother took me to live with my aunt and uncle, and I attended a local school during this time. My developing interest in railways was given some help by the fact that the house that we lived in was located in Ellesmere Road, Berkhamsted, a dwelling which faced directly onto the main trunk route of the London, Midland and Scottish Railway (LMSR) from London Euston to the Midlands and North. Here, I saw all the classic steam locomotives of the LMSR in action, hauling all manner of trains, ranging from express passenger to humble pick-up freights. The express engines, including Princess Coronations, Patriots and Jubilees, were painted in a mixture of LMSR maroon red and the less appealing wartime black. The never-ending procession of freight trains were in the capable hands of locomotives such as G1 0-8-0s and Austerity 2-8-0s, the latter being a type of engine originally designed for use with the military forces in World War 2. I can also recall that many of the local passenger trains were hauled by elderly 'George the Fifth' and 'Precursor' engines, top link locomotives in their day, but displaced as bigger and more powerful locomotives were brought into service. In September 1945, just after the end of hostilities, I was able to visit the site of a very bad train accident, which took place at Bourne End, between Berkhamsted and Hemel Hempstead. A 'Royal Scot' class passenger locomotive, no 6157 *'The Royal Artilleryman'*, was derailed on a crossover that had a speed restriction of twenty miles per hour (mph), the train itself travelling at no less than sixty-five mph when it left the tracks. The great engine had ended up in a field adjacent to the line, from where much effort had to be expanded in order to re-rail it. I shall never forget the sight of this tragic accident, at that time one of the worst that had happened for some years.

By the early part of 1946 I was almost fourteen years of age, and my compulsory education was coming to an end. During my adolescent years, my interest in railways had grown to the point where I had formed an ambition, rather like many other boys, to join one of the private railway companies in order to become an engine driver. However, an individual had to be sixteen years of age before he could begin the long apprenticeship which would culminate in him becoming a driver, therefore

Picture 3 The Weighbridge at Aylesbury High Street depicted during the 1950s (the late Geoff Williams).

I needed to obtain some other kind of work prior to this. Once my school days had come to an end, I made some enquiries as to what types of jobs and vacant positions were available. My efforts were soon rewarded with the offer of a junior clerk position in the goods office at Aylesbury High Street station, at the opposite end of the branch line from Cheddington. Prior to taking up the position, I had to undertake two exams, these being a medical exam that took place at Drummond Street, near to London Euston, and a clerical exam. For the latter, I had to travel to Rugby, whereupon the actual test took place in the District Goods Manager's office. Although I was successful in passing both exams, I did not take up my new position until January 1947. This was because the person who was currently holding the position that I had attained was awaiting his National Service call-up papers and, for some unknown reason, these had been delayed. Whilst waiting for my start date, I did two temporary jobs of a clerical nature, working in both the local Town Clerk's Office and the National Insurance Office, thus gaining valuable work experience.

After these delays, I was finally able to begin my railway career at the start of 1947, becoming a proud employee of the LMSR. My duties at Aylesbury

Picture 4 Also seen during the 1950s, the goods shed and offices at Aylesbury High Street (the late Geoff Williams).

High Street were based around the Weighbridge Office, which was situated in the Coal Yard. The main part of these duties involved recording, on a daily basis, all the railway wagons (both empty and full) which were parked in the yard at a particular time, the details obtained then having to be forwarded to a signal box lad, who worked in the 'No 1' signal box at Leighton Buzzard. This individual then had to send this information onto the Wagon Controller, who was based at London Euston. Other duties carried out included weighing road based commercial vehicles, the lorries being weighed twice – once when they arrived at the yard empty and, once again, before they departed with a full load. In addition, I had to count the numbers of sheets, ropes and sacks that were being used, again on a daily basis. This information was then sent by telephone, from the main Goods Office to the corresponding office situated at Northampton.

Even in this early part of my railway career, I was able to gain some unofficial time travelling on the footplate of either one of two trains which arrived at Aylesbury for unloading, sorting and re-marshalling. The first of these was a passenger train (this working, which arrived at 11.23, included freight stock as part of its formation) that had travelled from Cheddington, the goods wagons involved having previously been part of a pick-up goods train that ran between Willesden, in north-west London, and Bletchley. The second working was a freight train, which arrived at 14.05, and which was a weekday only working from Bletchley. Whilst the trains were being sorted

Picture 5 The Monday to Friday 11.00 am departure from Cheddington was a mixed train, and was allowed an extra eight minutes to Aylesbury. 41275 is seen in the spring of 1950 waiting to depart from Cheddington in 'push-pull' formation (the late Harold Clements).

for their respective return journeys, the footplate crews concerned allowed me to travel on the footplate – valuable experience for my later railway career. My main task, once these freight trains had arrived, was to write out and then deliver demurrage forms to local merchants. The merchants in question had goods delivered on one or another of the wagons that made up the incoming freight trains. The purpose of the form was two-fold – firstly to inform them that their goods had arrived, and secondly, to let them know that they had a two day period of time to unload their wagons. If the unloading was not completed within forty-eight hours, a daily demurrage fee would have to be paid for each subsequent day that the unloading was not carried out.

The start of my railway career coincided with the bitterly cold winter of 1946/7. The heavy snow encountered led to an amusing situation which came about one morning. As usual, I had gone out on my 'rounds', collecting all the wagon details. However, because of the bad weather, my work was taking a lot longer to complete than usual. Things took so long that an urgent telephone call was made from Northampton Goods Office to Aylesbury, demanding to know why the information required had not been sent. The Chief Clerk at Aylesbury could only reply that, as I had already started on my duties, he could only presume that I had got lost in the heavy snow! The frantic promptings of Northampton initiated a search to discover my whereabouts and general wellbeing. Fortunately, I was okay, and quite unaffected by what had gone on.

Although I enjoyed my duties as a junior clerk, my career goal, as far as the railways were concerned, was to become an engine driver. During the early part of 1948, having now become an employee of the newly nationalised British Railways system (the former LMSR having become part of the state-owned railway network, along with the Great Western, London North Eastern, and Southern Railways), I was approaching my sixteenth birthday. As I mentioned earlier in this narrative, this was the age at which would-be drivers could begin their long apprenticeships, the first rung on the ladder being the position of engine cleaner. In my particular case, I had applied for a transfer to the motive power department prior to my milestone birthday and, as part of the application process, I had to undergo a second medical, which included a very stringent eye test. I was pleased to find out that I passed this important examination, and found myself accepted as an engine cleaner, based at Bletchley Locomotive Depot. By a happy coincidence, my first day in my new role was on my exact sixteenth birthday, March 15th 1948. After attending an interview with the Shed Master on duty at the time, Mr Andrew Gillitt, I was thrown straight in at the deep end. (Incidentally, at the time of writing, Mr Gillitt is still happily with us, having reached the grand old age of ninety-three). Having then reported to the depot's Cleaning Foreman, I was issued with a set of overalls, given the necessary cleaning cloths, and told to begin work on an LMSR built tank locomotive that was on shed at the time, joining a group of cleaners who were already hard at work

Although the main part of my time at work was spent in the business of engine cleaning, it was realised that not only myself, but the rest of the cleaning gang of which I was a part, were all potential engine drivers. A very important part of this process were our classroom lessons. These covered things such as learning railway rules and regulations, the basics of firing a steam locomotive, understanding about signals and the various commands that they gave. One of the other tasks undertaken was that of a bar boy. Here, the boy in question had to crawl into a locomotive's firebox, and remove damaged fire bars, or parts of broken brick arches. When people today talk about the 'romance of steam', duties such as this particular task are largely forgotten. It was, however, one of many similar duties that had to be carried out in order to keep steam locomotives in tip-top operational condition. Unfortunately, it was also one of many reasons put forward for the demise of the steam locomotive fleet, and its replacement by more modern (and cleaner) forms of traction, before too many more years had passed.

Our engine cleaning gang was also utilised for all kinds of other tasks during the course of a normal week. One such task involved transferring a stack of coal from a siding into adjacent wagons, this being for the forthcoming Easter weekend workings. I well remember being asked by the cleaning foreman on duty at the time whether I would like to come in on the following Sunday to carry on this work in return for some overtime. My reply was, "six days thou shall labour, and on the seventh day, thou should rest." Owing to the lack of suitable trains, I would have had to make a forty mile round trip by bicycle to get to Bletchley from Aylesbury. The effort involved would not have been justified by the extra money that I would have earned in my wage packet.

An unusual incident occurred on one occasion when our gang was told to do an extremely thorough cleaning job on a mixed traffic steam locomotive, number 3002. This was the third engine of a new type of locomotive which had been designed by H.G. Ivatt, the last Chief Mechanical Engineer of the LMSR, the class itself being one of the last to appear whilst the LMSR was still in situ. 3002 had been given the prestigious job of hauling the empty stock of the Royal Train from Wolverton Works, near to Bletchley, to Liverpool Street via Cambridge. The Shed Master expected the engine to be cleaned to perfection, which is what we thought that we had done. However, the Shed Master decided to rub a clean cloth on the underside of the engine's boiler, and found a small piece of grime. Our gang then had to clean the engine all over again! It was a matter of pride that 3002 be turned out as clean as possible, a credit to Bletchley shed. As well as being cleaned, 3002 had its number altered to 3000, the prototype of this class, which became collectively known as the 'Flying Pigs'. I discovered that this process of altering numbers to suit a particular occasion was one that was practiced widely by the railway companies. During the 1930s, the LMSR had done this to two locomotives that were due to be exhibited in the United States of America, the engines in question being 'Royal Scot' 6152, which assumed the identity of class prototype 6100 *'Royal Scot'* (this event taking place in 1933), whilst in 1939, 'Princess Coronation' 6229 *'Duchess of Hamilton'* swapped names and numbers with its class prototype 6220 *'Coronation'*. Both original class leaders were unavailable at the time of the respective exhibitions.

After six weeks working with the cleaning gang, I was examined on my knowledge of the railway rules and regulations that I had been studying. I was tested by Locomotive Inspector Abey, this theory exam being the first section of a two part test, the second part being a practical exam, which involved the theory being put into practice. In my particular case, my practical exam involved firing a local passenger train on a return journey from Bletchley to Oxford Rewley Road. I was working alongside Driver Bewley and being tested, once again, by Inspector Abey.

From the above mentioned log, it will be seen that the locomotive was another of the 'Flying Pig' class, no 3005, and that the train departed Bletchley seven minutes late, but recorded a 'right time' arrival at Oxford. (It should also be noted that the station building at Oxford Rewley Road exists to this day, and has now become the Visitor Centre at the Buckinghamshire Railway Centre, situated at Quainton Road, not too far from Aylesbury). Following the completion of the uneventful return journey, I was 'passed out' for firing duties, thereby climbing a rung on the promotional ladder, becoming known as a 'Passed Cleaner', and obtaining a wage rise of a few shillings per week. My fledgling railway career was now well and truly under way.

CHAPTER TWO

ON THE FOOTPLATE

At the tender age of sixteen, having become a passed cleaner, I had taken a large step towards achieving my original goal when I had first joined the railways, this being to become an engine driver. At this particular time there was very little unemployment, a situation which meant, as far as British Railways (BR) were concerned, there were staff shortages in various areas of the company. For me, this was a lucky break. I was still physically based at Bletchley Depot, although officially my proper 'home' was Aylesbury High Street, which was a sub-shed of Bletchley. There was a shortage of firemen to cover the various diagrams and duties carried out at Bletchley – this meant that I was immediately put onto firing duties once I had passed the tests described in the previous chapter. My first job was to fire an LMSR built 'Jinty' type 0-6-0 tank locomotive, carrying out shunting duties in Bletchley North End yard. This type of duty was acknowledged in the railway industry as the bottom rung on the footplate ladder that would eventually lead to the top link, which was driving locomotives on express passenger trains. The general policy at this time was that most passed firemen and newly appointed drivers at Bletchley would go into what was known as the control link. The turns required were decided by the Control Office, and would cover all kinds of work. The yard shunt engine drivers that I found myself working with were older men who, for various medically related reasons, were not fit to drive engines on the main line. I spent only a few days working on this shunting diagram, and I was then transferred to a different job, helping to fire locomotives and moving them around the shed, in preparation for their regular crews to take them onto whatever passenger or freight train they were booked to haul.

As with the shunting duties, this new task was one that was mundane in the overall scheme of things, but one which was vital to the running and general well-being of the railway. Unlike diesel and electric locomotives, both of which can supply power straightaway, a steam locomotive required many hours of preparation, prior to taking up its duties. From being 'cold', the fire needed to be lit, and the pressure inside the boiler had to build up to what was known as 'working pressure', this being when the engine was able to move by itself. This task was performed by a member of staff who was known as a 'steam raiser'. In addition, many other tasks, such as coaling and oiling up various mechanical working parts, needed to be completed, this work being carried out by the driver and fireman who were taking the locomotive onto the main line. One drawback of this long preparation time was that many more steam locomotives were required to cover the same amount of work as the more modern forms of traction; in addition, more staff were required to be involved. With the increasing labour shortages of the early post war era, BR were able to use these scenarios as reasons for eliminating steam traction at the end of the 1960s.

My tasks in helping to fire and move steam locomotives around the yard at Bletchley included transferring engines from what was known as the 'ash road', this being a siding where engines had their fires dropped and their smokeboxes emptied of ash by staff members known as 'firedroppers', this after having completed their previous duties. Such engines would not have their fires relit, and would be moved to other parts of the shed under their own steam, should some still be available. If this was not the case, then a yard shunt engine would move them instead. Other duties that I undertook included firing engines to the coaling plant, helping the driver to turn locomotives utilising the shed's turntable, together with setting the shed up to the shed foreman's requirements, which could consist of a number of different tasks, for example, if a locomotive needed to be placed on the wheel lathe, or in a particular road for things such as a boiler washout, repairs, cleaning or a fitter's examination. A further duty that came under this 'umbrella' heading would be one where a certain locomotive would be needed for a particular duty, and had to be positioned accordingly, ready to go into service. An example of this would arise if a particular engine needed to go to workshops for heavy maintenance or a general overhaul. The locomotive in question would be rostered to haul a particular train which would enable it to get to its end destination.

On occasions, the drivers would allow me to perform both firing and driving duties, all of which was invaluable experience, useful for the driving career that I was after. On one occasion, I very nearly caused a derailment with a former London and North Western Railway (LNWR) 'Super D' 0-8-0 freight locomotive. This first of this family of engines entered service in 1893, towards the end of the Victorian era, and were so successful that several hundred were built, becoming the LNWR's standard heavy freight locomotive. Some were still in BR service well into the 1960s, and it is fortunate that a single example, 49395, has been preserved and returned to steam, after many years of inaction.

Returning to my escapade with the 'Super D', I had been allowed by my driver to move this engine from the ash road to the coaling road. I had to perform a manoeuvre, which involved reversing the locomotive from the ash road onto a line which backed onto the shed foreman's office, this being necessary to clear a set of points. Once this had been done, the engine was then moved forward onto the coaling road. My 'Super D' was low in steam and, in addition, had a boiler full of water. Whilst reversing the giant, I tried to close the engine's regulator, but found that it would not shut completely. As a result, the locomotive's brakes would not respond to what I was doing. My only course of action was to force the reversing wheel into forward gear. Having done this, I was lucky because the engine came to an immediate stand, just inches from the buffer stops and, more importantly, the shed foreman's office!

Apart from this somewhat traumatic experience, things were going well for me, and I was thoroughly enjoying life on the railways. My firing duties became more interesting as, the following week after the 'Super D' incident, I was put to work firing a locomotive that was employed on carriage shunting duties. This involved attaching and detaching parcels vans as and when required, and also sorting out coaches in the carriage shed itself. This diagram even involved a stint of firing along part of the former cross-country route between Oxford and Bedford, on a passenger train which had obtained the unusual nickname of the 'Whitehalls'. This curious title came about because this working had first been introduced during the Second World War for the conveyance of Government officials from Bedford to their place of work in Oxford. As far as my duties were concerned, my driver and myself would take over the afternoon return working at Bletchley, and crew it as far as its final destination at Bedford, from where we would travel back to Bletchley as passengers. The regular rostered steam engine for this duty was normally a Bedford based Midland Railway 'compound' 4-4-0 tender locomotive, more than two hundred of which had been built between 1905 and 1932. This miscellany of duties continued, as within a few more days I fired my first main line freight train, which was a return trip between Bletchley and Northampton down sidings. As well as my first experience of working with an LMSR Stanier-designed 8F 2-8-0 freight locomotive, I fired through a tunnel for the first time, as well as utilising the water troughs at Castlethorpe, just north of Wolverton. Although the northbound working was made up of empty wagons, the return trip was comprised of no fewer than sixty full coal wagons, something of a considerable task for an inexperienced fireman such as myself.

After three months as a passed cleaner, I was appointed a state registered fireman at the beginning of June 1948. However, before I was able to commence my duties at Aylesbury, where I was to be physically transferred, I was designated to cover a diagram based at nearby Leighton Buzzard shed for a period of one week only, this situation coming about because a fireman permanently based there was taking annual leave. The turn of duty involved booking on at Leighton Buzzard at 7.00 am, working the first return branch line train of the day to Luton Bute Street, and then coming back to Leighton Buzzard, finishing by taking the locomotive back onto shed. The train itself was made up of a mixed passenger and parcels vehicle formation. Our locomotive would be an ancient London and North Western Railway (LNWR) tank locomotive of either a 2-4-2 or 0-6-2 wheel arrangement, similar to those used on the Aylesbury–Cheddington line, which were soon to be replaced by more modern steam locomotives.

In total contrast, the second part of this same diagram consisted of firing a local freight train which travelled only as far as Dunstable. This particular section of line was noteworthy because there was a fearsome gradient of 1

Picture 6 The now preserved 58926 taking water, prior to going on shed at Leighton Buzzard, after having worked the 8.30 am train from Luton, circa 1949 (the late Harold Clements).

12

Picture 7 Leighton Buzzard (LB) engine shed seen during the late 1930s. Note the ex-Lancashire & Yorkshire engine 12105, an unusual allocation to LB's parent shed at Bletchley (courtesy of Bryan Cross).

in 40 on the outward run between Leighton Buzzard and the sole intermediate station on this part of the line at Stanbridgeford, which presented a formidable challenge to all trains, both passenger and freight. The locomotive that was used on this particular duty was a further example of the LNWR 'Super D' class, the rule being that a load of thirteen fully loaded coal wagons, together with a brake van, was the maximum this class of engine was allowed to take up Sewell Bank, as it was locally known. On one memorable occasion, I was rostered to fire the 10.25 am local freight train to Dunstable. On the particular day during the week in question, a very bad thunderstorm had arisen, and torrential rain was falling. My driver was determined to get the whole train up the bank to Stanbridgeford without having to carry out the time-consuming task of splitting it in two; in contrast, the train guard had already written out a 'wrong line order form', which would enable our engine and brake van to travel 'wrong line' to return for the second portion, should the need arise. After a nerve-wracking forty minutes, the complete train finally made it to Stanbridgeford. Sometime later, when we arrived at Dunstable Gasworks, both my driver and myself having been soaked to the skin by the heavy rain, we were forced to strip to our waists, dry out our clothes, and then repeat the process for our lower halves, before beginning the return journey. It was most certainly not our day as, on the return journey, with the engine running tender first (and with no protective tarpaulin to hand), the heavy rain returned, and we got soaked once again! Things were complicated by the fact that we were booked to call in at Grovebury Sidings. These were located just outside Leighton Buzzard and were exchange sidings with the network of narrow gauge railways constructed in conjunction with the sand mining operations that were carried out in this area at that time. Our duties required that we had to collect a mixed freight train of loaded sand and empty coal wagons, which would then be despatched elsewhere from Leighton Buzzard later the same day. During this period of time, chalk was also being mined in and around the village of Totternhoe, situated not too far from Stanbridgeford. This was another useful source of revenue for the railway, and many chalk carrying freight trains were run along this now closed and forgotten branch line.

After my two soakings, I was glad to discover that all the paperwork issues relating to my new state registered fireman position had been sorted, and I

Picture 8 An unidentified ex-LNWR G2a (or Super D) machine breasts Sewell Bank on a Dunstable-bound goods train, circa 1948 (the late Harold Clements).

was finally to report to Aylesbury High Street on a permanent basis the following week. At least I would be spared having to toil on my shovel, working heavy freight trains up and down the Stanbridgeford gradient! It was at this point in time that I was physically transferred from Bletchley to my permanent home shed at Aylesbury High Street. Here my firing duties were spent on the passenger services that ran up and down the single track branch line between Aylesbury and Cheddington, where connections could be made with trains on the main trunk route between London Euston, the Midlands and the North. My young age of sixteen had meant that special dispensation had had to be arranged between the local railway management, the appropriate trade union and a local staff representative, in order that I could take up my firing duties on these particular workings.

CHAPTER THREE

AYLESBURY HIGH STREET LOCO

With my transfer to Aylesbury High Street, my railway career was now gathering pace. As previously mentioned, all of my time was spent firing on the single track branch line between Aylesbury High Street and Cheddington. This route was very simple and straightforward in its layout. There was but one intermediate station, this being located at Marston Gate. In addition, there were a series of farm crossings that had to be negotiated, along with two public level crossings, these being situated at Mentmore and Broughton. Most other branch lines around Britain had their fair share of curves and gradients; however, the seven mile long Cheddington railway had been laid dead straight for no fewer than six of those seven miles.

Picture 9 A view of Aylesbury High Street engine shed (which was a sub-shed to Bletchley) taken in the 1950s after closure of the Cheddington branch (the late Geoff Williams).

The locomotive depot at Aylesbury High Street consisted of a shed situated on a single siding, the shed being equipped with doors at either end. One task that had to be carried out on shed was to coal the locomotives. In the case of a tender locomotive, this duty had to be performed in the open air, and only on the night shift, which could be very unpleasant during periods of bad weather, in particular heavy rain or frost. It took place after the locomotive which was to receive the coal had finished its work for the day. The engine would collect the coal wagon from the goods siding and take it on shed behind it. In the case of a tender locomotive however, the wagon would be placed on an adjacent road. The coal would then be transferred by hand from the wagon to the locomotive's bunker or tender as applicable. With regards to staff, there were two drivers, two firemen and a single passed fireman, together with a pair of guards, who were allocated to the depot. As Aylesbury was a sub-shed of Bletchley, a member of the latter shed's staff would cover periods of annual leave and sickness, as and when they occurred. The drivers would work alternate early and late turns, whilst the firemen were employed on early, late and night shifts. On the night shift, the fireman was responsible for coaling the engine, cleaning it and then raising steam for the first branch line passenger train working of the day, which he would work before being relieved by the day shift fireman. At this time there was no Sunday service on the branch, therefore on this particular shift, the night turn fireman would begin his spell of duty at midnight, lighting up the engine ready for the first train on Monday morning.

The regular steam locomotive that was used on the Cheddington service during this period of time was a former London and North Western Railway (LNWR) tank locomotive, 6604, which possessed a 2-4-2 wheel arrangement. This old timer had originally been one of 220 similar engines that were constructed by the LNWR over a period of years from 1879 to 1898. The class was designed by Francis William Webb, the Chief Mechanical Engineer of the LNWR between 1871 and 1903. When, as was necessary from time to time, 6604 had to go to Bletchley for general repair and maintenance work or a boiler washout, a number of engines from the same class would deputise, these being either 6601, 6666, 6699 or 6701. Another two Webb designed LNWR veterans, 0-6-2T 'Coal Tank' engines 7773 and 7799 (the latter subsequently renumbered to 58926 after nationalisation in 1948), occasionally took turns on the Cheddington service. (The class as a whole were known by the footplate crews who worked them by various nicknames. The ones that I personally knew them as were either 'mourners' or 'mourning coaches'. It is suggested that this name came about from their sombre appearance when they first appeared in a plain black livery, their melancholy appearance being reinforced by their large flat side tanks). In my experience, these latter engines had very poor braking properties and, as a result, were employed mainly on passenger workings. The first examples of this class appeared a little later than their 2-4-2T stablemates in 1881, and up to 1899 some 300 of the breed were built, 291 passing into LMSR stock at the time of the railway grouping in 1923, whilst no fewer than sixty-four became the property of BR upon nationalisation in 1948. They were known as 'Coal Tanks' because they were basically a side tank version of Mr Webb's 'Coal Engine', which was an 0-6-0 machine, built for use on slow freight trains. It is interesting to note that 58926 (7799), whose original number was 1054, escaped the attentions of the scrapman. At the time of writing, it is owned by the National Trust and is on permanent loan to the Bahamas Locomotive Society, this group being based at their Ingrow Works on the Keighley and Worth Valley Railway. 2012 saw this unique machine returned to full working order, following its third major overhaul since preservation. Whilst on a visit to the Worth Valley in February 2012 (during the annual 'Winter Steam Gala'), I had the pleasure of a short footplate trip on this fine veteran, reliving my time of actually working the very same engine during the 1950s while I was based at Aylesbury.

I well remember that if none of the LNWR veterans were available to run the branch line service, or in the case of a failure of the regular engine, then we would have to 'make do' with whatever Bletchley shed could come

Picture 10 Ex-LMSR 'Flying Pig' 43005 is depicted at Aylesbury High Street in 1948. This was the engine used when the author was passed out for firing duties, also in 1948 (Author).

up with. In general, these latter engines had not long finished their previous turns of duty, had 'dirty' fires, were low on coal and were not in the best of mechanical condition. Locos that found their way onto the Cheddington service ranged from 'Crab' 2-6-0 mixed traffic machines, ex-Midland Railway 3F and 4F locomotives, the famous 'Super D' heavy freight engines, former Lancashire and Yorkshire Railway 0-6-0 light goods types and much more modern London, Midland and Scottish Railway (LMSR) 2-6-0 locomotives. I also recall that, on a single occasion, a Midland Railway 2P 4-4-0 engine worked on the branch, a rarity on a railway that was originally deep in LNWR territory. Towards the end of the life of the Cheddington branch, the LNWR old-timers were finally retired and replaced by LMSR 2-6-2 tank engines, the duties mainly being in the hands of a trio of these newcomers, 41222, 41275 and 41272, the last named earning a place in history as the 7000th steam locomotive to be built at Crewe Locomotive Works.

As a newly passed fireman, I was keen to increase my own personal knowledge of railway practices and procedures in any way possible, and it was during my time at Aylesbury that I learnt how to drive an engine, as opposed to merely moving a locomotive around the shed, as I had done during my time working at Bletchley. Of the two drivers that were based at Aylesbury, one would only allow me to move whatever engine we were working a few feet to set it in the correct position for oiling; the other was happy for me to not only oil the engine in question, but to take it from the shed to the station and then couple up to the train. This generally happened on the night shift, and was a 'win-win' situation for both the driver and for myself; I gained valuable driving experience, whilst my driver was able to spend a little longer in his bed! On quite a number of occasions, this same driver would also allow me to drive the engine on a return trip from Aylesbury to Cheddington.

During this time, from mid-1948 to 1950, the passenger trains that were run on the Aylesbury to Cheddington branch were, in general, made up of a two coach formation. From every Monday to Friday, there were variations to this theme, in particular in the case of the mid-morning train from Cheddington back to Aylesbury. This was a mixed formation, the passenger coaches being joined by goods wagons, carrying supplies for various customers in the Aylesbury district. At Cheddington we had to carry out a delicate shunting manoeuvre, which involved crossing the fast running lines on the main railway trunk route between London Euston, the Midlands and the North, to a set of middle sidings. Here we had to pick up the wagons in question (which had earlier been detached from a Willesden to Bletchley pick-up freight train), move them onto the branch proper, run our engine round the wagons and then attach them to the rear of the branch passenger train. On arrival at Aylesbury, the wagons were then placed as required in either the coal or goods yards.

The 20.05 departure from Aylesbury back to Cheddington, in addition to the normal formation of two carriages, would also convey two parcel vans, which had been loaded with copies of the 'Readers Digest' magazine, these periodicals having been processed at the Hazell, Watson and Vineys ink/printing firm. In addition, goods were also conveyed from nearby Dominion Dairies. On arriving at Cheddington, the vans were detached, and were then taken northwards from Cheddington by a light engine that had itself come from Willesden Shed, in north-west London. Further vans were then added to the train formation at both Leighton Buzzard and Northampton; if my memory serves me correctly, I believe that the final destination of the complete train was Liverpool.

Wednesday was 'Market Day' in Aylesbury, and the farmers who lived along the branch would come into Aylesbury during the morning in order to carry out their business of buying and selling both produce and livestock. Regarding their return journeys, it became a recognised procedure for the guard of the lunchtime departure to Cheddington to go into the 'White Hart' public house (which was located opposite Aylesbury High Street station) in order to blow his whistle five minutes before the scheduled departure time. This was done in order to ensure that all the farmers would catch this train. The guard would then advise the train's driver and fireman (which would, of course, be myself on some of these occasions) as to which farm crossings that the farmers wished to be dropped off at. This we then proceeded to do, although it was strictly unofficial. A second, unorthodox example of close co-operation between the railway and its neighbours would happen every Friday and Saturday evening. Various residents of Cheddington would place 'orders' for fish and chips with the engine crew. Once the train had arrived at Aylesbury, whilst the driver attended to the needs of the locomotive, taking on water and running the engine round its train, the fireman would go into the local 'chippy' and pick up the orders. The fish and chips would then be placed on the small shelf on the front of the steamer's firebox. In this way, the food was kept hot until the train returned to Cheddington, meeting up with its hungry customers!

On a more serious note, a number of potentially serious incidents happened during the time that I was firing on the Cheddington branch line. The first of these took place during the first passenger working of the day to Cheddington. On a foggy autumn morning, we were travelling between Aylesbury and Marston Gate when we hit an obstruction on the line, the engine rocking violently, but fortunately staying on the rails. My driver was able to bring the train to a stand; we then looked around the engine to try and establish what it was that we had hit. Our first thought was that we had hit either a single cow or a herd of cows. However, we could not see any such animal in the locality, and as there was no obvious damage to the engine, we resumed our journey to Cheddington. At the terminus, we arranged for the local permanent way gang to travel back with us, so that the line could be cleared, if this was found to be necessary. By the time that we returned to the scene of the earlier incident the fog had lifted, and we discovered that we had hit a flock of no less than thirty-two ewes in lamb. Sadly, the strength of the moving engine had decapitated nine, whilst a further fifteen, each of which had sustained injury of one kind or another, ended up having to be put down. We later found out that they had been grazing in a field adjacent to the railway. An unknown person, who had used one of the foot crossings during the previous night or early morning, had left all the gates open; the ewes had wandered through the gates, and onto the railway line itself. They then fell asleep on the track, where they stayed until their sad and sudden demise.

Another incident which I well remember took place on an evening run when I was firing 7773, our train having left Marston Gate for Aylesbury. I had put a round of coal into the firebox when, without warning, there was a massive 'blow-back'. In a steam locomotive, a blow-back is caused when the engine's fire, together with the heat generated, blows back into the cab, instead of being drawn through the boiler tubes and exhausted through the chimney in the normal way. In a situation when the engine's blower is not turned on when entering a tunnel, this can have extremely serious consequences. Both my driver and myself were able to get out of the cab, and make our way onto the engine's outside frames, fortunately without any serious injury. We managed to stop the train after the flames incurred as a result of the blow-back had died down. On looking over our engine to discover why the blow-back had happened, we found that the locomotive's smokebox door had been burnt. Once the door had been carefully opened, we found that a section of the blastpipe elbow had broken due to the fact that it had rusted away. Obviously, the engine was by now a complete failure, and I then had the unenviable task of walking no less than five miles in the dark back to Cheddington, with the single line staff token, in order to obtain assistance. I was fortunate because, at Cheddington, the light engine from Willesden Shed that was ready to work forward the parcel vans that would have arrived on the 20.05 from Aylesbury, was available to assist us. This particular machine was an ex-LMSR 'Compound' engine. As far as I know, this was the only locomotive of its type ever to run over the Aylesbury branch. It pushed the failed 'Coal Tank' to Aylesbury, moved it to the shed, and then hauled the next working back to Cheddington. Once this locomotive had resumed its normal diagram, a second replacement engine (if my memory serves me correctly, this was a 'Crab' mixed traffic machine) was drafted onto the branch until one of the normal tank engines could be put back in service.

I recall a third incident where we as a crew did not adhere to proper procedure and, had senior members of the railway management been in attendance, we would have been in serious trouble. I was due to fire the first passenger working of the day from Aylesbury to Cheddington and, having coupled up the engine to the train, I then (for a reason which I cannot recall) took the coupling back off the locomotive. As a result, when the train began to move, the vacuum and heater pipes were immediately disconnected. A spare vacuum pipe was thus urgently required – however, none was to be had. After speaking with the train guard, it was decided to run to Cheddington, using only the engine brake and running the train as a loose coupled formation. Upon arrival at Cheddington, we were able to 'rob' a vacuum pipe off a stationary railway van and fit it onto our engine.

In a lighter vein, on many occasions I can recall when we would knock over wild game, such as rabbits, partridges or pheasants, mostly on late turns,

Picture 11 The day following the aforementioned blow-back incident, 'Coal Tank' 7773 is seen at Aylesbury High Street, before it was towed to Bletchley by ex-LMSR 44549 (Author).

when the darkness made it impossible to see these animals on the railway line. The procedure that we adopted was that the train crew would cut a set of playing cards to see who would 'bag' the spoil, which was then collected on the last train of the day.

We would quite often come into contact with the local Hunt who would cross various sections of the railway in the course of their activities. The practice was to stop the train and let them cross in front of us. When this happened, as a 'thank you' gesture, a ten shilling note would be left by one or other of the Hunt members – this was then split amongst the train crew. On occasions one of the Hunt members would give this to us at Cheddington.

Looking back, probably Cheddington station's most important passenger was Lord Roseberry who lived at nearby Mentmore during the time that I was firing on the branch. Lord Roseberry owned the Mentmore Estate, his place of residence being Mentmore Towers. His Lordship travelled to London from Cheddington on a regular basis, his chosen train being one of the few remaining 'Parliamentary' workings, the time of departure being just before 9.00 am. The 'Parliamentary' was a name that was given to certain trains which were designated to stop at particular stations in order to convey land owners of the area around the station in question. These land owners had originally allowed the railway company in question to build a section of line across their property. The land owners then used these trains to travel to Parliament in order to carry out their business. In the main they were members of the House of Lords.

On one particular occasion, Lord Roseberry was looking to catch his train, but arrived late at the station. It must be recalled that at this time Cheddington had two public entrances, one on the branch line side of the station, whilst the other gave access to the main line platforms. Both entrances were joined together by a covered passageway, along which was the entrance to both the station master's office and the booking office. On this day, the driver of the branch line train had been in the station master's office, using the internal railway telephone to talk to Bletchley engine shed, the purpose of his call being to summon a spare locomotive. By a sheer fluke, the driver, having finished his call, emerged from the office, and collided with Lord Roseberry. Over on the main line platform, the guard of the London-bound train, seeing no sign of His Lordship, gave the 'right away', whereupon the train commenced its journey. When he discovered what had happened, a furious Lord Roseberry demanded that the station master phone the line's General Manager in order to have the next

London-bound express make a special stop at Cheddington to pick him up! This was subsequently arranged – an extremely pro-active example of customer service!

A well-known landmark in the Cheddington area was the Roseberry Arms Hotel, this being situated on the right hand side of the branch line in the Cheddington direction of travel. (It could be thought that there is a connection between this establishment and Lord Roseberry; I can only assume that the hotel had at one time been part of the Mentmore Estate). I remember that the landlady, Ma Keppy, (as she was known affectionately to the locals) kept hens in the hotel's garden. Opposite the hotel was a field where wheat was grown. When this was harvested, she would let her hens loose in the field, in order to get some exercise. On a number of occasions, our train would knock down one of her precious hens – however, unlike the rabbits, pheasants and partridges mentioned earlier, there was no chance of doing a vanishing act with the deceased hen. Instead, if you returned the hen to its rightful owner, Ma Keppy would exchange it for a pint – just as good!

A final amusing incident that stands out in my mind from this time, was something that happened to a nurse, who we railwaymen got to know, as her father was a Shed Foreman at Bletchley depot. To protect her modesty, she shall remain nameless. On certain days, we used to allow her to travel on the engine's footplate, this being on the occasions when she had finished a turn of duty at Aylesbury Hospital. One evening, she came running up the platform at Aylesbury and said, "Congratulate me! I've just had my first baby!" Having stated this, she then realised what she had said, and turned crimson! What she had meant to say was that she had been working on the maternity ward of Aylesbury Hospital and had delivered her first baby.

I was enjoying my time working on the Aylesbury–Cheddington branch, but, as with everything else, all good things come to an end. Having turned eighteen early in 1950, in June of that same year, like all young men of my age, I was called up to do my National Service. I was conscripted into the Royal Air Force (RAF) and, having been initially sent to Padgate on the Wirral Peninsular, I was then transferred to nearby West Kirby, where I did my basic training. On completion, I was then drafted to somewhere much closer to home, this being RAF Henlow in neighbouring Bedfordshire, where I spent the rest of my two years working in the Receipts and Despatch Section of the Radio Engineering Unit that was located there. One condition of doing National Service was that your civilian job

<u>*Picture 12*</u> *The author with ex-LNWR 2-4-2T 46601 at Cheddington in 1948. Also in the picture are Driver Waller and Footplate Inspector Abey (Author's collection).*

<u>*Picture 13*</u> *Former LNWR machine 46601 is seen at Aylesbury High Street in 1949 with a passenger working to Cheddington (the late Harold Clements).*

(whatever that might be) was held open for you until your time in the military was completed. This was true in my case, although in September 1950, Aylesbury High Street shed was closed, and the train crew duties on the Cheddington branch moved to Leighton Buzzard shed. My work colleagues were all transferred to the neighbouring Aylesbury Town depot, with the exception of the elder of the two drivers, who took early retirement. I too was transferred to Aylesbury Town which, in an internal re-organisation, had been moved from the Eastern Region to the London Midland Region. This was not the only change at this time for, in January 1953, the Aylesbury–Cheddington branch was closed to all traffic, due to falling receipts. On the last day of that particular month a farewell special was run, and I managed to travel aboard this train, this time as a passenger rather than on the footplate. With the passing of the old branch, a chapter in my expanding railway career had come to an end. However, good times lay ahead.

CHAPTER FOUR

AYLESBURY TOWN LOCO

Having completed my two years National Service in the Royal Air Force in 1952, I returned to my full time employment on the railways. However, as mentioned in the previous chapter, my former home shed of Aylesbury High Street had been closed, and the majority of the staff employed there (including myself) were transferred to the neighbouring establishment of Aylesbury Town depot. Because of the fact that Aylesbury had been served, prior to the nationalisation of the railway system in 1948, by trains belonging to the GWR and the London & North Eastern Railway (LNER), the footplate crews based there were a mixture of former employees of these companies. In addition, there were three drivers who had worked for the Metropolitan Railway (MR) prior to its merging into

Picture 14 A mid-1950s illustration of Aylesbury Town shed with an unidentified Riddles 4MT 76XXX engine on view (Author).

London Transport during 1936. Since nationalisation, the depot itself had been transferred from the Eastern to the Midland Region, and was a sub-shed of Neasden depot in North London, although the latter was also subsequently moved between regions, from the Western section to the Eastern.

The train services which Aylesbury Town was responsible for providing motive power for were divided between two links. The first of these links was made up of a total of eight turns which comprised those duties previously covered by the MR. Firstly, there was the intensive local commuter service between Aylesbury and Rickmansworth. Until 1960, all trains between Aylesbury and Rickmansworth, in both directions, were worked by steam traction; beyond Rickmansworth and into London these same trains exchanged their steamers for an electric engine. These latter machines were known as the 'Metrovick' class, because they had been constructed by the Metropolitan-Vickers Company of Barrow-in-Furness, and were a group of twenty new locomotives, using some parts that had previously belonged to a similar sized group of engines that had been built for MR passenger services between 1904 and 1906. What gave these locomotives something of a personality was, apart from their appearance and sound, that they were all given names of people associated with the areas through which they worked. They were used to help run the intensive MR passenger train service from their entry into service during 1922 until the early 1960s, when they were replaced by electric multiple unit trains. Following this decision, four 'Metrovicks' were retained by London Transport (LT) for departmental use. It is very fortunate that two examples of these fine machines are still in existence today; *'John Hampden'* can be found as one of the premier exhibits in the LT Museum at Covent Garden, whilst *'Sarah Siddons'* is still in working order, and occasionally hauls special excursion trains on the London tube network, her fine dark red MR livery providing a striking contrast with the off-white, red and blue finish, which is the present day standard for the remainder of London Underground's passenger rolling stock fleet.

I recall that, in addition to the staple diet of passenger trains covered by the Metropolitan link, there was a comprehensive freight service as well. It may surprise some people to realise that such workings ran on what was, to the casual observer, a suburban passenger railway. However, the owners of the pre-1936 MR were nothing if not ambitious and always considered their organisation a full-blown main line railway, one of the results of this positive outlook being the running of many freight trains. In my time working at Aylesbury these were mostly coal trains, either full or empty, which ran between Quainton Road, just north of Aylesbury, to Harrow-on-the-Hill and Neasden. Such workings would also call at the numerous goods sheds situated at many of the former MR stations.

The second link that existed at Aylesbury was comprised of twenty-four turns, and covered the non-MR workings. These included passenger trains to and from Aylesbury and Marylebone over both the ex-MR route, passing through such places as Wendover and Amersham, as well as part of the former GWR main line from Birmingham. In addition, crews were utilised on London-bound through trains over the branch line between Aylesbury and Princes Risborough. The branch line passenger service itself over this useful route also made up part of this second link. Amongst the more unusual workings that were covered by Aylesbury was a passenger train that traversed part of what was the Great Central Railway in the course of its journey to both Brackley and Woodford Halse. I can also recall there was a night parcels train that ran from Marylebone to Bletchley, travelling via Claydon and Winslow, taking in a part of the cross-country route between Oxford and Cambridge and, in the course of its journey, passing Verney Junction, which was the terminus of the old MR, some fifty miles from its original headquarters at Baker Street. To add to this rich mix of workings, the shed also covered a cross section of auto-car turns and weekend ballast trains between Princes Risborough and Banbury, together with a single return working through from Banbury to High Wycombe, although the latter was covered for only a short period of time. In addition, MR duties were regularly worked on rest day cover turns.

Having become used to firing a miscellany of passenger trains in my previous duties, working on the Aylesbury to Cheddington branch line, I was somewhat taken aback when, upon arriving at Aylesbury Town, I found myself working on a light duty turn. This diagram covered shunting duties in both Aylesbury and Princes Risborough goods yards, both 'up' and 'down' yards having to be covered at the latter location (in a working railway context, the terms 'up' and 'down' refer to the direction of travel on a running line, 'up' being in the direction of London, whilst 'down' is away from the capital). In addition, a freight working was made along the Little Kimble branch, the return train from Princes Risborough being made up of wagons that had previously formed part of a pick-up goods working from Banbury. On this diagram, whilst the working hours of 10.00 to 18.30 (Monday to Friday) were quite mild, compared with other shifts, I had to wait for a period of several weeks before the situation was rectified, and I could take my rightful place in the main line link. At the time I was looking to get married, and the fact that the main line link included eighteen booked Sunday turns, together with the possibility of a further three, enabled me to add to my savings prior to this major event in my life.

Looking back, my memories of the miscellany of steam locomotives that found themselves allocated to Aylesbury Town depot was that they were mainly tank engines, tender locomotives being something of a rarity. Although an LMSR 'Flying Pig' 2-6-0 mixed traffic machine did find its way

Picture 15 *Former GCR A5 69829, seen at Aylesbury Town during 1952, hauling a passenger working to Marylebone (Author).*

onto the shed's books towards the end of my time working there in 1955, it was generally the case that any tender engines seen were usually locomotives that belonged to other sheds. In the early 1950s, the majority of the passenger services to and from Marylebone were in the capable hands of the A5 tank locomotives. The A5 engines had originally been constructed by the Great Central Railway (GCR) in three batches between 1911 and 1917; following the railway grouping in 1923, a fourth batch was built by the LNER during 1925/6, production finishing at a total of forty-four. The GCR had originally designated them 9N. What was unusual about the A5s was that they featured a 4-6-2 type wheel arrangement – something very rare amongst British tank engines. They put in many years of reliable service before the final examples were sent to the breakers yard in 1961. During my time at Aylesbury they were gradually superseded by another type of tank engine, the L1s. A total of one hundred of these latter engines were built between 1945 and 1950, but they were never as

__Picture 16__ Also at Aylesbury Town, but in 1954, is ex-LNER L1 67772, once again with a Marylebone-bound passenger working (Author).

successful as the GCR machines due to the fact that their driving wheels, which had a diameter of 5' 2", were too small for the passenger train work upon which they were employed. They did not outlive the A5s by too many years, with the final example being sent for breaking up in 1962. In addition, some former MR tanks were also allocated to Aylesbury, these veteran engines finding employment on the pick-up goods trains that traversed their old stamping ground between Quainton Road, Harrow-on-the-Hill and Neasden.

In the case of the L1 locomotives, they were not allowed to work trains over the Aylesbury to Princes Risborough branch line because of weight restrictions. However it would sometimes happen that an L1 would be allocated to one of two evening passenger trains that commenced their journeys at Marylebone, ran to Princes Risborough, and then used the branch via Little Kimble to access Aylesbury. Should this happen, the L1 was detached from its train at Princes Risborough, and the locomotive that had previously worked the 18.26 departure from Marylebone to Aylesbury, but via the former MR route, was substituted. The engine in question, which on most occasions was either an A5 or even a B1 4-6-0 tender locomotive, would work light engine over the Little Kimble route as far as Princes Risborough, where it would then work the train to Aylesbury, whereupon it terminated. The poor old L1 was then left to make its way back to Aylesbury, but via a much more roundabout route, heading north from Princes Risborough as far as Ashendon Junction, before accessing the former GCR route, via Akeman Street and Grendon Underwood Junction. From here, the errant machine would then run in a southerly direction back into Aylesbury.

For the previously mentioned workings to Woodford Halse, Brackley and Bletchley, we were usually fortunate that a B1 locomotive (or similar) was booked to work them. These engines were the LNER's equivalent of the LMSR's 'Black Five' mixed traffic machines, being designed by Edward Thompson, the LNER's Chief Mechanical Engineer between 1941 and 1946, succeeding Sir Nigel Gresley in this position. From 1942 to 1952, no fewer than 410 of these rugged, two cylinder engines were built, and a fair number lasted until the end of steam workings on the Eastern Region during the late 1960s. The B1s that I fired on these duties were usually machines that were allocated to our parent shed at Neasden.

On a number of occasions when a suitable B1 was not available, Neasden shed would turn out either an A3 express locomotive or a V2 engine, both these machines being representatives of types that had been designed by Sir Nigel Gresley. There were occasions on the Bletchley parcels working when the allocated B1 would fail upon arrival at its destination. Should this happen, then either a 'Black Five' or one of the 75xxx locomotives from the-then new 'Standard' range of steam locomotives would take over. As far as I was concerned, I found both these alternative engines a much better steaming machine than the B1. The parcels train was a heavy one; I found that both the 'Black Five' and the 75xxx were more adept at handling the train over the heavily graded Metropolitan line part of the journey.

Whilst working at Aylesbury, it is true to say that I became used to handling a miscellany of locomotives from a cross section of the former private railway companies. A good example of this was when I was firing on the auto-car workings between Princes Risborough and Banbury. These trains commenced with the first train starting from Aylesbury, and finished with the last one returning through to Aylesbury. It was then the case that the locomotive used was shedded overnight at Aylesbury, for coaling and servicing purposes. The usual motive power for these duties was a GWR 14xx 0-4-2 tank locomotive, seventy-five of which had been built for workings of this kind from 1932 onwards. The engines were allocated to Banbury Shed; on the occasions when a 14xx was not available, a 94xx pannier tank engine was usually substituted, although I did have a week working these trains with a 'Manor' class 4-6-0 tender locomotive. Whilst both myself and my driver would appreciate the abundance of extra power available, the drawback was that we had to run tender first for half the time, there being no adjacent turntable available. In times of bad weather, in particular rain, this made for a most unpleasant trip.

I mentioned earlier how the freight workings covered by the Metropolitan link went no further north than Quainton Road, and that this link also covered the Baker Street-bound passenger trains between Aylesbury and Rickmansworth, the latter station being where the former Metropolitan Railway (MR) electric locomotives took over from the steamers. I can recall a number of amusing incidents with various Met link workings. One of these took place at Rickmansworth where there was a wooden sleeper crossing laid across the 'up' working line (this line being for those trains working towards London), the idea of having the crossing being that the shunter, whose job it was to couple and uncouple the locomotives, had a firm surface to stand on. In addition, a stop board was provided, this being for the benefit of the train crew, who would know exactly where to bring their train to a halt. In ninety-nine cases out of a hundred the steam engine working from Aylesbury would haul its train bunker-first. However, on the day of the incident in question, the locomotive had been coupled to its carriages chimney-first instead. As a result, when coming into Rickmansworth, the driver misjudged his stopping point and passed the crossing. He was disciplined for this error by his supervisor, the details of the incident being recorded on what was known as a 'form one'. However, the driver managed to have the charge against him dropped due to the wording on the form. This stated that he (the driver) had personally passed the stop board, when in reality, it was most of the engine, and not he himself. As the accused driver was able to prove exactly what had happened, the charge was quashed!

Another amusing happening that I can recall from this period also took place at Rickmansworth, but this time on the opposite line that ran in the direction of Aylesbury, and points north. Trains leaving the station had to contend with a ferocious 1 in 113 gradient, the difficulties being added to by the fact that then, as now, the station was situated on a curve. It became common practice that some train guards would walk from their own compartment or brake van to the engine cab, in order to give the 'right away'. They reasoned (quite correctly) that the time taken by the engine to begin its journey, and to overcome the wheels slipping, gave them plenty of time to jump aboard the train as it gained speed very slowly. One guard, however, had the fright of his life. His driver and fireman put sand on the rails in front of their engine in order to counteract any slipping. When they backed down onto their north-bound passenger train, they left the engine's driving regulator slightly open, then reversed the motion with it still open. This in turn meant that there was no slipping and the train got off to a brisk start, forcing the guard to have to run and jump aboard his charge before it vanished from the station! It taught him a lesson – he never came up to the engine's cab again.

One less amusing happening, which could have had potentially fatal consequences, concerned a north-bound freight train, which was stopped at Wendover in the early hours of one morning when the duty signalman drew the attention of the engine's driver to the fact that his train was incomplete. The driver, one of the former MR employees, had originally been working a train made up of forty empty four wheeled wagons. At first he was adamant that the signalman was mistaken and that his train was complete. However, on carrying out the necessary checks, he was taken aback to discover that he had been pulling only three of his original forty wagons! To this day, I fail to understand how both driver and fireman could have been unaware of this fact, especially having just climbed the steep gradient from Great Missenden, the previous station on the line. Fortunately the second portion of this train had come to rest in the dip between Great Missenden and Wendover. In order to collect the rogue wagons, the driver was authorised to set his train back and recouple the two halves. Once this was done, the whole formation then continued onto Quainton Road, stopping at Aylesbury to change crews as originally booked.

On a normal day, this particular working was an easy one for the main line rest day crews. I remember that you would book on at 3.00 am, relieve the MR men who had bought the train from Harrow, and then take it as far as Quainton Road. The wagons were then backed into the 'down' yard sidings, ending up with the engine standing on what had been the former 'tramway' route to the nearby hamlet of Brill, the line itself having been closed by London Transport as early as 1935. We would then remain here for more than three hours awaiting an 'up' goods train that had commenced its journey from Woodford Halse. On arrival at Quainton Road, the Woodford crew would back their train into the up sidings, cross over and work the empties (which we had previously bought in) forward to Woodford. We would then sort their train into destination order and, together with other wagons that had arrived from Bletchley, take it as far as Aylesbury, a further crew then relieving us to take the train to its final destination at Harrow. It would have been quite feasible for the Aylesbury main line link men to have crewed the original working as far as Woodford Halse as well as the return trip; however, as the duty fell within the MR link, this was not possible.

A more amusing happening occurred at Quainton Road whilst on another rest day working. I had fired an empty freight train, following which our engine was uncoupled and moved across to the 'up' yard in order for it to be coaled. This was the job of a local labourer, however, both my driver and myself would always give him a hand to complete this heavy and dirty task. There was a good reason for wanting to get this job done quickly. Whilst waiting for our return path back towards London, we would go to a nearby pub (which in reality was no more than the parlour of a house) and have a drink with the labourer. One evening we took things a stage further by coaling the engine ourselves, without the labourer's help, taking the coal direct from a railway wagon on an adjacent road. We had noticed that our engine's coal was of somewhat better quality than normal and, being somewhat inquisitive, we decided to check the appropriate labels, to see which colliery that it had come from. To our horror, we discovered that, far from being normal railway coal, it was a consignment that had been destined for the Harrow branch of the Co-Operative Coal Company. The wagon itself had been detached from a previous train with a hot axle box. It goes without saying that we did not put it back! I can only imagine that the local section of the railway claims department had some paying out to do!

At this time all freight trains had very easy schedules over the Aylesbury to Rickmansworth line. To the footplate crews, including myself, this became something of a source of frustration, as we could complete our workings much quicker than the timetable allowed. This caused many arguments between the footplate crews and the relevant signalmen. In spite of the fact that we were 'beating' our schedules very easily, it was still very difficult to convince our colleagues in the signal boxes that we would not cause any delays to the passenger trains. However, it was well known that the ex-MR drivers would always take the full schedule when working their freight trains, even if their load consisted of merely the engine coupled to a lone brake van. Goodness knows where they got to!

CHAPTER FIVE

MAIN LINK MEMORIES

As I mentioned in the previous chapter, all the various diagrams covered by Aylesbury Town shed were split between one of two links, these being either former Metropolitan Railway (MR) workings or those that were not. Focusing just on those duties covered in the non-MR link (which was known as the 'Main Link'), these were then sub-divided into three separate areas, these being:

a) The diagrams that covered workings to and from London Marylebone, either over the former MR lines, or via the ex-Great Western/Great Central Railway joint line via High Wycombe, and over the branch from Princes Risborough to Aylesbury.

b) The auto-car branch line trains that worked between Aylesbury, Princes Risborough and Banbury.

c) The diagrams that covered trains that ran to and from London Marylebone to either Woodford Halse or Bletchley.

To and from Marylebone

In the previous chapter, I made reference to the fact that the local passenger services that ran from Aylesbury to Marylebone via the former MR route were hauled generally by either the veteran Great Central Railway (GCR) designed A5 class tank locomotives or their more modern successors the L1s, although as time went on the L1s became more common on these workings. With the L1s, I found it remarkable that the steaming quality varied between different machines, this in turn affecting the amount of coal that was consumed. I can recall that on some of these locomotives it was possible to bank the fire prior to leaving Aylesbury, this being adequate to run as far as the northern outskirts of Harrow, before having to pick the shovel up again. On other engines of the same type, you would need to fire them again before arriving at Stoke Mandeville, which was the first station south of Aylesbury. In normal railway practice the fireman would make up a good base fire, to which coal would be added on a 'little and often' basis. To bank the fire meant that once the base fire was made up, the firebox would then be filled up with coal. As the bunker had also been filled up prior to the engine departing on its diagram, and extra lumps of coal had been placed on the footplate itself, more coal could be carried than in the normal way, which in turn meant that the locomotive would not have to return to the coaling stage later during its shift to refill its bunker.

Upon arrival at Marylebone during the morning and evening peak periods, the normal practice as regards the disposal of the passenger stock that had been used on the commuter workings was that, once all the passengers had alighted, a second locomotive would be attached to the other end of the now-empty stock, and it would be drawn forward so that the original train locomotive could then be released and attached to a second set of carriages. This would then be pulled into Lords Tunnel (this being the first tunnel encountered upon leaving Marylebone, and which had been originally constructed in the late 1890s as so to avoid any damage to the hallowed turf of Lords Cricket Ground), the train then being brought to a stop by one of the local shunters, by means of the train brake valve. The shunter would then release the brake valve, following which the train was shunted back and round into the adjacent goods yard. This situation came about because, with all the smoke hanging around in the tunnel, it was impossible for the footplate crew to locate the 'set-back' signal (a signal of this type was a standard ground signal which, when cleared, authorized the driver to set back in the direction that he had originally come from, but onto another line or into a siding), which also meant that the crew were unable to see when the signal was cleared for them to set back into Marylebone goods yard, where the coaches were stabled, ready for the evening peak services.

As can be imagined, there were times when the effectiveness of the work that we did was hindered by the ever-present smoke made by the steam locomotives. For example, there was always smoke hanging around the exit from Canfield Place Tunnel, this being situated opposite the MR station at Finchley Road. Some of us Aylesbury crews would add to this, as on one of our afternoon turns we would exit the tunnel en-route to Princes Risborough, just as another of our Aylesbury turns, returning from High Wycombe, was about to enter it. We used to put a fresh firing of coal on, and the driver would almost close the regulator, just before getting to the end of the tunnel. The idea was to fill the entrance with thick black smoke, this almost choking our mates as they entered the tunnel. Later, during the same evening, these same two crews would cross each other again, this time at Beaconsfield – there was, therefore, great rivalry to ensure that you were running to time!

I can recall that, in the course of our duties, there was even a chance for some unofficial 'racing', the scene of this happening being Northolt Junction. This was where the former Great Central route from Marylebone linked up with the ex-Great Western Railway's main line from London Paddington to Birmingham Snow Hill and points north. By a strange coincidence, the 16.10 local departure from Marylebone to High Wycombe reached Northolt Junction at the same time as the 16.10 express passenger train working from Paddington to Birkenhead. As the two trains were running on parallel lines, it was feasible for our local to 'race' the express over the four mile section of line to West Ruislip. In spite of the fact that we were booked to stop at this particular station, we managed to win our race on quite a number of occasions!

On one memorable occasion in September 1954, my driver and myself nearly fell foul of the powers that be, because of an oversight on our part. We were in the process of preparing an A5 in order to work the 17.29 passenger train from Marylebone to Princes Risborough. This involved cleaning the fire from the engine's previous duty and filling the firebox with coal, prior to the engine being coaled in the normal way (as mentioned earlier, the idea of this latter procedure was to save time by not having to return to Marylebone depot later). Once this preparation work had been completed, we found ourselves with an hour to spare before we had to back down onto the Princes Risborough train. We got into deep conversation with a footplate crew who were normally based at Woodford Halse, and who were spending the day road (or route) learning. Our idle gossiping nearly had dire consequences for us, as when we got back onto the A5's footplate, we discovered that the fire had gone out, and that there was only 80lb of steam raised, hardly enough to pull our train. Panic stations! We found as many old wooden sleepers as we could in order to build a new fire, the resulting smoke produced blacking the sky out. The shed foreman helped the situation by arranging for our machine to swap duties with the locomotive due to work the subsequent departure from Marylebone, which was timed to leave at 17.42, the destination being High Wycombe. We were fortunate in that we raised just enough steam in order to take this latter working out on time.

The reason why I can easily recall the date in question was that it all occurred on the day prior to the opening of the 'New Woodhead Tunnel'. This massive structure was located on the steeply graded route that ran over the Pennines between Manchester London Road and Sheffield Victoria, a line that had been part of the Great Central Railway (GCR). From the start of its life, many freight trains were worked over this route, and the section through the original Woodhead tunnel was one of the most difficult pieces of railway anywhere in Britain for the footplate crews involved. The steep gradients ensured that the goods trains took around fifteen minutes to cover the two mile section; in addition, as can be imagined, the smoke produced by the locomotives used caused problems for the crews, not only a lack of visibility, but also breathing difficulties being encountered. The London and North Eastern Railway (LNER), the successors to the GCR, had drawn up plans during the 1930s to electrify the route – however the Second World War brought this ambitious scheme to a temporary halt, and it was not until 1954 that the newly electrified railway was brought into public service. As part of the scheme, a new tunnel was built at Woodhead, replacing the old structures.

At this time, one of the premier express trains on the former GCR route from Marylebone was the 'Master Cutler'. This train ran from London to Sheffield Victoria, and on the day of our troubles with the A5, it was carrying the-then Transport Minister, The Right Honourable Alan Lennox-Boyd, and other important officials who were going to open the new tunnel. Our 17.42 working was timed to arrive at High Wycombe just two minutes before the 'Cutler' was due to pass. We were warned by the Neasden Shed Master (who was in attendance at Marylebone), in no uncertain terms, that we would be in serious trouble should the 'Cutler' be delayed because of what had previously happened with the A5's fire. If no delay occurred, he decided that he would overlook the entire incident. The whole journey to High Wycombe was a struggle, but our gallant veteran A5 did not let us down, and our train arrived at its destination on time, leaving the 'Cutler' free to proceed on its way.

One feature of those far off days (which now, thankfully, is no more) was the appearance of the notorious 'London Smog', or 'Pea-Soupers'. I remember that I once had a five day period of time working trains in and out of Marylebone during one of these thick fogs, an experience I would not wish on my worst enemy. It was at Rickmansworth where you first encountered the fog, although, because the line as far as Harrow-on-the-Hill was protected by colour light signals (these particular signals also being equipped with London Transport fog repeaters), it was possible to keep reasonably near to time. From Harrow onwards it was back to the more traditional semaphore signals. There were fogmen on hand to help the footplate crews; even so, I can recall that at Neasden South it was necessary to stop the train, and to climb the junction signal post located there to check whether the signal itself was set at off (or clear). Once you had arrived at Marylebone, and begun the process of taking your engine to the loco sidings for servicing, you had to be led there by a man walking in front of the locomotive carrying a flare lamp. I never want to experience anything like that again. It was during the five days mentioned previously that I also had an experience at Harrow when, because of one of these dreadful fogs, we had encountered a problem in locating the end of the platform. Our train guard, who could only find his way from his brake van to the engine by holding onto the handles of the carriage doors, demanded to know from my driver and myself why we had spent so much time getting to Harrow from Marylebone. The reply he got from my driver and myself was sufficient to turn the air blue, I can assure you!

A fogman was a railway worker who belonged to the permanent way department. On days when there were poor weather conditions, his job was to stand at certain locations where there was a semaphore signal. A detonator would be placed on the line, and the fogman would exhibit a yellow hand signal to an approaching train should the signal itself be a 'distant' that was showing caution. This same procedure would apply at a 'home' signal, except that the hand signal would be red. If either signal showed a proceed aspect, the fogman would remove the detonator, and show a proceed hand signal.

On Sundays, Aylesbury crews had two diagrams which involved working lunchtime departures from Marylebone, one being a return working to High Wycombe, and the second a return working to Princes Risborough. One of the Aylesbury drivers that I knew had a liking for ale and, when working the latter turn, arranged with the landlord of a public house situated near to the station at Princes Risborough to have two pints-worth of his favourite tipple left in bottles under the said pub's doorstep. This was always organised the day prior to the driver in question working this particular duty – the reason being that the train arrived at Princes Risborough after the pub had shut! He had an easier time organising similar refreshment at High Wycombe, because the time spent at this latter location between the outward and return runs allowed him to visit another favourite local. Mind you, he had to scale a fence in order to get there!

As regards signalling, all railways are split into sections, each with their own set of signals. In the area covered by Aylesbury footplate crews, one such section governed the line between High Wycombe and Beaconsfield. During my time at Aylesbury, it was decided to shorten this by adding in a colour light intermediate section at Tylers Green. This was an intermediate block section between High Wycombe and Beaconsfield. One day I was firing a train that was approaching this section, with both distant and home signals showing green, thus indicating that the line immediately ahead was clear. As we were about to pass the home signal, it changed back to red, whereupon we made an emergency stop, although, by the time that the train was brought to a stand, it had passed the signal in question. I stepped down from the engine's footplate and contacted the relevant signalman, using the internal railway telephone. The signalman was somewhat surprised at what I told him; according to his indications, the errant signal still showed green. He then asked if I could wait for a short while, so that he could make some enquiries. Whilst on the phone, I heard him speak to a third party. He then came back to me, advising that my driver and myself should ignore the red aspect and proceed as normal. What had happened was that a signal engineer was working underneath the signalman's box, and had disconnected the wrong circuit wire just as we were passing.

For me, the saddest thing that happened during my time at Aylesbury took place on February 8th 1955. Whilst working the 18.26 train from Marylebone to Aylesbury, Bert, my driver, to whom I had fired for no less than seven years, collapsed and died on the footplate. We had just departed from Harrow-on-the-Hill and were dropping down to the junction signal in order to cross over to North Harrow. This signal came into my view first and I called out to Bert that it was "a red" (or at danger). Somewhat unusually, Bert did not respond to my call and, when I looked across the footplate, he was slumped over the controls. I quickly managed to pull on the steam brake and halted the train just short of the signal. I walked along our train calling for a doctor, of which there was one on board. Sadly, after examining Bert, he confirmed that my old driver was dead. After a delay and a discussion with the duty signalman at Harrow, I clipped the trap points behind our train, and set back into the station proper. Here an ambulance had previously been called; this then took both Bert and myself to a nearby hospital. Eventually, following these traumatic events, I arrived home at around midnight, some three hours later than I normally would have.

Auto-Car Workings.

Picture 17 'Flying Pig' 43067 is depicted at Aylesbury Town in 1954, working an ex-GWR auto-car on the service to Princes Risborough, after the failure of the regular GWR 14XX engine (Author).

Prior to the nationalisation of the railway network in January 1948, the working of push/pull type branch line train services differed on the GWR, LMSR and LNER as regards what sort of fireman could work them. On the GWR, the fireman had to be someone who was 'passed for driving'. With the LMS, the ruling was that the fireman had to be examined and passed out for push/pull working, whilst on the LNER, any fireman could be utilised on these workings! Whilst the private railway companies were still in existence these rulings did not cause any problems; however, once crews from the different organisations found themselves working together under the nationalised system, problems could, and did, occur. At Aylesbury, for example, this caused a kerfuffle with former GWR drivers if they discovered that a fireman, other than one that was passed for driving, was rostered to work these trains. To overcome this situation, a letter was issued to the former GWR drivers at the depot, authorising them to work with any fireman who was booked with them on auto-car workings.

I well remember one incident that was caused as a result of these different methods of working, which happened when an ex-LNER footplate crew travelled over the single line between Princes Risborough and Aylesbury, having previously been given the wrong single line token. This was a device (of which there was only ever one example per section) which was given to the crew of a train that was travelling over a particular section of track. This gave the train permission to proceed, and was surrendered by the crew once they had completed the said section. In the incident related, a signal box lad working at Princes Risborough had placed the wrong token in the Aylesbury holder (this being a post upon which the single line token was placed in such a position so that it could be picked up by an engine's fireman as his train moved slowly past, rather than someone having to stand by the side of the track and physically hand it to him). The system employed was that the single line token was always carried on the locomotive. As far as the GWR rule book was concerned, once the fireman had received the token, he would check that it was the correct one and inform the driver of this by sounding the engine's whistle. In the corresponding LNER rule book there was no such instruction, therefore, during the happening in question, the error was only discovered by an ex-GWR train crew who were working the local Thame service, and then by the Aylesbury South signalman once the train arrived there. It was not until the crew of the branch line train to Thame (which was due away shortly after the Aylesbury-bound working, and which was heavily delayed by the happenings described above) collected and checked their own token that the error came to light.

In addition to the services worked over the Aylesbury to Princes Risborough branch, the footplate crews at Aylesbury also covered a morning and afternoon turn, which ran as far as Banbury. The morning turn in the down direction towards Banbury was usually uneventful. The return working was booked to follow the London-bound Cambrian Coast Express (CCE). However, if the CCE was running late, we would leave on time and would normally be held at Bicester, so that it could pass us. This in itself was no problem, and usually the opportunity would be used to top up the engine's tanks with extra water. The ex-GWR 14xx tank locomotives used would normally only have enough water to reach Princes Risborough if we had a clear run. I can remember one particular occasion when, because the CCE was exceptionally late, we were signalled to proceed by the Bicester signalman so, as on previous occasions when this happened, we were expecting to run in front of the express right through to Princes Risborough, therefore we did not take on any water. In the meantime the express regained some lost time, and we were held at Haddenham to let it pass. This turn of events had left us dangerously short of water so we were left to make a human chain, this being made up of my driver and myself, the train guard and a station porter, all passing buckets of water to quench the thirst of the 14xx!

The afternoon working was more interesting. During the course of this journey we would be held at Aynho Junction, just south of Banbury, in order so that we could follow a cross-country express train into our final destination, our local train being a booked connection to the main line working. We followed this train into the station using permissive station working call on signals. This signal was of a type that was a subsidiary to the main signal, and was placed underneath the latter. Once a train had come to a stand at it, the signal would be cleared, and it was therefore safe for the train to proceed as far as the line was clear. This system of signalling allowed two trains to use the same section of track. Before this train had departed (and before we could move forward), a London Paddington to Birmingham Snow Hill express train, often worked by a former GWR 'King' class locomotive, would utilise the same platform, slowly pulling up to the rear of our train.

Marylebone to Woodford Halse and Bletchley

Looking back, I suppose that our most 'ex-Great Central Railway (GCR)' turn began at Aylesbury at 3.00 am. We started by bringing an engine off the shed, and would couple this machine to an overnight parcels and fish train from Grimsby, which was already standing in Aylesbury station. Having detached and run round three fish vans, we would then work the train forward 'all stations' to Marylebone, via the ex-MR route. On arrival at Marylebone, we would drop down onto the train from which we detached the vans from Aylesbury, and draw the whole formation up to the 'neck' of the carriage sidings. The three vans were then detached, and the remainder of the train would be shunted into their respective roads within the sidings. We had to be very careful when handling our train brake as, with a mixture of four and six wheeled vehicles, some of which possessed quick action brakes, it was easy to snap a coupling. This same turn was also the time when one or two of the crews did a spot of poaching, setting their snares on the railway bank between Great Missenden and Amersham during the course of the morning, and collecting their spoils on the next trip!

Our next booking on this link was at 6.00 am, when we would relieve the train crew who had worked the overnight parcels train to Bletchley, and who had then come back to Aylesbury with a stores van. After putting this van away, we would proceed to the nearby carriage sidings to pick up the stock which would form the 6.58 am passenger service to Marylebone, via Princes Risborough and the GWR/GCR joint line. Having taken on water before setting off, we used to gain sufficient speed approaching West Ruislip and 'put the bag down' on the troughs located there. The reason that we did this was to save taking more water on at Neasden locomotive shed, where we would subsequently take our engine, dispose of it and then prepare it for its next duty. The only trouble was, more often than not, the outer home signal would be at danger and, because of the speed that we had built up prior to the troughs, it would mean that we would have the greatest difficulty in stopping at it. Fortunately the signalmen there knew what we were doing and, when we spoke to them, would tell us to wait for the signal to clear. We were very lucky as we were never reported for over-running this signal.

On these particular duties, we would always find that, when our train ran onto what was known as the 'direct line' at Neasden South Junction (this being the start of the southern-most extremity of the former GCR main line into Marylebone), we would be running parallel with an electric train that was travelling from Watford (Met) to Baker Street. We would 'race' this train up the incline as far as West Hampstead, our whistle being answered by the 'hoot' of the electric. We really had to open up our engine to keep up with the electric, even more so if we managed to overtake it.

Around this particular time, I can recall that my driver (who was a passed fireman) and myself fell foul of a B1 mixed traffic locomotive that had fallen into a very poor mechanical condition and, as a result, was very rough riding. On one of our afternoon turns, we would work up to Marylebone on a local passenger train from Aylesbury over the former MR route. Once having arrived at the terminus, we would be relieved by another footplate crew, then in turn we would take over from a set of Neasden men who had brought a light engine from that particular depot in order to work the 18.10 semi-fast passenger working to Woodford Halse. The usual motive power was a B1; however, on occasions we would find ourselves with either a V2 mixed traffic type, or even an A3 express engine. It was whilst working this train that we came face-to-face with B1 61009 '*Hartebeeste*', one of a pair of the very earliest B1s built, and one of two badly maintained machines that had been transferred from Stratford to Neasden.

After having been given 61009 for two nights running, my passed fireman and myself got somewhat fed up with its deplorable mechanical condition, and advised the Neasden shedmaster that, should we be made to use it again, we would refuse to work the train. Typically, the following night we were issued with it again, together with not only the shedmaster, but a spare footplate crew. We refused to work it and were booked off duty, with a letter to report to the Neasden shed office the following morning. We then travelled back to Aylesbury 'on the cushions' (in railway terms, this meant that we travelled as passengers rather than on the footplate); during the course of the journey, 61009 lost much time, and at Aylesbury our replacement footplate crew refused to take it any further, and failed it! At that time, there was a lot of press interest in the declining state of steam locomotives and of the railways in general. Being aware of this, my mate phoned the 'Daily Mirror' and told them the whole story. In conclusion, later that same night, we were told to book on as normal the next day, and we heard no more about the earlier incident. As far as I am aware, the errant 61009 never worked on any more passenger trains. Her place was taken by sister B1 61028 'Umseke' which was a machine that had been well looked after. Later still, we were issued with a third B1, 61164, and it was with this engine that I managed to get in some unofficial driving, achieving a speed of no less than eighty-six mph whilst working a stores van from Woodford Halse to Aylesbury.

Picture 18 Thompson-designed B1 61028 'Umseke' seen awaiting departure from Marylebone during 1953 with the 18.10 semi-fast passenger working to Woodford Halse (Author).

On a typical working day, the footplate crew that booked on at Aylesbury at 21.40 relieved those men who had been working the stores vehicle from Woodford Halse. This was one of my regular turns of duty, and it would begin by uncoupling the stores van from the train formation, running round it, placing it on the loco shed, and then working the engine only as far as Neasden shed, where we would firstly dispose of it, and then prepare it again, before running light to Marylebone. (As far as steam locomotives were concerned, the term 'to dispose' meant that the engine in question would have its fire emptied or completely cleaned out. The ash pan would be emptied and the cinders would be removed from the smokebox. The task was completed when the engine's small tools, handbrush and oilcans would be returned to the shed storekeeper). From Marylebone we would work the 3.00 am parcels train that had Liverpool as its final destination, although we only worked it as far as Bletchley, before handing over to an engine and crew that were normally based at Willesden in North-West London. I recall that one of the shunters based at Marylebone had an arrangement with all the footplate crews working this particular turn that, in exchange for leaving us two pints of milk and the morning newspapers outside his cabin, we would, in return, couple up to the train ourselves, so saving him having to leave the warmth of the cabin, and having to walk the length of the station in order to do so!

On foggy or frosty nights (or early mornings in some cases) whilst working the 3.00 am parcels over the section of line between Claydon LNER Junction and Swanbourne (these being located on the cross-country route between Oxford and Cambridge), and in order to observe the signals on this part of the line, we footplate crews would have to constantly change over positions to do so, first one of us looking out of the driver's cab window, and then the other. The reason for this was in order to try and keep warm! After a spell looking for the signals, the next step was to stand in front of the engine's fire to thaw out; once this was done, the whole process would be repeated.

This particular train would normally be loaded to around 300 tons; however, around Christmas time, this would go up to 400 tons, with up to no less than twenty vehicles making up the train formation. Such a figure gives an idea of the amount of traffic of this type that used to be carried by rail; sadly this is a commodity that, by and large, has been lost to other modes of transport. I found that the B1s would struggle with the heavier loads on the gradients encountered. In contrast, on the occasions when we had a Riddles-designed BR Standard 4 4-6-0 engine, I found that they coped with the train formation much better. The other working that we had over this section of line was a Saturday-only lunchtime service from Marylebone to Brackley, and then back just as far as Aylesbury.

Other incidents of interest

On Sundays, in addition to our booked passenger turns, we did quite a lot of ballast train workings over the Princes Risborough to Banbury line. The normal practice was that we would work out from Aylesbury with only an engine and brake van. We would pick up the permanent way men (or 'pway men' in railway language) en-route, and then we would attach the wagons as required at Princes Risborough, making our way to the actual site of work from there. To relieve us, a light engine and crew would be sent, again from Aylesbury, making its way via Ashendon Junction, Grendon Underwood Junction and Quainton Road. On one particular occasion, to save time when disposing of our engine when we got back to Aylesbury, we ran the fire down very low after passing Quainton Road, estimating that we would still have sufficient steam to reach 'home'. To our horror, we then came across a hand signalman out with a red flag and detonators, who advised us that a pway gang were changing a broken rail just in front of us! It was fortunate that we were only held up for only a few minutes, and we just made it back to Aylesbury.

During the early 1950s, the standard of the coal used was variable at best, and poor at worst, a situation emphasised by the fact that, although there were two coal hoppers located at Neasden sheds, they both contained the same, low grade of coal. I was on the shed one day with my driver when a crew that had worked down from Leicester brought an engine on shed, asking us which hopper contained the passenger engine coal. We replied, "Take your pick – there is no difference here," a sarcastic reply, which did not go down very well with them. The poor coal caused other problems as well, one such incident coming about as the result of the badly designed bunker door on the L1 tank locomotives. This left much to be desired, and if you had a number of large lumps of coal, they had a habit of getting jammed in the doorway. Occasionally, when trying to clear them, you either broke the shaft of the pick used, or even the shovel handle itself. This in turn created a need for a new shovel. If you did this whilst in a depot (for example at either Neasden or Aylesbury), it was a simple matter of taking one off an adjacent engine. However, if the breakage occurred elsewhere, this would cause major problems.

Despite all the difficulties encountered in the normal course of events, there were 'fringe benefits' that could be gathered in more unorthodox ways. I can recall that, at Ardley, which was situated just north of Bicester, there was a fresh water spring on the southern end of the 'up' platform (this being used by trains travelling in the direction of London) which was very refreshing during the course of the summer months. It had its uses during the rest of the time as well! On arrival in the platform, the fireman would nip off the engine and fill the tea can up with the water, the driver then picking him up as the engine passed by. No need to go to the bother of finding a tap! In the course of our ballast train duties, we found that Blackthorn (which was situated between Brill and Bicester) was an ideal location for picking blackberries, whilst a plentiful supply of wild strawberries could be found at Wendover. When working a night goods train from Aylesbury to Harrow-on-the-Hill, we would be shunted into Wendover Goods Yard in order to allow a following passenger train to pass. We were then signalled out of the yard as far as the starting signal where, before it was 'cleared', there was time available during which many strawberries could be picked. At other places in the locality, one could find a good mix of apples, plums and other fruits. In addition, the long upside shunting neck situated at Quainton Road gave access to a couple of adjacent fields, where one could always find a plentiful supply of mushrooms!

CHAPTER SIX

A CHANGE OF CAREER

At the beginning of 1955, I was in the fortunate position of having become well-established within the two sets of links that were covered by Aylesbury Town shed. I was doing a job that I loved, and things were looking even better for me as in March of that year I got married, my wife Pat and myself electing to live in the area surrounding the county town of Bedford. As far as my work was concerned, I had decided to arrange a transfer from Aylesbury to the motive power depot at Bedford itself. How things can quickly change! Due to the fact that a group of workings that were covered by Bedford were moved north to Wellingborough shed, my transfer unfortunately fell through. This left me in an impossible position, as there was no way that I could travel from my home to Aylesbury Town on a daily basis. I was forced to leave the railways and take up employment at the Stewartby Brickworks, these being located alongside what was then the Oxford to Cambridge cross-country railway route. Today, only the Bedford to Bletchley section is still operating, as a branch line. Even whilst employed at the brickworks, I was drawn back to the railway, spending my lunch breaks with the crossing keeper who was based at Stewartby station itself. One day I was conversing with a relief signalman who was covering this particular duty, when he suddenly suggested that I should apply for a job as a signalman, as there was a severe shortage of staff in this particular grade throughout the surrounding area. I therefore applied for a signalman's position shortly afterwards, this taking place in person at the Station Master's office at Bedford Midland Road. I was lucky as my application was accepted, subject to the required medical examination, my previous railway service being taken as a reference. More good luck followed as I only had to wait a couple of days for the medical, and I was then able to start my training programme the following week, the actual date in question being May 16th 1955.

At this moment in time, the normal procedure for training new recruits to the signalling department was to undergo a classroom-based theory course, before moving onto the practical side of the job. However, in my particular case, I was designated to be trained 'on the job', rather than attend classroom sessions. I believe that the fact that I already had eight years railway experience had a bearing on this. I was to be trained by a senior relief signalman, and my new place of work was to be the London and North Western Railway (LNWR) Junction signal box located at the Bedford end of the branch line to Hitchin, a route that was sadly closed in December 1961. This box controlled the section of line between Ouse Bridge box (this being located nearer to Bedford itself) and Bedford St Johns Number 1 box, which was situated in the Hitchin direction. The box was very busy, being open from 22.00 hours on a Sunday to 22.00 hours the following Saturday. It controlled two through running lines (up and down directions respectively) to and from Hitchin. In addition, there was a coal yard situated on the up side of the running lines, whilst the down side was host to a group of sidings collectively known as Ampthill Yard (sometimes they were referred to as Holding Sidings). There were also other connections and sidings located here, serving the nearby Britannia Iron Works, together with Mitchell and Butler's brewery depot. Finally, there were through roads linking the Hitchin branch to the Oxford–Cambridge route at Bedford St Johns. Freight traffic was big business within the locality. There were regular exchange trips of traffic between Ouse Bridge and Bedford St Johns, whilst shunting operations were conducted in the brewery sidings each morning and the coal yard late each afternoon. As for the iron works, workings into and out of these premises were organised on an 'as required' basis.

The District Signalling Inspector (DSI) used to pass my box each morning and made it his business to see how I was progressing. In addition, I also had to visit his office each Friday in order to take a more formal examination of the knowledge that I had gained thus far. When the DSI felt that I was ready, he arranged for me to attend the Divisional Office at London St Pancras for a thorough examination on the Rules and Signalling Regulations. My examiner was Mr George Walton, who was the Assistant Divisional Manager (Operating) for the London Midland Division at the time. After an exam that lasted some three to four hours, I then had to go and see the Divisional Manager, Mr J.C.R. Rodgers , who asked me a further series of related questions. (A few years later, Mr Rogers became President of the Locomotive Club of Great Britain, the railway study group that I had previously founded in 1949). Having satisfied both these gentlemen of my competence, I was pleased and proud to be appointed a temporary Signalman (Class C), my location of work being formally confirmed as the previously mentioned LNWR Junction box, and I took charge for the first time on June 27th 1955, covering the late shift. My new railway career was under way!

<u>Picture 19</u> A 1966 view of the LNWR (London and North Western Railway) Junction signal box, where the author trained as a signalman during the mid-1950s. This box was located at the Bedford end of the former Hitchin branch (Author's collection).

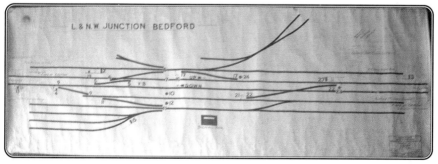

<u>Picture 20</u> The route diagram inside the LNWR Junction signal box (Author's collection).

I remained working here until March 1956, when I applied for (and was appointed) a permanent Class C Signalman at Bromham box, which was located on the Midland main line to the north of Bedford. Prior to taking up my new position, I had to go to the Divisional Office at St Pancras for a 'further rules' exam. Bromham box was even busier than the Junction box, being open continuously 365 days a year, and controlling movements on both the fast lines and goods lines. When travelling north, the next box was Oakley Junction, this controlling all train movements onto the branch line to Northampton, via Turvey, Olney and Piddington. Bromham itself had junctions from both down fast to down goods lines, and from up goods to up fast. The advantage of having these junctions was that freight trains could bypass Bedford station when the platforms were occupied by either commuter trains running to and from London St Pancras, or by one or another of the various branch line passenger workings. Once the freight trains had passed Bedford, they were routed back to the goods lines at Kempston Road Junction.

My box was lacking in some quite basic facilities, as I recall. For example, there was no running water, a situation which was resolved by cans of water being dropped off from the daily Bedford to Northampton pick-up goods train, this working also bringing me notices and working timetables. In addition, the toilet that I used was a chemical one, which had to be emptied into a pit on a weekly basis! One other odd chore which I remember doing during this period of time was to retrieve stray golf balls that had come from the nearby Bedford golf course. My doctor was a keen golfer; once things were quiet on a Sunday, I would search the embankment for these balls, which I would then pass onto him!

There were two incidents that stick in my mind from my time working at Bromham. The first of these concerned an occasion on a foggy night, when I was crossing an empty goods working from Cricklewood to Wellingborough, a train which could be anything up to no less than one hundred wagons in length. The freight was making its way from the down fast to the down goods line, and I was watching for the train's brake van to pass my box, so that I could place the junction signal back to danger. Out of the gloom came a brake van; however, this was not the end of the train. I should have checked to see if the van had the train's tail lamp fixed to it, as this would confirm that this was the last vehicle in the train formation. Rather than carrying out this check, once the brake van had passed the signal, I immediately put it back to danger, this then setting off the detonators placed at the signal, because the rear of the train had not passed it. Even though the train engine was at least sixty or seventy wagons further on, both driver and fireman clearly heard the explosion. The train was subsequently brought to a stand, whereupon the train's fireman had to walk back to my box in order to see what the problem was. Apart from the obvious hold-up to the long freight train, two following workings, an early morning London-bound express train and a fitted freight, were also slightly delayed. I got a 'please explain' form request, and a visit from the local Signalling Inspector, for this misdemeanour.

The second incident took place one morning when, because of a problem on the down fast line, Control had instructed me to introduce absolute block working on the down goods line, and divert the 'Thames Clyde Express', one of the most important trains on the Midland route, onto the goods line, the express being the next train due. I brought the express almost to a stand at the junction signal, as laid down in the signal regulations, and then cleared it, along with the section signal. The express train's driver accepted the route and drew the train onto the goods line. However, instead of proceeding, he stopped at the section signal, and walked back to my box to inform me that he had not signed the road for the goods line. I explained to him what the situation was and decided to get him to speak to Control himself. After a heated phone conversation he decided to take his train forward.

Before I go on with my story, I would like to explain what two of the terms mentioned in the previous paragraph meant, in relation to the operation of a signal box of the time. Absolute block working is a method of signalling trains whereby only one train is in a block section of track (this being between two signal boxes) at any one time. The phrase 'signed the road' in railway terms meant that each driver had to learn the various routes that he would be working over. Once this was done, the driver in question then had

Picture 21 *Taken in 1956, Bromham signal box was situated north of Bedford on the Midland main line (MML). This was the first main line box that the author was assigned to (Author).*

to sign a route card to acknowledge that he was fully conversant with them, hence the term 'signed the road'.

By 1957 I had been a signalman for some two years and I was enjoying my work once again. I was fortunate enough to be promoted to a 'Class 2 Relief Signalman', my home station being Bedford Midland. In railway terms the word 'relief' means that the person in question does not have one permanent work location, but can be sent to work at one of a number of places within a set area. Prior to taking up my new position, I had to undertake a further set of examinations, these including regulations for working trains over single track lines utilising both tablet working and electronic tokens. Like the absolute block working system mentioned previously, the tablet working and electronic systems ensured that only when a train was in possession of either tablet or electric token could it proceed over the relevant single line section. I had to learn about these devices because I would be working boxes located on both the Bedford to Hitchin and Bedford to Northampton branch lines, both of which used these items. In addition to the more normal signal duties, I found myself undertaking other jobs, these including 'lamping' (this being the collective term for cleaning, trimming and replacing lamps) and the occasions when I had to cover the issuing of tickets at Piddington station.

Upon taking up my new position, the first two signal boxes that I learnt were at Houghton Conquest and at Elstow, both of which were situated not too far from Bedford. The former opened only for a period of one hour each morning. This was to control the freight operations run in support of the Coronation Brickworks, one of the largest of the many such establishments that were at one time situated around Bedford itself, and which have now completely disappeared. The latter box was opened only in the afternoons, once again for brick traffic. As well as operating these two boxes I carried out similar duties at Wilshampstead. I also had the job of cleaning, trimming and replacing the lamps in situ at all three locations.

Wilshampstead signal box was situated on the Midland main line south of Bedford. On this section of the Midland, the sequence of signal boxes was Bedford South, Kempston Road, Elstow, Wilshampstead, Houghton Conquest, Millbrook and then, following a tunnel, the sequence was completed by Ampthill. Wilshampstead was first opened during the Second World War, in conjunction with the operations that were carried out in support of a newly built munitions factory at Elstow. Not only were there extensive sidings at this location, but a platform was also constructed for the benefit of the workers who were employed in the factory. A passenger service running to and from Luton brought the workers in for the start of the morning shift and returned them to their respective places of residence at night. Following the war, these sidings were then used for the purpose of marshalling goods trains that carried the produce of the two brickworks located nearby. There was a nine lever ground frame situated in the marshalling yard which, when its working days at Wilshampstead were over, was dismantled and taken away for use on a preserved narrow gauge line, the Sittingbourne and Kemsley Railway.

The other area where I found myself carrying out 'lamping' duties was at Luton. Here there should have been both an early and a late turn, with each shift looking after all lamps based at Luton South, Luton North and nearby Limbury Road boxes. Because of staff shortages, I did a twelve hour turn opening Limbury Road box during the lunchtime hour, this enabling a Cricklewood to Wellingborough freight to call there. In the evening I would then open the same box again, this time to let in the 'trip' engine that came from Luton to set the coal yard up, and to sort the empty wagons out. In a railway context, the term 'trip' was used to describe a train that was working from one yard or siding to another. Details of such workings

Picture 22 An example of 'lamping' duties being carried out in the Glasgow suburban area, circa 1948 (Author).

were listed in an internal document known as the 'London Division Trip Workings Publication'. Once this engine was 'inside' (this term being used to notify that the locomotive in question was 'inside' the yard and therefore off the main running lines), the box was closed, and the signalman then became a shunter, assisting the trip train's guard. What used to happen was that the driver, fireman, guard and myself, as relief signalman, would take turns in doing each other's jobs. For me, this was a chance to get back on the footplate and relive earlier days.

Over a period of time, in the course of my relief duties, I learnt and worked a wide miscellany of signal boxes. As far as the main line was concerned, in addition to the boxes already mentioned, I worked at Millbrook, Ampthill, Flitwick, Harlington, Sundon and Leagrave. I also covered both Southill and Shefford on the Bedford to Hitchin branch, together with Turvey, Olney, Ravenstone Wood and Piddington, on the route from Bedford to Northampton.

My most vivid memories of the branch line based relief work concerned the very bad winter of 1957/8. To get to the various signal boxes, I had to cycle from my home at Wootton. At Southill box, which was located on the Bedford to Hitchin route, I had a ten mile bike ride to reach my workplace. The box would open at 05.00 each morning, this being in readiness for the 05.15 freight train, which ran from Bedford to Hitchin. Normally, this journey would take me an hour – however, because of the snowy weather, I found myself having to push or even carry my bike and, as a result, it was nearly 06.00 before I was able to get there. This in turn meant that it was too late for the early freight to be run in front of the first passenger train of the day. When I arrived, the station master was already in the box, demanding to know why I was late. Despite explaining the situation to him, and pointing out that on the road out of Southill village there was a bus that had been stuck overnight in a deep snow drift, he replied by saying that he would have to report me to the Divisional Office for being late on duty and delaying the freight train. What annoyed me was the fact that he, as a station master, should have been able to have worked the box and drawn the single line tablet out of the machine for the freight train. The truth was he had not a clue what he should be doing!

Later that same day, the empty stock for a troop train working for the RAF camp at Cardington was brought to Southill, in order to run round. I asked this same station master if he could allow this train to wait for a total of fifteen minutes so that I could get a lift back to Bedford. He refused to do this. I was fortunate inasmuch as that the train crew had other ideas. They found a fault with their locomotive, which delayed the train until such time as my relief arrived – therefore, I managed to get my lift back to Bedford after all. It was interesting that, because of the bad weather, my relief had had to walk along the railway line from Shefford to get to Southill. However, he wasn't the only member of staff who had a difficult journey to work that snowy day. The early turn Running Shed Foreman at Bedford Motive Power Depot, who lived in Southill was, due to impassable roads, unable to get into work until the first passenger train of the day returned from Hitchin!

CHAPTER SEVEN

SIGNALLING MEMORIES

By this time, the early part of 1958, I was well established in my new signalling career. During this time, I gained many special signalling memories, some of which I would like to relate during the course of this chapter. One of the most unusual things about my work was that I was required to carry out many duties which, to the casual eye, would not seem to have anything to do with the normal work of a signalman.

An example of this was at Piddington, which was on the branch line from Bedford to Northampton. Here, instead of a separate signalman, the post was known as a 'porter/signalman', the member of staff in question working a regular early turn. The signal box was only opened 'as required' during

Picture 23 Piddington station, depicted in the late 1960s, on the occasion of an excursion train. This was on the former Bedford–Northampton route from which passenger services were withdrawn in March 1962 (Author).

the late morning for a local pick-up goods train which would call and service the adjacent sidings, these leading into an Army maintenance depot. I found that when I had to relieve the regular signalman here, I had to travel out on the first passenger service of the day from Bedford. On arrival at Piddington I quickly had to open the booking office, in order to issue tickets to any people who were joining the train that I had just alighted from! Until the signal box was opened, the rest of my time would be spent carrying out general porter-type duties and selling the odd ticket to would-be passengers. Looking back, it would seem that the low numbers of travelling customers was a major contributing factor to the sad demise and closure of the branch not so many years later.

The regular porter/signalman made the best possible use of his time during the course of his shifts. In conjunction with his wife, he grew chrysanthemums on a commercial basis! I recall that if you were rostered at the signal box during the course of the winter months, you would have great difficulty working the lever frame as he would store all the boxes of cuttings in the box, heated courtesy of British Railways (BR). In addition, he would also keep poultry, and every Friday the District Signals Inspector would drop by in order to collect his eggs! The closure of much of the secondary and branch line railway network has seen the end of such unusual practices which, in their own small way, contributed to the well-being of the railway and of the local economy.

A somewhat more unpleasant memory from this same time took place at Sundon, which was situated roughly one mile south of Harlington and which, at one period, was host to a large cement works. The signal box concerned covered the shunting carried out within some sidings which were known collectively as Inns Sidings. These served a large rubbish tip. Each day, a train would arrive from London, this being made up of no fewer than forty wagons full of general rubbish. Despite the fact that each wagon was sheeted over they were always accompanied by many flies, irrespective of whether it was a warm or cold day, and of course there was always the 'stink' (or dreadful smell).

It was known amongst the signalmen in the Bedford area that Sundon and Wilshampstead boxes were notorious for the extreme coldness encountered whilst working within these establishments. In the case of the latter location, as it was normally closed from each Saturday lunchtime to midnight on the following Monday morning, and as no heater had been used during this time, it was necessary to keep one's overcoat on and operate the levers wearing gloves, until the time came to be relieved at

07.00 the same day. In addition, Wilshampstead also had the most lever movements of any of the boxes in the surrounding area. As an example, to enable a train to cross from the adjacent sidings to the down fast line required no less than seventeen movements. This was alright if everything went okay; sometimes however, the required signal for the move wouldn't clear, which meant in turn that you would have to go through the whole procedure again which, with the heavy equipment that you were using, would be quite exhausting.

One way in which I was able to help my fellow signalmen, and where my previous experience of working on the footplate came in useful, was when a number of fitted freight trains found themselves losing time at night between Bedford and Millbrook on the up fast line. (A fitted freight train was one that had its vacuum brake operative throughout the whole length of its formation). As a result, a series of 'please explain' notes were issued to some of the signalmen, the reason for the delays being alleged that the signals on this section of track were not being cleared in time, thus delaying the freights in question. The method of signalling was that, on receiving the 'train on line' signal from Wilshampstead box, Millbrook box would then offer the train onto the next box, Flitwick, (Ampthill being closed at night), at the same time clearing their own signals. At this time, Millbrook had a colour light 'distant' signal which could be seen from quite a distance away.

Trains that were approaching from Wilshampstead would see this signal and shut off steam, thereby causing a delay. After a night visit from the District Signalling Inspector, who saw all that was going on, the method of working was altered. What then happened was that when the 'train on line' signal was received from Kempston Road, (this latter box being located two miles north of Wilshampstead. As far as the Midland main line was concerned, it was the next signal box that was open on a continuous basis, other than during the period of time each afternoon from Monday to Friday, when the intermediate box at Elstow was also fully operational, its main function being to look after brick traffic) Wilshampstead now sent the 'train approach' signal to Millbrook box. In turn, Millbrook then offered the train in question to Flitwick, at the same time clearing their signals. The adoption of this new way of working solved the problem, and speeded up the journey of the freight trains concerned.

It will be recalled that one of the reasons that I originally became a signalman was because of a serious shortage of suitably qualified staff of this kind within the Bedford area. In the late 1950s, this situation still persisted and, as a result, on occasions I would be asked by one of the local signalling inspectors to go to a particular box, carry out two twelve hour shifts, and then be 'passed out' to cover the box in question, in a situation where the regular signalman would be on sick leave or if there was a vacancy. In this particular railway context, if you were 'passed out', this meant that, in the opinion of the inspector concerned, you were competent to operate the signal box in question. It was fortunate that I was able to pick up the workings of these boxes quite easily. On a number of occasions, due to no relief being available, I would be asked to stay on for a further four hours beyond the end of my normal shift. I would agree to this providing Pat, my wife, was informed, and that arrangements were made for food to be sent to me. Most times, Pat would bring such a meal to Bedford station, and it would be put on a train that was issued with a 'stop' order, to deliver my meal. If I was working a box that was near to my home, Pat would cycle instead, bringing the food directly to me.

After some fifteen months working as a relief signalman, there was a re-organisation of the relief requirements. As a result of these changes, I was unfortunately made redundant. It was lucky that at the same time there were two vacancies at Millbrook box and I was allocated one of these. What was good about Millbrook was that it was only some three miles from my home and, as a result of this, I was able to use my bicycle. This journey was not without its problems; as the last half mile going to the box was along the up slow line cess, when travelling after dark, I always had to remember to turn off my rear bicycle light, otherwise any train coming from the Bedford direction would see my red light and think that someone was exhibiting a danger signal. (The 'cess' was the name given to an area that was normally levelled, and which was located next to the outside of the running lines, usually on one side only. The track layout was normally as follows: cess, up slow line, down slow line, up fast line and down fast line. In railway terms, the running lines themselves were known as the 'four foot', and the space between the two set of running lines (slow and fast) was known as the 'six foot'). After two months based at Millbrook, the regular signalman who was working there retired. To cover the various shifts, the workload was then divided between myself and another signalman who had previously been based at Tadcaster, which was north-east of Leeds. We were asked (and agreed) to work twelve hour shifts – this then became the normal pattern of working for the following six months.

Although officially it was not permitted to listen to a radio whilst carrying out our work, my colleague and myself procured such an item, via the hire purchase method. We would only use it during the quiet periods of our shifts. In addition, we also had the company of a crow that had a damaged wing. This bird would come into the box through an open window and feed from a dish on our table. We were lucky to receive some fringe benefits during this time, courtesy of a Derby-based driver by the name of Packard. When this individual was passing Millbrook whilst returning from St Pancras to Derby, he would throw off a bundle of newspapers, with a few sweets wrapped in them. He also included some good horse racing tips. The reason for this was that on a previous occasion, he had lost a hat whilst passing the box, and the signalman then on duty had been kind enough to return it to him. The papers, sweets and tips were his way of saying 'thank you'.

On a more sombre note, one incident that could have had quite serious consequences took place on a Sunday afternoon. On this particular occasion, I was crossing a north-bound train consisting of loaded wagons of spoil from the down fast to the down slow line. The freight had come out of Ampthill tunnel, and the driver was whistling furiously. What had happened was that the weight of the train had caused the driver to lose control, and the train was running away. Normally, I would have ensured that the train was almost at a stand before clearing the junction signal, prior to crossing it over. Realising what was happening, and not being able to reverse the points in order to keep it on the down fast line, I immediately cleared the signal, and just hoped and prayed that it would get safely over the junction. The fireman on the train was very brave as he had managed to get off the locomotive's tender and onto the front brake van. Once there, he was screwing the handbrake on as hard as he could. For my part, having sent the 'train running away on the right line' signal to Kempston Road (which was the next box open to the north of Millbrook), there was nothing else that I could do, other than hold my breath, and hope that all would be well. Fortunately, the goods train crossed the junction safely, and stopped further down the line.

At Millbrook you were able to cross trains from the down slow line to the down fast via the up fast. On occasions, we had to do this if problems were occurring in the Bedford station area. This needed co-operation on the part of the train guard in question – at night, we as signalmen often had to throw a lump of coal at the brake van of the train we had crossed over, to remind the guard to change the position of the red rear train light, once the train itself had crossed from slow to fast line! Sometimes we also had to throw a lump of coal at the brake van when we crossed a train from fast line to slow line (or vice-versa) to make sure that the guard was awake and would change his lamps!

Picture 24 Millbrook signal box (P. Butler).

After working at Millbrook for a little under a year, a vacancy came up at Bedford South, which was a higher graded box, the signalman therefore being paid more money. In those days, each signal box was graded by their respective workloads and lever movements. Bedford South was a much busier box and had more levers than that at Millbrook. I applied for this vacancy, and was successful in my application, thereby beginning a happy stay of some three years. As well as being located just over the River Ouse bridge, Bedford South box was quite different to Millbrook, in that it had two separate lever frames, one being located on the fast line side of the box, and the other on the slow side. Every train movement, from fast to slow, or vice-versa, meant that you had to cross the box twice over. In addition, Bedford South also controlled movements over the main line to enter both the locomotive depot and the gas works sidings, and also a group of lines that were collectively known as the South Sidings. There was also a through middle road from the Bedford Junction box, which led out onto the up fast line, this being mainly used for light engine movements into the depot, and workings in and out of the gas works sidings.

In those days, all main signal boxes were open continuously, 365 days a year. I was fortunate that in my time at Bedford South, I was rostered to work the night shift during each of the three Christmas periods. The last overnight train was an 'up' (in the direction of London) mail train that had commenced its journey at Sheffield, and which called at Bedford at 3.45 am. Following this, there were no further trains due until I was relieved at 7.00 am that morning. By this time, I had become a father and, working this particular shift, I was able to get home and see my children opening their Christmas presents, as well as enjoying my Christmas dinner. There were very few trains about until the local services started to run again on Boxing Day.

As I mentioned earlier, my time at Bedford South was a very happy one, although I had one or two differences of opinion with the Bedford Station Master. This was over what I called sensible regulation of trains (which in general railway terms meant that you did not run either a slow passenger train or a freight working in front of an express) or, being more specific, a single passenger train, this being the 17.00 departure from London St Pancras, which was due into Bedford at 17.42. On occasions, I felt it better to delay this train by a couple of minutes, as it had two minutes recovery time between Bedford and Wellingborough. I did this because the alternative would have been to delay, for anything up to five minutes, the next north-bound local passenger train, which was timed to arrive at 17.48. This latter working terminated at Bedford and was due to return to London at 17.53. A partially fitted freight train was due to pass through Bedford on the slow lines at 17.35; sometimes it was delayed by a few minutes waiting for a clear run through the station. On occasions, as the result of such a delay, I would refuse it permission to run through Bedford from Kempston Road, signalling the 17.42 express in its place. By the time that the express departed Bedford on its north-bound run and cleared the station, and after the freight train had recommenced its journey from its stand, it was inevitable that the local passenger train would be delayed. In order to avoid as much delay as possible, if there was a good chance that the goods working could get through even by delaying the 17.42 by two minutes, then I would have no hesitation in giving the freight priority. Although I felt that I was keeping the trains in question moving well by adopting this policy, the Station Master disagreed because the express in question brought many businessmen home from their work in the city of London, and he felt (rightly) that the timekeeping of such a prestigious train should be a top priority. On most evenings he would meet this train, and no doubt if it was late he would be taken to task by those same businessmen.

Picture 25 A July 1960 view of Bedford South signal box, looking towards Bedford station (Author).

Picture 26 The interior of Bedford South box, also depicted in July 1960, showing the signal frame that covered the slow lines on the Midland trunk route (Author).

Picture 27 *Taken from Bedford South box, an unidentified 'Jubilee' class locomotive (with a Fowler-designed tender) heads a north-bound passenger working , crossing over from the fast to the slow lines (Author).*

Picture 28 *As the steam era drew to a close, many top-link machines found themselves on more mundane duties. An example of this is a fitted freight seen hauled by ex-LMSR 46139 'The Welch Regiment', passing Bedford South on the up slow line (Author).*

Picture 29 *'Jubilee' class engine 45619 'Nigeria' is shown crossing from the up slow to the up fast line at Bedford South during 1960 (Author).*

Picture 30 *Also in 1960, 46100 'Royal Scot' makes an appearance at Bedford South (Author).*

Picture 31 47279, a 'Jinty' class tank locomotive, passes Bedford South whilst crossing the MML fast lines with a freight train bound for the nearby gasworks (Author).

Picture 32 The new railway age. The 'Midland Pullman' diesel train approaching Bedford South on the up fast through line (Author).

CHAPTER EIGHT

FROM WAGES STAFF TO SALARIED STAFF

Towards the end of my three year period of time from 1958 to 1961 working at Bedford South signal box (a period of time which also saw the demise of steam locomotive traction within the Bedford area, and the introduction of diesel multiple unit trains on the local passenger services between Bedford and London St Pancras), I had a visit one evening from the Assistant Divisional Operating Superintendent (ADOS), Mr Dennis Holyfield, whose job it was to assist the Divisional Operating Superintendent in all operational matters. I offered him a cup of tea and, whilst drinking it, he asked me how long had I worked on the railway, and what my previous railway service had been. When I told him, he was very interested in what I had to say, in particular about my time as a junior clerk in the Goods Department at Aylesbury High Street, and also the part of my life working on the footplate. After talking over what I had done so far, he suggested to me that, as a way of moving up the promotional ladder, I might like to apply for a Relief Station Master (RSM) position. Mr Holyfield asked me to think about what he had said, adding that he would call and see me again in a fortnight's time, to establish what my answer would be.

I thought through Mr Holyfield's idea at great length. To help me make the correct decision, especially as it would mean a cut in pay, I decided to ask the Bedford Station Master for his opinion. He felt that I was not the right person for the job and, as a result, was not prepared to put my name forward. Fortunately for me, a fortnight later, he went on annual leave. I seized my opportunity, and asked his temporary replacement, the senior Relief Station Master, what I should do. He asked me to let him have my clerical post application; he then promised to send it through with his recommendation. As it happened, there was at that moment in time a vacancy in Bedford Booking Office, which would give me valuable accountancy experience, which I could then use in a subsequent application for an RSM position. As with the relief signalman's post that I held prior to working at Millbrook, a relief station master could be sent to a wide miscellany of stations within a set location. He would be expected to undertake a cross-section of activities, of which running a booking office would be but one – this being especially so at some of the smaller branch line stations.

Having decided to go ahead and apply, I was disappointed when the regular Station Master (SM) returned from leave and came to see me, saying that he had stopped my application. It will be recalled from the previous chapter that I had had a number of disagreements with this person concerning train regulation. It may well have been that this was partly the reason for him turning down my application. However, it was lucky for me that Mr Holyfield, the ADOS, came to see me once again and, as a result, he overturned the SM's decision, thus enabling my application to go ahead. My next step was to report to the Divisional Office at London St Pancras for a further examination. This time however, the exam in question was not about relevant rules and regulations, but to do with the clerical work that I would be undertaking. I was pleased to say that I passed this latest examination, and I was told to report to the Chief Clerk at Bedford Booking Office, the date in question being Monday January 8th 1962.

In my new role, I discovered that there were a number of differences between what I was now doing and what I had been used to. To begin with, in the course of my work, I was now meeting the public face-to-face on a daily basis. Prior to starting, I procured some new clothes to enable myself to look as spick and span as possible. Although once fully trained I would still be doing shift work, these consisted of early and late turns, rather than nights as well as days, the booking office of course being closed during the night. During my time as a signalman I operated the various boxes on my own; in the booking office, for the greater part of each day, I was now working as one of a team of people. I also found out that the new role used my brain to a greater extent whereas, of course, working in the signal box and on the footplate was much more physical.

In those pre-computer days, I discovered that booking office work consisted of much more than selling tickets to the travelling public. At the end of each shift, I had to cash up all the money that I had taken, and carry out a check of all the tickets that I had sold, ensuring that the latter balanced with the revenue on hand. In addition, there was then 'end of the day', weekly and monthly balances to be reconciled. It was necessary to be well aware of how much stock was on hand of each type of ticket – you had to be an inventory controller, making sure that fresh supplies were ordered once on-hand stocks had got down to a certain level. If no printed tickets were available, it became necessary to have to hand write out every single ticket of that particular type, a separate record then being kept of each ticket issued. There was a considerable number of tickets available for customers to buy. These included normal singles and returns, cheap day and evening returns (the latter being valid only for journeys into London), and military forces singles, returns and warranty tickets. Then, as now, reduced rate (or privilege) tickets for railway staff were available to procure, as well as weekly and season tickets, which could be bought to cover set periods of time, mainly a series of months and even odd days. The mix of tasks undertaken included having to answer questions about times of trains, these either being verbal (whilst selling tickets at the booking office window) or on the telephone. Although I enjoyed the variety that the job entailed, if you found yourself working on your own (as happened outside of office hours) things could get a little hectic.

As mentioned before, correctly balancing the money that was received was arguably the most important part of the whole job. If a loss was incurred that was less than £1.00 per shift, you had to inform the Chief Clerk of the booking office. If the loss was greater than the same amount, you were required to submit a full written report. If this state of affairs occurred more than once, you would be interviewed, and could face disciplinary action. I recall that on one occasion, I was working on a late shift with a trainee. At the finish of our turn of duty, when we were balancing the money taken, we discovered that we were no less than £2.00 short. During the course of the shift, we had sold a Forces ticket to a destination in the north of England, although I could not remember the exact location. The cost of the ticket in question was £2.00, which accounted for the loss incurred. As the rules stipulated, both my trainee and myself had to make out written reports to the Chief Clerk, as a result of which we were both told to be more careful in future. However, this tale had a happy ending. A few weeks later, when undertaking a ticket stock check, the missing ticket was discovered – it had fallen down a tube, which was part of the rack upon which the Edmondson-style railway tickets were kept in. Therefore, the ticket in question could be brought back into office stock and the month end balance adjusted accordingly.

During my time working at Bedford Booking Office, a new evening return ticket, priced at 7/6 (or in decimal money 37½ pence), was introduced. The odd thing about this particular ticket was that it was cheaper than a London-bound single, and we as booking office staff would always point out to a customer that to procure the return ticket would be cheaper than the single. It was surprising how many people needed to be convinced of the validity of this cheaper alternative!

Season tickets made up a large part of the booking office's business. At that time the office would request their customers to pre-order their 'seasons', and they would then be prepared during the course of the weekend. Many of our regular passengers would make a point of coming to the station on a Sunday evening, collecting them prior to the beginning of their working week. Other people, having previously been advised of the price of the ticket, would collect them early on the Monday morning, paying for their purchase by means of a cheque. On one occasion, just after I had 'cashed up' my day's takings late on a Friday night, I had a passenger appear at the booking office window, who demanded that I make out an odd day's season ticket for him, while he waited. I pointed out that this would not be possible, as I had finished my shift, and was in the process of locking up the office. It was obvious that the irate passenger was well under the influence of drink, and he began to get very aggressive. He reiterated his demand for the ticket, stating that he was a retired RAF squadron leader. My reply was that, "I am Corporal Turner, and I am very sorry, but you must pre-order your ticket, and collect it at the weekend, like everyone else." With this, our conversation came to a somewhat abrupt end and, grumbling, this passenger left without his season ticket. Subsequently, he reported me to the station master (SM). When the SM then spoke with me about the incident, I was fortunate in that he backed my stance, having told the irate customer that what I had stated was correct, and that I was right to refuse to make out the season ticket.

Being one of the 'public' faces of the railway could be rewarding, but, as in the situation mentioned above, it could also be something of a drawback. I found that whenever fares were increased, there was a never-ending string of complaints from numerous customers, despite the obvious fact that we would have no control whatsoever over these increases, which were decided upon by some of those much more senior in the railway organisation to myself and my colleagues. On one occasion, we decided on a novel approach to the problem. We drew up a large notice which stated 'Please do not blame the poor booking clerk – it isn't his fault', and put it up in the booking hall. We thought that we were being clever, but when the Station Master saw it he was far from happy and made us remove it!

Altogether, I spent a total of fourteen happy months working in Bedford Booking Office. I enjoyed the work that I was doing. It was something very different from the signalling and footplate roles that I had undertaken before, and I relished the challenge that was placed before me. However, I was still looking to apply for a Relief Station Master's position, and in fact I was offered the chance to apply for the RSM's job at Bedford a mere nine months after I had begun work in the booking office. However, as I wished to add to my clerical experience, I decided not to send in an application, but to wait for the next suitable opportunity, which came about once I had completed a full year working as a booking clerk.

CHAPTER NINE

MY DAYS AS A RELIEF STATION MASTER

As mentioned in the previous chapter, my time working in the booking office at Bedford had been both constructive and positive. For me, it was a different side of the railway industry, contrasting greatly with my work both on the footplate and within the miscellany of signal boxes that I had covered. I appreciated the fact that my latest position had added to my all round railway experience, standing me in greater stead for possible future job opportunities. It will be remembered that the whole point of my working in the booking office was to enable me to be better qualified should a suitable Relief Station Master (RSM) vacancy become available. It was fortunate that, not long after the beginning of 1963, such an opportunity did appear, and I immediately put in what turned out to be a successful application.

So, yet again, I was off to St Pancras Chambers for an interview, this being with the Assistant District Operating Superintendent (ADOS), the Commercial Manager and the Staff Assistant. Having satisfied these three people of my competence and suitability, this was followed by a very thorough rules and regulations examination, the questions being put to me by the ADOS. Finally, I then had to sit a second interview, this time with the District Operating Superintendent himself. One of the questions that he asked me concerned the resetting of the passenger communication cord on the-then new diesel multiple unit (DMU) trains, which at that time were in the process of taking over the Bedford to London St Pancras passenger services, replacing the veteran steam locomotives previously used. Looking back, I believe that I was asked this particular question because, at that time, there had been an incident where a passenger travelling on one of the new trains had pulled a communication cord. After the passenger's problem had been sorted out, a further delay had occurred because the train driver had been unaware of where the reset cord was located. I was lucky because, prior to my interview, I had discussed what had happened with a driver friend of mine, who disclosed the location of the reset cord. (For the record, it was situated in the driving cab, just above the driver's head, to the right of where he sat whilst working the train). My examination and interviews were successful and, following the results, I was appointed to the position of Relief Station Master (Class 3), the date in question being March 25th 1963, and my home 'base' being Bedford Midland Road.

At this moment in time, the grading system for Relief Station Masters was divided into three sections. Special Class RSMs looked after duties located at major stations, for example London St Pancras, Leicester and Derby. Class One RSMs covered (in my area) Bedford Midland, Luton, St Albans City, the freight managers at both London St Pancras and Brent, together with the depot manager based at Cricklewood Carriage Sidings. Class Three RSMs were used to cover all other stations, this including the numerous operating clerk positions. In practice, Class One and Three RSMs intermixed, depending on what cover was required and the availability of particular staff.

Although I was officially titled 'Relief Station Master', I was expected to cover a wide miscellany of jobs and positions. Examples of these occupations included operating clerks who were situated at Bedford, Luton, St Albans City and London St Pancras. In addition, the pool of RSMs found themselves acting as clerical staff in different 'freight yard masters' offices, these facilities being found at Brent and St Pancras Goods Depots, together

Picture 33 Flitwick signal box. The author made daily visits to this location (P.Butler).

__Picture 34__ Ampthill signal box. The author would make weekly visits here in the course of his work. Signalman G. King looks out of the window (B. Cross Collection).

with the Yard Master's office at nearby Cricklewood Carriage Depot. (One of the main functions of the freight yard masters office was to deal with all personnel-related matters to do with staff based in the yard in question and also freight train guards, these including turns of duty, leave, pay and discipline-type situations. The office also doubled up as a booking on point for the guards. In addition, records were kept of all traffic movements both into and out of the yard). As well as this variety of posts, at weekends the RSMs would be utilised as Operating Inspectors on engineering work. During my time in this role, I personally covered two further positions, the first of these being a Junior District Signalman's Inspector at Bedford, and the second, in complete contrast, being a Yard Master at the previously mentioned Cricklewood Carriage Depot. For some reason which now escapes me, I also found myself on duty on various Saturdays at Wembley Central (which was located on the main line running north from London Euston), this being on occasions when major sporting events were held at the old Wembley Stadium. In the fullness of time, I deputised for station masters at all the stations along the Midland main line from Bedford to Kentish Town. (I even had periods of time working within both the operating and parcels offices at London St Pancras). I carried out the same duties at Bedford St Johns, Millbrook, Woburn Sands and Fenny Stratford, all of which were situated on the Bedford to Bletchley route. It is good to know that all these stations remain in use to this day.

Before commencing my new duties, I had a week's training with one of the senior RSMs, who was working at Radlett station, just south of St Albans City. He gave me much useful advice, one such valuable lesson being that if any incident should occur, it was best not to rush straight into dealing with what had happened, but to stand back, and weigh up all the pros and cons before making any decisions. However, it was also necessary to bear in mind that the well-being of the railway was to come first and, in the case of derailments (as an example), the prime task as an RSM was to get the trains moving again as soon as possible. I was to find that my new job contained much variety, and that I had many unusual situations to deal with. Sadly, during my first six months as a relief RSM, I encountered no less than three fatalities, two of which were fellow railwaymen.

Once I had finished my training at Radlett, my first job as a fully qualified RSM was at Flitwick, which was situated south of Bedford on the Midland main line between Ampthill and Harlington. Here, the regular station master was on annual leave for a fortnight. In those days, the Flitwick station master had a dual role, as he also acted as the station's goods agent (as far as grades went, the goods agent would be the equivalent of a station master). In addition, the station master had a considerable number of staff serving underneath him, these consisting of a booking clerk, a goods office clerk, early and late turn porters, together with no fewer than nine signalmen, who were split equally between Ampthill, Millbrook and Flitwick signal boxes. At this time, Ampthill still possessed a goods yard which was used for the removal by rail of ex-Army vehicles, including tanks. At Flitwick, as well as the regular passengers, a considerable amount of parcels traffic, both for distribution and collection, was dealt with at the station. A road van that was normally based at Bletchley took care of consignments that arrived at Flitwick for delivery around the local area, and would then bring back in traffic for despatch. Only small packages of livestock and other odd parcels were collected from the station. Other duties that I covered in my role as Flitwick RSM included overseeing the booking office when the regular clerk was taking tea and meal breaks – here my previous experience working at the booking office at Bedford came in extremely useful. In addition, I answered passenger queries, both face-to-face and via the telephone. Another one of my duties involved making not only a daily visit to Flitwick signal box, but also weekly ones to both Ampthill and Millbrook – the latter being a location which I knew very well from my period of time working there. There were other tasks which to the untrained eye might seem nothing to do with the general running of a railway station, but which I was expected to undertake. One such job was to visit tradesmen in the area adjacent to Flitwick, the idea being to generate business from them for the railway, both passenger and especially freight. Working as an RSM also meant that you would be 'on call' on alternative weeks with the station masters working at the stations either side of whichever location you happened to be covering. The idea of this particular arrangement was that you were available to sort out incidents that occurred outside normal working hours.

A number of unusual situations that occurred during this period of time still spring easily to my mind, around fifty years after they happened. One such problem arose as the result of a telephone call that I received one day from a locally based GP. He informed me that there were a series of 'deadly nightshade' bushes growing beside the railway line in the area near to Ampthill. As he considered that they were a danger to children living in the locality, he demanded that the railway should take responsibility for moving them. In the course of our phone conversation, I pointed out that the said bushes were situated in a farmer's field, outside the railway boundary fence, which was metal. This meant that the farmer would be responsible for moving them, rather than the railway authorities. However, the doctor still stuck to his original stance, insisting that the railway remove the offending bushes, going on to state that if I would do nothing about it, then he would report me to my superiors. It would seem that if he did indeed report me, his argument must have fallen on stony ground, as I heard no more about this problem.

Another incident involving land located adjacent to the railway concerned a couple of donkeys which from time to time kept getting onto the running lines. A local individual rented a piece of ground near to Ampthill, within which the two donkeys resided. It seemed that the grass on the railway side of the boundary fence situated there was of a more tasty variety than that in the field itself, and as a result the animals kept breaking through onto railway property. Of course, when this happened, it caused delays to the main line services. Eventually, after a long drawn out argument, the field's owner was persuaded to move his donkeys away from the area, and onto pastures new.

The other animal-related incident, which was rather amusing, and which happened during my time at Flitwick, came about as the result of a local public house selling off 'Broiler' hens, the only condition being that the new owner had to kill them and then pluck them. I should mention at this point that a broiler hen was one that would have been kept for laying eggs, rather than for eating, and which was coming to the end of its laying days. I was lucky in that I had a relief signalman who was covering the early turn at

Flitwick signal box, and who in his spare time kept a smallholding. Having procured one of the said hens myself, I asked him if, once he had finished his turn of duty, he would do the necessary killing and plucking for me. There was a coal bunker situated at the end of the 'down' fast platform at Flitwick (for trains running north from London), and it was here that my signalman colleague decided to do the plucking. It was most unfortunate for him that, when he had almost finished his grisly task, a north-bound express passenger train thundered past, the feathers concerned flying everywhere as a result. To this day, I do not know what any waiting passengers witnessing this somewhat unusual activity thought was taking place!

A much more serious incident that I was required to deal with in the course of my normal duties took place on a Saturday afternoon, the exact date being October 10th 1964. On the day in question, I was supervising train movements in Ampthill Yard, this being in connection with the loading of surplus Army tanks. Whilst carrying out this task, I received a message stating that a diesel multiple unit train had caught fire at Wilshampstead and that, unfortunately, a female passenger had for some unknown reason jumped from the train and had lost her life as a result. The District Operating Superintendent (DOS), Mr J.C.R. Rogers, contacted me from Bedford Midland Road, and asked me to board the next north-bound train from Ampthill station as far as Millbrook, carefully examining the track in order to see whether there were any parts that could have detached themselves from the diesel train in question. Mr Rogers himself was carrying out a similar exercise between Bedford and Millbrook, and as a result of his investigations, he found the broken driveshaft that had caused the fire, the errant article being located just north of Millbrook. On having completed my part of the task (and having found nothing of value), I then checked the train register (this was used to record all movements and incidents within the said signal box's area – in addition it was where all signalmen signed on and off duty) and found that the signalman at Wilshampstead signal box had failed to send the 'obstruction danger signal'; this was something he should have carried out when it was obvious there was an obstruction of the line. This was a duty that was laid down in the railway rules and regulations – failure to carry out this procedure could have put those dealing with the broken-down train in severe danger of being hit by other trains on the adjacent lines. At the subsequent enquiry that was held about the incident, this very point was raised by the Investigation Officer, as a result of which the signalman in question was severely reprimanded for his omission. This was the fourth fatality that I had been involved with during my time as an RSM. As mentioned earlier, the first three occurred during the six month period that followed my promotion into the RSM grade, the locations being Scratchwood Sidings (these being situated between Elstree and Mill Hill), Harlington station and Luton station. I mentioned earlier that there was much variety in my latest role – however, these unfortunate deaths were variety that I could do without.

Relief Station Master memories – Station by Station

As stated previously, during my period of time working as a Relief Station Master (RSM) along the Midland main line, I was called upon to deputise for permanent station masters at a wide variety of locations throughout my designated area. Each station, large or small, was different to its neighbours. I will relate some of the ways in which each station covered its operating obligations later in this chapter. Before that however, I would like to give a little of the background to what was happening on the railways in general, and also to highlight some more of the seemingly never-ending miscellany of tasks that RSMs were not only asked to do, but expected to carry out as part of a normal working day.

The 1960s were a time of great change on the railway network. To the general public, the most obvious change was the elimination of steam locomotives, and their replacement by diesel and electric traction. Another indication of the fact that the 'old' railway was fading into history was the closure of many miles of line, in particular amongst the branch line network of the nation. A change that was going on 'behind the scenes' was one that directly affected me in my work as an RSM. This was the setting up of the new 'Area Manager' organisations. Previously, each station had functioned as a more-or-less self-contained operation, each with its own station master (SM) and a miscellany of staff working for the SM. The new area manager tier of organisation was usually located at the biggest station within a designated geographical area, the higher managers being based in the Area Manager's office (or area headquarters), whilst the stations became devoid of their station masters, the staff concerned coming underneath a station supervisor. Such a move was designed to streamline the railway organisation, trim 'red tape' and eliminate duplication of staff.

The setting up of these 'areas' involved a period of consultation with the railway staff involved. As far as those consultations taking place on the southern end of the Midland main line were concerned, I found myself working as an RSM for short periods of time in odd locations, bridging the gap between the end of the old station master type set-up and the starting of the new area manager organisations. For example, in addition to my work on the Midland main line, I worked for short periods of a few days covering Gospel Oak and West Hampstead stations, both of which were situated on the North London line between Broad Street and Richmond. On the Bedford to Bletchley branch line, I was requested to work at Woburn Sands, this being when the permanent station masters at both Woburn Sands and Millbrook were moving to their new positions, the former within the Watford set-up, and the latter becoming part of the Luton area. I spent no less than six months at Woburn Sands, a task which, during the last month, involved overseeing Millbrook. Not long afterwards, I carried out a similar 'caretaker' role, this time looking after both Hendon and Mill Hill. Here my main task was to oversee (from an operational point of view) the work that was taking place next to the running lines in conjunction with the building of the London extension of the M1 Motorway.

No matter what station you were working at, as an RSM there were a number of tasks that were carried out as routine. One such job was the rostering of the staff working underneath you, making sure that all the shifts that were required to keep the station working were covered, utilising the available personnel in the most constructive way. Another role that you were required to do was to visit your station's signal box on a daily basis, and other affiliated boxes (such as those at Ampthill and Millbrook, mentioned previously, which were part of my domain at Flitwick) had to be paid a visit, either on alternate days, or even just once a week, depending on the location. As mentioned before, as an RSM, depending on where you were covering the regular station master, you could find yourself 'on call', looking after out of hours emergencies for two to three weeks running at a time. However, it was usually the case that one of the neighbouring permanent station masters would cover for you, should you have something special on.

Some of the more unusual tasks that I carried out on many occasions took place at stations that did not have their own chief clerks working in their respective booking offices. Clerks of this particular grade were only found at the largest stations along the southern end of the Midland, these being London St Pancras, St Albans City, Luton and Bedford Midland. In their absence, one such task that I carried out on a daily basis was the transporting of a day's takings from the station to the local bank. In addition, on each and every Friday, I also had to draw the staff wages (again from the local bank) and obtain the National Insurance stamps, also for the staff, from the nearby post office. When I carried out this duty at Cricklewood, I could find myself carrying between £6000 and £7000 at a time, fortunately with the aid of a plain clothes policeman. At all the other stations, the money carried totalled hundreds of pounds: on these occasions, I walked by myself.

I have set out below special events and unusual happenings that occurred at each of the following stations, all of which I covered in my role as an RSM. I worked at these locations at various different times and, as such, what I am about to describe is not set out in the order in which they happened. However, I have laid out the stations in their correct geographical order, heading north from London St Pancras on the Midland main line.

LONDON ST PANCRAS

I found myself covering a miscellany of positions in the regular station master's office at London St Pancras, usually during the week leading up to Christmas. I generally found that, for me, the busiest day of all was Christmas Eve. On that day, after lunchtime, all the temporary staff (these in the main being students who had been working at the special parcel post depot at Kentish Town) had to be paid off and their National Insurance cards stamped, a tax certificate being issued to them at the same time. During this part of the day, I had to undertake this work by myself, as the regular members of the station staff had all gone out for a Christmas drink. The arrangement that I had was, having dealt with the business surrounding the casual staff, and once the regulars returned to work (after the pubs had shut, usually around 15.00), I was able to finish my shift earlier than rostered. On a subsequent occasion, when I was no longer required to work at St Pancras as an RSM, I was temporarily put in charge of a parcels office that had been specially opened during the time when neighbouring Euston station was being rebuilt, and my office, together with Marylebone, looked after all of Euston's parcels traffic.

KENTISH TOWN

On the occasions when I covered the regular station master, I found that one of my main duties was to pay regular visits to the large number of signal boxes located in the immediate area of the station. From the north, these were as follows: Carlton Road, Engine Shed Junction, Kentish Town Junction, Kentish Town West and Islip Street. In addition, I also needed to keep an eye on the activities of Mortimer Street, which was situated on the branch line to Junction Road Junction. As well as the regular passenger and freight movements, Kentish Town also dealt with a considerable amount of homing pigeon traffic, something which is no longer seen on the modern railway. The birds themselves would arrive in special trains from the north of England, be released on arrival at the station and then the empty baskets would be returned to their senders. To the best of my knowledge, I have been unable to ascertain why Kentish Town was chosen as a base for this unusual activity. Another victim of changing railway working patterns has been the decline of mail trains, for many years a source of considerable revenue. At Kentish Town, during each and every Christmas, the former cattle dock sidings would be utilised as a temporary GPO mail depot, for receiving, sorting and despatching letters and parcels.

WEST HAMPSTEAD

Many of the stations in this southern-most part of the former Midland Railway main line were opened in 1868 at the time when the Midland's London extension finally reached its goal. However, West Hampstead did not come into operation until 1871. It was constructed by the Midland to serve a newly built hamlet that was evolving in the locality, this being known as West End. The original name of the new station was indeed West End, this title being amended to West End and Brondesbury in 1904 and, a year later, the present name was adopted. When I worked as an RSM at West Hampstead, not only was I responsible for the safe running of the passenger station, but also for the wellbeing of nearby West End Sidings and the Finchley Road loading sidings. I mentioned in a previous chapter about a daily rubbish train that travelled from London to Inns Sidings, at Sundon. West End and Finchley Road sidings were the starting point for this dirty, but necessary working. One of my many duties was to sort out the paperwork generated by these workings.

My 'patch' also included a fair number of signal boxes (in the days before technology allowed a few large signal or 'power boxes' to take over the duties of the many smaller establishments), the ones around West Hampstead including Finchley Road, West End Lane and West Hampstead itself. The West End Sidings had a connection into a further set of sidings, serving the adjacent Cadbury factory. As can be imagined there was a considerable amount of traffic generated by this famous company, which arrived from Bournville. One day, whilst paying a visit to West End Sidings, I found a number of boxes of Cadbury chocolates and chocolate bars under a bridge abutment leading into their depot. It appeared that someone had obviously stolen them and hidden them away, ready to move at a later moment in time. I made my way to the Cadbury office, and reported my finding to the depot manager. To my surprise, he mentioned merely to, "leave it with me." I thought at the time that he might at least have offered me a bar of chocolate for advising him of what I had found, but he never did. Thinking about it subsequently, the chocolate may well have been put where it was deliberately, in order to catch someone who was stealing this traffic on a regular basis. Who knows?

The booking office at West Hampstead was fortunate as it possessed a lovely open coal fire. This reminds me of a silly thing that I did once on a Friday – this being the day set aside for making up the staff insurance cards. On this particular occasion, I had earlier procured the National Insurance stamps from the local post office; once I returned to the station, I began the task of sticking them to the insurance cards. Typically, as I was engaged on this important task, I was called away to attend to another duty. For safety's sake, I decided to put the remaining stamps in a bank cash bag. In those days, bank cash bags were not transparent, and this was very nearly my downfall. Returning to the booking office after finishing the secondary task, I saw this particular cash bag and, thinking it was empty, threw it on the coal fire! Fortunately, I suddenly realised that there were still stamps inside it, and I managed to pull it out of the fire in the nick of time. I was lucky insomuch as only two N.I. stamps had been scorched – however, I then had to purchase replacement stamps out of my own pocket!

CRICKLEWOOD

From when it was opened to traffic in 1868, Cricklewood was known as Childs Hill and Cricklewood, and this situation lasted until 1903 when it was shortened to its present day name. Cricklewood was also home to a large motive power depot, the first part of which was completed in 1882, and a marshalling yard. For many years, this was 'journey's end' for the common coal trains that made their way down from Toton, near to Nottingham. From 1927 until the late 1950s, many of these immense trains were worked by the thirty-three members of the London Midland and Scottish Railway (LMSR) 'Garrett' class steam locomotives, these possessing an unusual 2-6-0 + 0-6-2 wheel arrangement. Although popular on railways in numerous parts of the world (a fair proportion of which were constructed by the various British private railway locomotive builders), 'Garretts' were very rare in Britain, the LMSR examples forming easily the largest class of their type.

As with Kentish Town and West Hampstead, signal box visits took up a large part of my time here, working as an RSM. Coming from the north of London, in geographical order, these were Brent Numbers 1 and 2, Cricklewood itself and Watling Street on the main line, whilst on the branch line that ran from Cricklewood to Acton Wells Junction on the

North London Line, there was Dudden Hill, Neasden, Harlesden and Acton Canal Wharf. From Acton Wells, trains could either 'turn' right at the junction to join the Great Western system at Acton, or continue straight on to South Acton Junction, where they would then head to Kew East Junction – here the trains in question could access the south-west division of the Southern Region. Mention of these latter three boxes reminds me of a highly embarrassing moment that occurred one day around this time. To get to the boxes in question, I travelled on the footplate of a local freight service, which ran from Brent to Acton. The first time that I did this, I noticed that we were passing some rather run-down looking 'two up and two down' terraced houses. Without thinking, I mentioned to the train driver that there was no way that I could live there, whereupon he pointed out one of these dwellings, stating that he resided there! I felt about an inch tall, and was most profuse in my apologies. Needless to say, I did not attempt to get a lift back from this train on its return journey!

I mentioned previously that one of my less well publicised roles was to collect the money from a local bank that would then be made up into staff wages. On the commercial side of my duties, Friday was the major day when this happened. At 09.00 a plain clothes British Transport (or BTP) policeman would join me and we would walk along Cricklewood Broadway to the bank in question, and collect the monies (or rather the notes). Usually, I found that I would be carrying between £6000 and £7000 back to the station about my person. This money would then be used to make up the pay packets of all the staff in all the departments within the Cricklewood area, these including personnel working in the carriage sheds, the freight yards and the locomotive department. I had the help of clerks from both the freight yards and carriage sheds to assist me in making up the wage packets. In addition, change from ticket sales would be kept in the booking office for a period of one week, and used for the payment of wages.

HENDON

As with many of the stations listed in this section, Hendon was originally opened by the Midland Railway in 1868, as part of its extension into London St Pancras. During my time working there it was a very busy station with regards to parcels traffic. There were no fewer than four or five road lorries used to deliver incoming parcels to their end destinations in the area surrounding the station, these vans then being utilised for outward-bound traffic, all of this happening within the course of each single working day. As regards signal boxes, I had only two to look after, these being the station box and Silkstream Junction Box, the latter being situated on the slow line between Mill Hill and Hendon. It controlled train movements on and off the goods lines, together with just the slow lines. These goods lines crossed over both slow and fast lines, and were located on the right hand side of the fast lines going towards London. Hendon was also the starting point for a special freight train service called the 'Condor' (the word 'Condor' being short for 'Container Door to Door' traffic), this being a forerunner of the more recent 'Freightliner' trains that can now be seen all over the domestic railway network. This train ran daily between Monday and Friday, commencing its journey each evening, and running as far as Gallashields, near to Glasgow, returning the following morning. It conveyed produce from the numerous factories that were situated in North-West London. Motive power for these trains was generally a pair of class 28 diesels. There were only twenty of these machines built. They were very unreliable from a mechanical point of view and, after the early demise of the 'Condor', were reallocated to the Cumbrian Coast line, which ran from Carlisle to Carnforth, via Workington and Barrow-in-Furness. They met an early demise, although a single example, D5705, escaped the cutter's torch, and is now being restored on the heritage East Lancs Railway.

I was present at the final run of the 'Condor', when a special send-off was arranged. The factory produce that was the Condor's staple diet had declined and the service was brought to an end. Later on, BR tried a similar experiment, with a new working called the 'Tartan Arrow Service'. A terminal was constructed and opened at Kentish Town for the new train, which was an overnight express parcels service running from London to Scotland.

Whilst covering Hendon, I was involved in the making of a security film by the Post Office (or GPO), and I was even fortunate enough to have a small part. The production itself was made for internal viewing by GPO staff. It was designed to make them more security-aware and urging them to be more protective of the work that they were doing. My role took place at the start of the film when the first shots depicted a parcels train arriving on the 'up goods' platform at Hendon. Following this, the GPO traffic carried was then unloaded onto barrows. At this point, I had to walk along the platform, wishing everyone, "Good Morning," and asking if everything was okay. The next scene showed a GPO van being loaded within the parcels depot, an operation that was being watched by a member of a gang who were going to rob the vehicle en-route to the nearby GPO depot. His job was to tell his fellow robbers when the van had set out on its journey. To ensure that the van had a clear road when leaving the railway depot, the film crew 'tipped' a lollypop lady, whose job it was to stop the traffic on the main road passing the depot. This took either three or four takes, which was quite amusing to see.

Picture 35 A scene from the GPO security film 'Mad Thursday'. The author is seen on the right of the picture in his railway uniform (Author's collection).

On the final Saturday of the filming, as well as keeping an eye on the goings-on with the GPO staff, I found myself also having to deal with a derailment elsewhere in the yard. Much of my working day was spent to-ing and fro-ing between film and derailment! I have to admit that I have never seen a copy of this particular film, although I do have some stills in my possession. If anybody reading this book knows if and where a copy of this production still exists, I would be very interested to know. If contact could please be made via the publishers, I would be extremely grateful.

MILL HILL

This station (which was opened in 1868, being known simply as Mill Hill until 1950, when it was renamed Mill Hill Broadway) was a very busy suburban passenger station, and the majority of its takings were made from this traffic. Things got extra busy when a nearby boarding school was 'breaking up' for holidays, and the pupils were returning to their respective homes. What would normally happen was that a day or two before the end of each term, the booking clerk would visit the school and sell all the required tickets in advance. At the same time, all luggage would be collected, taken to the station and sent to their individual destinations.

An unusual feature of Mill Hill at this time was the double-framed signal box that was in situ here. Because of the space that was available between the fast and slow running lines, the signal lever frames were built at an angle to each other, instead of one directly behind the other, as was the case in most boxes. I mentioned previously about the work of the Operating Inspectors who looked after what was happening with the construction work taking place on the adjacent M1 Motorway. During my time at Mill Hill, this work made up the bulk of my daily activities.

I recall that, one Christmas Eve, major problems came about as the result of a derailment that had occurred at Islip Street, which was just to the south of Kentish Town, the outcome being that all four running lines were blocked by debris. This brought all services to a standstill. At the time that this happened, a St Pancras-bound express train was standing at the Mill Hill home signal. The train was then drawn forward into the station itself, my staff and myself then setting about the major task of detraining all the passengers and their luggage. It was fortunate that Mill Hill bus station was situated directly underneath the railway station. We made sure that all the passengers caught buses that were heading for Edgware from where they could transfer to the Northern Line of the London Underground, this route then taking them directly into central London.

ELSTREE

On being opened by the Midland Railway in 1868, this station was known simply as 'Elstree'. In 1950, after nationalisation, it was renamed 'Elstree and Borehamwood', and in 1959 it was rebuilt to a more modern design and layout. As with Mill Hill, I remember that it was a very busy station as regards local passenger traffic. There were booking offices situated on both sides of the station, the respective platforms being joined by a connecting footbridge. Problems were caused to the running of the train service by children who lived on a housing estate that was located adjacent to the London-bound 'slow' line. These individuals used the railway as a short cut to the fields on the opposite side of the tracks; in addition, they were on occasions, not only crossing the tracks in front of trains, but throwing stones at the trains themselves. This problem was worst at weekends and during the school holidays. When such an incident occurred, and it was reported by a driver, all services had to be run at 'caution' until it was confirmed that all lines were clear of unwelcome intruders. The problem only eased off after a series of operations involving high profile police presence.

During my time at Elstree deputising for the resident station master, I was involved in the arrest of one of the booking clerks who, it was discovered, was taking individual tickets from the racks of tickets that were not to be sold in the immediate future, selling them and pocketing the money. In theory, when the right time came to sell one of these tickets, he would put back some of the money that he had stolen, and report the loss of a smaller value ticket. In addition this clerk had also been falsifying cash returns. He had been under suspicion for some time and, while I was there, the local British Transport Police (BTP) decided to set a trap for him. I was asked to call him over to my office on a separate matter; however, he must have guessed what was happening, because he made to go to the lavatory on his way, but was prevented from doing so by a plain-clothes BTP officer. On arrival, he was confronted by the BTP, and a marked ticket (the trap in question) was found on his person. It was fortunate for me that he admitted what he had been doing and pleaded guilty. This meant that I was not expected or required to go to court and give evidence.

RADLETT

Radlett, together with Harpenden, was known for the many 'Senior City Gents' who used its services to commute to their places of work in London. Bowler hats and rolled up umbrellas were the norm. I had a most embarrassing experience here on the occasion of the very first day that I was deputising for the resident station master. I was aware of the fact that I had to see out the 08.15 departure to Moorgate and, prior to this, I had arrived at the station in good time, left my briefcase in my office, donned my station master's hat and made my way to the appropriate platform. I had hardly got onto the platform when a bowler-hatted 'Senior City Gent' came up to me and said, "That's a damn stupid poster you have up in the booking office." Having no idea what he was referring to, or having seen the offending article, I replied to the effect that I was sure that it would have been okayed by the railway publicity department before it was put on public display. The 'gent' then carried on his line of conversation, stating that the government were trying to cut down on crime (in particular burglary), but that the railway were undermining things by displaying inappropriate posters, such as the one in my booking office. It was fortunate that at that moment, the 08.15 train ran into the station, before I had to think of another answer. I then decided to study the errant poster for myself. It depicted a row of suburban houses. On one of these houses, there were two bottles of milk on the doorstep, a newspaper in the letterbox, and a cat resting on one of the window ledges. The caption for the poster was 'They have gone out for the day – why not join them on one of our *Awayday* tickets'.

Needless to say, I kept out of the way of my angry passenger for the rest of that week.

CHAPTER TEN

MY DAYS AS A RELIEF STATION MASTER
Part Two

As I mentioned earlier in this part of my story, talking about my time as a Relief Station Master (RSM), my 'base' was Bedford Midland and therefore I was rostered to cover at many stations between there and London St Pancras. In this new chapter, I have included some anecdotes about life working at those establishments in the northern part of the southern section of the Midland main line, together with the secondary route between Bedford Midland and Bletchley.

ST ALBANS CITY
Today St Albans City station has been shortened to plain 'St Albans'. For many years it was the biggest of three stations in the city, the others being St Albans Abbey, which still remains the terminus of the branch line from Watford Junction, and London Road, which was on the route between St Albans Abbey and Hatfield. Although the last section of this latter branch was closed in 1968, most of the trackbed has been turned into a public footpath, whilst the main building at London Road station has been refurbished and now serves as office accommodation. The majority of my time at St Albans City was spent covering the station's operating clerk and, on odd occasions, the permanent station master. The former had a miscellany of tasks to undertake, including sorting operating-type correspondence, rostering staff, dealing with paybill matters, updating staff discipline records and producing annual leave rosters. When I covered the latter position, I discovered that I had no fewer than four signal boxes under my care. These were located at Sandridge, St Albans North, St Albans South and Napsbury. It is good to know that St Albans South has now been preserved by a local group of volunteers, and much good work has been carried out, restoring it to its former glory.

HARPENDEN
When working as an RSM at Harpenden, one needed to have good legs as

not only were you responsible for the well-being of the Midland station, but also Harpenden East, which had originally been built by the Great Northern Railway, and which served that company's cross-country branch between Hatfield, Luton and Dunstable, the latter location being where it formed a connection with the London & North Western Railway's route to Leighton Buzzard. It was a mighty long way to walk between the two Harpenden stations. I was required to pay a visit to Harpenden East on only one day per week unless an emergency of some kind came about which required my attention. Matters of a routine nature were dealt with by the resident station clerk. I also had to keep an eye on the goings-on at Harpenden Junction signal box, which again was a long walk from the Midland station.

Harpenden was also the starting point of the branch line to Hemel Hempstead, which has become known within railway history as the 'Nickey Line', although the origins of this unusual name have been debated by historians ever since the line first opened in July 1877. It had lost its passenger service as early as 1947 due to a gradual decline in receipts and increased bus competition. Freight traffic lingered on after this date, although by the time that I began working as an RSM at Harpenden, the section of line between Redbourn and Heath Park Halt (which was just beyond Hemel Hempstead, and the terminus of the branch) had been closed to all traffic for two years, even though the track was still in situ. Rather naughtily on one occasion I, together with Sam Newbold the local goods guard, and the two-man crew of a class 25 diesel locomotive, made an unofficial journey to Heath Park from Harpenden, the whole situation arising because I had previously mentioned to Sam that I had never travelled over the line. During our journey we had to push our way through young saplings that were growing in the four-foot section of track between the two rails, and lift a whole series of level crossing and farm gates off their respective hinges, this being because, since the closure these gates had been closed against the defunct railway line. We completed our round trip and arrived back at Harpenden more-or-less in one piece. I was grateful for this: should the diesel have become derailed, we would all have been sacked!

LUTON

The majority of the time that I spent at Luton (which for some years was known as Luton Midland Road to distinguish it from nearby Luton Bute Street, the latter being on the same branch line as Harpenden East) was utilised in covering the permanent Operations Clerk. This post involved working on a miscellany of tasks other than purely operating matters. Each Monday was spent on working out and balancing the station staff wages paybill, whilst every other Tuesday was set aside for the task of completing the salaried staff paybill. I also found myself calculating bonus payments for not only the platform and parcel porters, but their supervisors as well.

In addition to my work at Luton Midland Road, I also spent a week covering the duties of the Goods/Parcels Clerk who was based at Luton Bute Street. During this particular week, a 350 horse-power 0-6-0 diesel engine became derailed whilst shunting the station yard. I was working in the operating office when this occurred and I was asked by Mr Dennis (who was the permanent station master at Luton Midland Road) to deal with this derailment, having previously confirmed that I was not too busy. He was of the opinion that to sort out the problems caused by the derailment would be good experience for me. Once the breakdown vans had arrived from Hornsey Depot, and I had them positioned correctly, it did not take too long for them to rerail the unfortunate diesel. One of my tasks, as the 'on-the-spot' representative of the operating department was to establish the cause of the derailment. After speaking to various parties, the Permanent Way Department (the section tasked with looking after the well-being of the railway lines) accepted that the derailment had been caused by a track defect.

LEAGRAVE

Leagrave was normally a quiet station except for the single fortnight each year when the workforce from the Vauxhall Motors factory based at Luton took its annual holiday. Leagrave was the starting point on the first Saturday morning of the fortnight for a number of holiday special trains heading off to various resorts, conveying parties of Vauxhall employees to all points of the compass. This meant that, during the week leading up to the Saturday, the station staff would be busy with people sending luggage in advance. In addition, on the preceding Friday evening, the booking office stayed open to a later than normal hour so that Vauxhall employees could buy their travel tickets, having previously collected their holiday pay. This was so that they merely had the task of catching their particular train, all of which left Leagrave early on the following Saturday morning. As a result of this activity, arrangements were made with the local bank for them to open on the same Saturday so that all the money could be safely deposited.

HARLINGTON

Picture 36 Harlington station during the early 1960s, looking north (Author).

When I attended Harlington in my capacity as an RSM, I discovered that, unlike Flitwick for example, Harlington did not possess its own permanent goods clerk. This meant that in addition to the normal station-type duties, I had to sort out all the paperwork that related to all goods traffic dealt with by the station, in particular the daily rubbish train which commenced its journey at Finchley Road in London, to the Inns Sidings at Sundon, a total of some forty wagons per day. The Sundon Cement Works also had a small amount of traffic going into and out of its premises at this time. The details of all freight traffic was brought to me by the porter/shunter who was on duty at the time. I can recall that I often had to cover Harlington at short notice. The reason for this was that Mr Alf Armitage, the regular station master, had had the misfortune of being the signalman on duty in the Harrow & Wealdstone 'Number 1' signal box at the time of the infamous double-collision in October 1952, as a result of which no fewer than 112 people lost their lives. Unfortunately he suffered from nightmares about the accident and, as such, often had to take sick leave without too much warning.

THE BEDFORD TO BLETCHLEY BRANCH
The origins of this particular railway route (which is still very much alive

and well to this day, being run by the 'London Midland' train operating company) go back as far as 1846, when it was first opened. By July 1862 it had become the central section of the important seventy-seven mile long cross-country line between Oxford and Cambridge. However, both the Bletchley–Oxford and Bedford–Cambridge sections were closed in the late 1960s due to falling traffic receipts.

The first time that I worked on this line was to cover the regular station master at Bedford St Johns, the first establishment on the route after leaving Bedford Midland. This was for a short period of only two days whilst my colleague attended meetings held in connection with the forthcoming area manager re-organisation. During my short time there, I managed to take the ticket money cash to the wrong branch of the local bank. This was because I misunderstood the directions that had been given to me by the booking clerk. Having finally deposited the money safely, I subsequently discovered that it did get into the right account, but took a few days to do so. Fortunately, no harm was done.

WOBURN SANDS

As I mentioned previously, when the permanent station master (SM) at

Picture 37 *Woburn Sands signal box, looking towards Bedford, and depicting the adjacent level crossing (Author).*

Woburn Sands took up his new position in the Watford Area Manager Organisation, I was asked to cover the SM vacancy for a period of no less than six months during the mid-1960s. My responsibilities included not only Woburn Sands itself, but also Bow Brickhill Crossing, Apsley Guise, Berry Lane Crossing and Ridgemont. In contrast to the situation today, where all stations along the branch itself (apart from both Bedford and Bletchley) are unmanned, I had a number of staff working for me at Woburn Sands – these consisting of both early and late turn porters, together with a goods clerk, a goods porter and two signalmen. Parcel traffic was large enough to warrant a road vehicle coming from Bletchley and delivering consignments to customers in the neighbourhood. Other staff which came under my control included crossing keepers at both Bow

Picture 38 *The newly restored station building at Ridgemont. Note that the signal frame is no longer in situ, having been replaced by a signal panel at the same location (Author).*

Brickhill and Apsley Guise, together with 'out of hours' crossing keepers at Apsley Guise and Berry Lane. In addition there was also a relief crossing keeper. Ridgemont station also had a full complement of staff – these were made up of a porter, two signalmen and a goods shunter. I can recall that, with no less than four different categories of crossing keeper under my control, it was quite a job working out their weekly wages!

By this time steam traction had been displaced by more modern machines. All passenger services were operated by diesel multiple units, whilst the parcels and pick-up goods trains (as well as those freight workings run for the benefit of both Stewartby and Ridgemont Brickworks) were all hauled by diesel locomotives. As I have already mentioned, I had a fair number of staff under my control with whom I established an excellent rapport. In addition, I also got to know many of the train crews that worked the line. I can honestly say that I thoroughly enjoyed my time working at Woburn Sands. I can still recall some of the good and unusual things that happened to me during this period of time. For example, on one of the weekday signalling shifts at Woburn Sands at 10.30, both myself and the goods porter would join the signalman on duty for a cup of tea and a piece of treacle tart, which the porter had previously procured from a cake shop situated not too far from the station.

At Apsley Guise, the resident crossing keeper and his wife had previously lived at Buckie, in the North-East part of Scotland. They moved from Buckie to Buckinghamshire after the Second World War and had made a new home in the railway crossing house, also at Apsley Guise. They possessed a large garden, within which they kept both chickens and geese. On the run-up to one Christmas, I was offered the chance to purchase one of their geese in order to make an appropriate dinner. I accepted their kind offer, and subsequently found myself on Christmas Eve in their kitchen sat on a chair, being offered a 'wee dram', whilst plucking the bird's feathers into a tin bath!

My goods clerk was a keen gardener in his spare time. He once offered me a clump of Michaelmas daisies for my own garden. You can imagine my surprise when, whilst handing them over to me he said, "That'll be two shillings please." I was told afterwards by a third party that he was a real skinflint!

Unfortunately there were also some unpleasant tasks to perform within my RSM role. One such occasion presented itself when I received a phone call one morning from the Bletchley police, stating that the former station master's father-in-law had just collapsed and died suddenly in a nearby street. I was asked if I could go to the station house and break the news to the former station master's wife, then requesting that she should accompany a policeman to her mother's house, to tell her what had happened. When I knocked on the door of the former station master's house, who should answer the door, but the wife's mother. Before I could say a word she said, "It's my husband, isn't it?" This was a duty that you wouldn't wish to do if you could help it.

On a far happier note, the most pleasant happening during this time was the retirement celebration of Sam, the goods porter at Woburn Sands, this taking place on the occasion of his seventieth birthday. Apart from a spell in the military forces during the Second World War, Sam had worked at Woburn Sands for the whole of his life. The local paper reported this momentous event, with a good article being accompanied by a picture of myself handing Sam his retirement gift and long service certificate. Despite his advancing years, Sam was still as fit as a fiddle. Every morning, before having his meal break, he would go for a swim in a nearby lake. He would do this even if it meant having to break a layer of ice before doing so!

During my time at Woburn Sands I found that Friday was a busy day, this being when I would organise the paying of my staff's wages. The day began with a visit to the post office to procure National Insurance stamps, and was followed by a visit to the bank to collect the money involved. I would then return to Woburn Sands to make up the wage packets. Having done this, I then had to get the wages to their rightful owners. I did this by catching a

Picture 39 Millbrook station building on the Bedford – Bletchley branch. This is still in existence, but in private ownership (Author).

train to Bow Brickhill to pay the crossing keeper. I then returned on the corresponding service as far as Apsley Guise, to pay the staff located there. On occasions, I would then walk along the line to Berry Crossing to pay the crossing keeper's wages – sometimes, she would walk up and meet me half way. I would then return to Apsley Guise, take a train to Ridgemont, and pay the staff there. Once I had finished, I would then go into the staff canteen at Ridgemont Brickworks to have lunch with the person there who dealt with the rail traffic. At least I did until one day, whilst having lunch,

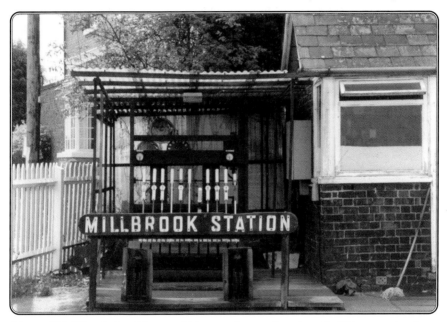

Picture 40 Millbrook signal frame, which was subsequently replaced by Ridgemont signal panel (Author).

one of the directors of the brickworks appeared and, not recognising me, asked who I was. Having told him, he then made it quite clear that he wasn't going to subsidise a railway employee's meal in his canteen!

In order to change this somewhat complex Friday routine, I would sometimes send the cash for both Bow Brickhill and Ridgemont by train in a sealed bag. I would then travel to Apsley Guise by train and pay the wages to the staff there. I would take my bicycle on the train and, once my wage paying duties were completed, make my way up into the village and have lunch in a local public house, before cycling back to Woburn Sands.

As mentioned previously, for the last month of my six months working on the branch, I also took over the running of Millbrook station. Here I had another goods clerk working for me. His main responsibility was to deal with the brick traffic that ran from both Stewartby and Lidlington, together with the inward-bound spent railway ballast, which at that time was being disposed of in a disused clay pit, also at Lidlington. Covering Millbrook meant that I also had responsibility for Kempston Hardwick Halt, Stewartby and Lidlington Stations, together with nearby Forders Sidings and its signal box. Two level crossings were also monitored by myself – these were at Wootton Broadmead and Lidlington, the latter crossing being of the then-new 'half barrier' type.

In addition to my duties at Woburn Sands, my only other time spent as an RSM on the branch was for a two day period of time working at Fenny Stratford (this being situated at the Bletchley end of the line); the duty in question normally being looked after by an RSM from the Euston relief staff.

CHAPTER ELEVEN

PITY THE POOR RSM!

By now the reader will have realised that the typical relief station master (RSM) covered a wide miscellany of duties at a cross-section of locations within his 'home' area. In this latest chapter, I will describe some of the more unusual duties, all of which I covered during the period of time that I worked as an RSM.

In those days, the RSM would be informed of what duties that he would be covering during the following week by means of a phone call on a Thursday afternoon, this call being made by one of the roster clerks that were based in the appropriate Divisional Staff Office. On occasions, you would then get last minute alterations to your duties – however, these were generally the exception, rather than the rule. If I had been on annual leave, I would make a point of calling into Bedford Booking Office on the Sunday evening to get my orders for the following week. I recall that on one such occasion, I was informed that I was required to go to Cricklewood Carriage Depot in order to cover the Depot Manager, Frank Goodchild. I queried whether these were the right instructions – however, I was assured that these were the orders left for me.

Next morning I made my way to Cricklewood, still convinced that Bedford had given me the wrong information. I knew that the Depot Manager's position was a class one grade (it will be remembered that I was a grade three RSM). When I arrived in the depot office, there sat one of the grade one RSMs. I made a comment to the effect of, "Now I know that I was given the wrong information by Bedford – I am in fact required to cover one of the clerical positions." However, my fellow RSM replied that my original orders were correct, and that Frank Goodchild had specifically requested that I cover him. The RSM went on to state that he was quite happy to do a clerk's job, working under me. He mentioned that, although Frank had never asked him to cover the depot manager position, he was not in the least bothered. On my previous visits to this particular location, Frank had been most insistent that I shadow all that he had been doing. I now realised why he had done this.

At that time, Cricklewood was the main carriage servicing depot for the southern end of the Midland main line, together with the suburban services into and out of London St Pancras. The main line stock included one of the premier passenger trains on the route, the 'Thames Clyde Express', together with a trio of overnight sleeper services, one of which went to Leeds, and the other two which travelled up to Scotland. It was the depot manager who was personally responsible for the cleanliness of each of the sleeper trains and that they were fully equipped. In fact, this was the last job that was required to be carried out before going home each evening.

At a depot like Cricklewood there was a very cosmopolitan mixture of staff. In addition, there was a high turnover of both carriage cleaners and shunting staff. In my time at Cricklewood, I found that much of it was spent interviewing new recruits and with matters of discipline. I am pleased to say that I didn't let Frank down, and that there were no complaints about the cleanliness of the passenger trains during my fortnight in charge of the depot.

In contrast to the duties at Cricklewood, I found myself working on occasions at St Pancras Goods Depot. My time was spent located within the general office here, working as a general clerk. The miscellany of tasks covered included dealing with staff questions and queries, and working out bonus payments. The formula for calculating the latter was worked out on the basis of the number of wagons that were dealt with by each member of staff during each of their shifts. In addition to the shunting staff on hand, St Pancras also had a complement of guards who worked the north-bound freight services out of both St Pancras Goods and Somers Town. As can be imagined, with staff working all round the clock, there was a three shift staffed time office. It was unusual for our pool of RSMs to cover these time clerk positions. This was because there were already three regular time clerks (together with a rest day relief clerk) who were permanently based at St Pancras. They would cover each other as regards annual leave and sickness.

One week at St Pancras, I was rostered to cover a 'late' shift at the time office, from 14.00 to 22.00 hours. It was unfortunate that, on the Friday of the week in question, the Bedford Branch of the Locomotive Club of Great Britain (LCGB), of which I was chairman, was holding its annual dinner. During this period of time, the LCGB President was none other than Mr J.C.R. Rogers, who, it will be remembered, was the St Pancras District Operating Superintendent. Mr Rogers had arranged for the London Midland Region Motive Power Officer, Mr Tildesley, to be our principal guest. Needless to say, I was anxious to be present at this important occasion and, in order to ensure that my work would be covered, I had previously spoken to (and obtained the agreement of) the two regular time clerks. They had told me that they were both quite happy to each work a twelve hour shift in order to make sure that everything was covered. However, when I spoke to my roster clerk (who was a young lady who had only recently been appointed to the position), she would not agree to this and informed me that she would be sure that Mr Rogers would understand that I had to work and would, therefore, be unable to attend the dinner. I then told her that I would have to phone Mr Rogers, and make my apologies at not being able to attend the event, at the same time explaining the situation to him. I concluded by pointing out to the roster clerk that I was sure that Mr Rogers would have something to say to her about what had happened. After the roster clerk had been seen by Mr Rogers, she rang me up and reluctantly advised me that I could, after all, have the Friday off, this being done in an extremely rude manner. In conclusion, I then pointed out to her that she could have saved herself all the hassle by giving me the time off in the first place!

Another location within which I found myself working on occasions was the Yard Master's Office at Brent. This place was a hive of activity, being the main marshalling yard for cross-London goods traffic. As with both Cricklewood and St Pancras, I found when working at Brent that I had a lot of staff matters to deal with. In common with St Pancras, many staff either worked as guards or shunters. A bonus scheme was operated here and, as at St Pancras, if the monthly gross payment of the staff, coupled with their bonus entitlement, came within a certain figure of the Yard Master's salary, he became entitled to a differential payment. It was somewhat galling that, although in the course of our duties we were required to calculate all bonuses and differential payments with this scheme, we were not included in it.

My duties as an RSM ranged from the mundane to the exceptional. One of the latter occurred when I spent a two week period of time covering the Assistant District Signalman Inspector at Bedford. This situation came about as the result of the permanent job holder covering the senior inspector whilst he was on annual leave. Having been a signalman in the area myself, with considerable knowledge of the local box workings, the two of us, together with a relief signalman, took the opportunity to carry out a number of annual rules and regulations examinations of some of the regular signalmen within the Bedford area.

In addition, providing we as RSMs were not covering any 'on call' duties, we could find ourselves being utilised on weekend engineering work, our specific responsibility being the on-site Operations Department Representative. Once again a wide range of tasks would be covered as part of this role. I can recall that, in my case, these roles included such things as travelling on a track relaying train from Bedford Ballast Pit to the site of work. When travelling out with the relaying teams, the RSM's job was to set the works train up on site, as required by the Permanent Way Department. This train would arrive on site with the tracklayer or cranes, together with a mix of both empty and loaded prefabricated wagons. These wagons would then have to be positioned ready for the work to start. The tracklayer or cranes would be placed adjacent to the line being worked on (that is, on a section that was not being relayed), the empty prefab wagon would be located ahead of the first panel of track to be lifted, and the loaded prefab wagons would be situated to the rear of the final panel.

To follow, what was known as 'safe working' was put in on the adjoining open running lines. In railway language, the term 'safe working' means that the open line (this being the line that normal services would be using during the duration of the engineering works) was not being fouled by movements taking place on the lines within the possession. If any work that needed to be carried out in conjunction with the track relaying exercise involved fouling (or obstructing) the open line, the open line would have to be blocked by the protecting signal being kept at danger and a hand signalman stationed at it, exhibiting either a red flag or red lamp. When a train was due, this signalman would contact the operating inspector on site, who in turn would stop the work being carried out. When he had done so, he would authorise the signalman to clear his signal, and to exhibit a green hand signal. A hand signalman would also be positioned at the actual site of work. When the train had passed clear of the worksite, unless another one was closely following it, the line would be blocked again and work recommence.

On occasions, things did not go as straightforward as they should have done. For instance, during one particular day, almost at the point of the completion of the relaying of a section of track, the 350 horse-power diesel shunter that was being used in conjunction with a track laying machine became derailed on a short length of temporary track. This in turn caused an overrun to the planned completion of the work by more than six hours. For me, this meant that instead of finishing at 18.00 hours I did not arrive home until well after midnight! On another track relaying job, a delay was caused by the steam locomotive (a Stanier-designed 8F 2-8-0 freight locomotive) running short of water. The upshot was that the errant engine had to leave the site of work to refill its water tanks.

On most occasions, prior to the track in question being relayed, the existing ballast was either completely removed by diggers, or merely cleaned of all the dirt by track mounted ballast cleaning machines. The procedure was that the cleaning blade (which was in two halves) was lowered below the sleepers, joined together and then the machine itself moved slowly forward. The ballast was raised up on a conveyer belt, the dirt was riddled through, loaded into wagons on an adjacent track and then the cleaned ballast would be returned to the track. I remember that one weekend, when such a ballast cleaner was operating on the down fast line (the train running direction being away from London), just to the north of Radlett, the cleaning blade hit a solid block of concrete which brought the machine to an abrupt stop. The machine operators then started to clear the ballast around the block – however, in doing this, they discovered that the block was no less than four foot square in dimension, and went deep into the ground. It was fortunate that the local permanent way inspector was able to recognise what this strange object was. It was one of a set of similar items constructed early in the Second World War and placed under each of the four tracks on this part of the main line. If a German invasion of Britain had taken place, a steel cap would have been placed on each block, the cap then disabling any enemy tank that would have tried to use the lines as a method of getting from one place to another. The only thing that could be done as far as the track renovation work was concerned was to dismantle the blade, move the machine forward of the concrete block, and the blade would then be refitted. Once this was done, the work required continued.

I also oversaw testing and maintenance work that was being carried out by the Signal and Telegraph Department within one or other of the many signal boxes that could be found within the Bedford area at that time, along with the supervising of work carried out as the result of either raising or replacement of bridges.

During this period, one of the most interesting under bridges that was being replaced and strengthened was that located just north of Luton station, on the slow lines at Welbeck Road. The work required took place over a long weekend, starting early on the Saturday evening and going through to the following Monday morning. The work carried out involved the main bridge beams being replaced by strengthened ones. This involved the use of two seventy-five ton steam breakdown cranes, one of which was based at Wellingborough and the other at Willesden, these being assisted at ground level by a road crane. Because of the noise and extra vehicle traffic generated by the work that was required, the residents who lived closest to the work site were offered hotel accommodation for the duration of the weekend. All accepted this kind offer, except for one lovely old lady. She refused to budge, saying, "I have lived here all my life, and I am not moving out now, noise or no noise." I believe that the contractors bought her a large bouquet of flowers when the work was completed.

Picture 41 *Replacing a bridge that took the Midland main line over a road north of Luton during the mid-1960s. A road crane can be seen, as can a railway steam crane which had come from Wellingborough (Author's collection).*

Having previously been a signalman, I was occasionally given the job of overseeing the testing and maintenance of the lever frames of signal boxes that had been repaired by the Signal and Telegraph Department. As well as being interesting work (and one that I could draw on my previous experience to help me do), it always took place in the warm and dry of the box in question – as opposed to other track relaying tasks which, of course, were always in the open!

Although I was a London St Pancras District Operating Superintendent RSM, there were times when I was called upon to carry out work within the equivalent area at London Euston. One such occasion came about as the result of a booking office in the London area having been broken into. I was sent, with a fellow RSM, the day after the break-in had occurred, in order to carry out a complete ticket stock check, to ascertain if anything valuable had been stolen. This not only covered the tickets in the racks, but all the stock in the office, which could be a tedious job. At stations such as Kenton or Harrow and Wealdstone this could take all day. Another duty that I was asked to cover on occasions (and which I mentioned earlier in this narrative) was to assist with detraining people, and getting trains away from Wembley Central, when there were special events at the old Wembley Stadium. These included both international and domestic football games (such as the Cup Final), the Rugby League Cup Final, international schoolboy football fixtures and women's hockey finals, when trains would arrive from all over the country. I will describe this in more detail in a later chapter.

By late 1968, I had spent almost five happy years as an RSM, enjoying the miscellany of tasks involved which added to my now-considerable all round railway experience. However, the railway itself was being rapidly re-organised during this time. It will be recalled that in an earlier chapter I made reference to the fact that British Railways were setting up Area Manager Organisations (AMOs) across the whole of the system. This programme had been completed by the end of 1968 – as all relief staff were provided from within these AMOs, there were now no requirements for RSMs. The result of this was that I was made redundant, along with all the other RSMs. At this time, London Euston was being rebuilt, and all the parcels traffic that would normally be dealt with there was being re-directed to either Marylebone or St Pancras. Once my RSM duties had come to an end, I was then given a temporary job working in the St Pancras Parcels Office.

CHAPTER TWELVE

OPERATING ENGINEERING SECTION

As mentioned at the end of the previous chapter, the creation of the Area Manager's Organisation within the London Midland Region spelled the end of the line for the Relief Station Masters and, on a personal level, I was put in the position of having to look for alternative employment. It was fortunate that I was not redundant for too long as a position became available, this being based within the parcels office at London St Pancras. My job was to supervise those staff whose work involved sorting the parcels out on arrival. Then when either firms or private individuals came with their paperwork to collect their goods, the parcels would be handed over to them, a signature being obtained from these people to confirm that they had received their consignments. Even while working here, I kept an eye on the vacancy lists and, after a couple of months, a job came up in the newly combined Divisional Office (this organisation having been created as a result of the merging of the former St Pancras and London Euston Divisions) which was located at Eversholt House, just to the rear of Euston Station itself. Within the Divisional Office (DO) a new section had been created to deal with the combined operating engineering programme and, as part of this section, a position for a clerk to cover the Midland lines of the former St Pancras Division had come into situ. I applied for this position and was selected to fill the post. As can probably be imagined, the Operating Engineering Section (OES: the name given to the group within which I would be working) covered many different areas of railway work. Before going into my specific role within the organisation, I would like to give you an idea as to what was meant by the OES.

During the course of each calendar year, a programme of infrastructure renewals was drawn up to be carried out over the majority of weekends by the various technical departments. To ensure that these programmes of works did not disrupt the scheduled train services more than necessary, the Operating Department had what was known as a 'Rules of the Route' publication. This book laid down how many line blockages, 'weaves' (these being the locations where a train should change tracks, for example from either fast to slow, or from slow to fast running lines) and route diversions could take place over a particular section of a line. The publication also laid down the number of speed restrictions which would be necessary as a result of the work that had to be done, restrictions that were then built into the normal timetable.

The various technical departments would submit their proposed Annual Programme of Work for agreement at a meeting with the relevant Operating Manager. In the case of the lines running south from Crewe to London Euston, the Operating Manager's Office (OMO) was based at Crewe itself, whilst the southern-most Midland lines were under the watchful eye of the OMO that was located at Derby. Quarterly meetings would then be held at District Level between the technical and operating departments. At that moment in time the overall regions (such as, in this case, London Midland Region) were then sub-divided into geographical regions, for example one such sub-region being at Crewe. These would then be broken down further into districts, an example of this being the London district. Such gatherings would be chaired by a representative of the Operating Manager, and a programme of work would then be agreed, as would a schedule of blockages and isolations of the overhead electrical line equipment if these were in situ on the line in question. In addition to the quarterly meetings, the next stage would be a follow-up meeting which was held once every six weeks, this being of a more detailed nature, when other departments added additional work that required carrying out. This work included things such as bridge examinations, station painting, signalling equipment maintenance, cable repairs and minor track work. The meetings relating to work that was to be carried out on the Midland were usually held at Leicester, whilst those for the Crewe–Euston line took place at Rugby. This meant that I would be away from my regular 'base' at Eversholt House for the whole of that particular day. However, if the main weekend work involved resignalling, a meeting would be called by the Signal & Telegraph Department at either Nottingham or Birmingham.

My own position at Eversholt House was one of a team of three similar roles, the areas covered in addition to the Midland main line section from St Pancras to Sharnbrook being the West Coast main line to a point just north of Rugby and the North London line, together with the suburban routes between London Euston and Watford Junction. Once I had been appointed to my new role, I was given a short period of training. This enabled me to carry out fully the duties of my new position – in addition, I was able to deputise for my two colleagues in the event of annual leave or sickness. My knowledge of the Midland lines was of great assistance when determining the actual blockage points for the work in question. This came

Appendix 1 *Two sample pages of a ballast programme as described in the adjacent text (Author's Collection).*

WESTERN LINES ENGINEERING PROGRAMME
(DISTRIBUTION LIST 'A')

AS FROM 11-6-84 ENQUIRES REGARDING THIS PROGRAMME T№ 050 2234

PROGRAMME OF ENGINEERING WORK ON THE LONDON DIVISION FOR THE FOLLOWING LINES:

    (A)   EUSTON TO NUNEATON AND COVENTRY VIA WEEDON OR NORTHAMPTON AND BRANCHES
    (B)   BROAD STREET TO KEW EAST JCN AND WEST LONDON LINE AND BRANCHES
    (C)   MARYLEBONE TO CLAYDON (LNE) JCN

FOR WEEK COMMENCING SATURDAY 9 JUNE 1984. UNTIL FRIDAY 15 JUNE 1984 INCL.

NOTES:

1. ALL WORK IN THIS PROGRAMME MUST BE REFERRED TO RESPECTIVE ITEMS IN THE CURRENT WEEKLY TRAFFIC NOTICE 'WE1' AND ANY ASSOCIATED SPECIAL NOTICES SHOWING DIVERSIONS AND POSSESSIONS FOR ENGINEERING WORK.

2. PERSONS IN CHARGE OF POSSESSIONS MUST LIAISE WITH DIVISIONAL CONTROL REGARDING ANY LIKELIHOOD OF POSSESSIONS OVER-RUNNING, AND IN THE EVENT OF THIS OCCURRING, FULL DETAILS AND REASONS ARE TO BE GIVEN TO THE D.C.C (VIA THE AREA SUPERVISOR IF NECESSARY) ON RELINQUISHING THE POSSESSION.

3. IN ORDER THAT WORK COMMENCES AT THE TIMES SHOWN IT IS IMPERATIVE THAT TRAIN CREWS WORKING ENGINEERS TRAINS MAKE KNOWN TO THE NEAREST SIGNAL BOX THAT THEY ARE READY TO DEPART AND MUST NOT WAIT FOR TECHNICAL DEPT STAFF UNLESS PREVIOUSLY ADVISED TO THE CONTRARY. ON ARRIVAL AT SITE IT IS THE GUARDS RESPONSIBILITY TO REPORT THE ARRIVAL OF THE TRAIN TO THE ENGINEERING SUPERVISOR IN CHARGE AND AWAIT FURTHER INSTRUCTIONS.

4. ATTENTION IS DRAWN TO THE OVERLOADING OF WAGONS WITH SPOIL. SUPERVISORS TO PAY PARTICULAR ATTENTION TO ENSURE CORRECT LOADING.

5. D.C.E TIMEKEEPERS TO LABEL ALL WAGONS AND ADVISE GUARD OF DESTINATION OF ANY WAGONS WHEN ALTERED FROM THAT SHOWN IN THIS PROGRAMME.

6. AS FAR AS THE TRAIN MOVEMENTS SHOWN IN THIS PROGRAMME ARE CONCERNED, THE CLASS 9 LOADING QUOTED FOR EACH TRAIN IS THE MAXIMUM GROSS LOADING (INCLUSIVE OF LOCOMOTIVE(S) AND BRAKE VAN(S))FOR THE CLASS OF LOCOMOTIVE(S) ALLOCATED.

   GUARDS ARE RESPONSIBLE FOR ENSURING THAT THE TONNAGE OF THE ACTUAL TRAIN DOES NOT EXCEED THE QUOTED MAXIMUM LOAD SHOWN AGAINST THE TRAIN IN THIS PROGRAMME. AS FAR AS POSSIBLE TOPS TRAIN PREPARATION FORMS TO BE PRODUCED BY A.F.C.s AND PASSED TO GUARDS BEFORE TRAINS DEPART. THE LOADS PUBLISHED IN THIS PROGRAMME ARE TO BE ENTERED IN THE T.R. HEADER CARD SO THAT INDICATIONS ARE PRODUCED ON THE TRAIN LIST OF ANY OVERLOADING. GUARDS TO PRODUCE DRIVER'S SLIP.

   GUARDS MUST IN THE CASE OF ANY OVERLOADING REDUCE THE TRAIN TO COMPLY WITH THE LOADS PUBLISHED IN THIS PROGRAMME.

   ON RETURN FROM SITE MANUALLY PRODUCED TRAIN PREPARATION FORMS ARE TO BE MADE OUT AND DRIVERS' SLIPS ISSUED. IN THE EVENT OF ANY OVERLOADING, THE PERSON IN CHARGE OF POSSESSION MUST BE INFORMED, TO ARRANGE FOR THE TRAIN TO BE REDUCED TO MEET THE MAXIMUM LOADS PUBLISHED IN THIS PROGRAMME.

   THIS PROGRAMME DOES NOT ABSOLVE STAFF FROM THE REQUIREMENTS OF THE WORKING MANUAL FOR RAIL STAFF, SECTION 6 (WHITE PAGES).

7. THE USE OF TRAFFIC BRAKE VANS MUST BE RESTRICTED AS FAR AS POSSIBLE TO WEEKENDS AND FOLLOWING THE COMPLETION OF ENGINEERING WORK ARRANGEMENTS MUST BE MADE TO RETURN THE BRAKE VAN TO TRAFFIC AS SOON AS PRACTICABLE.

8. CANCELLATIONS TO THIS PROGRAMME WILL BE WIRED OUT TO ALL CONCERNED BY THE THURSDAY PRECEDING THE DATE OF COMMENCEMENT.

9. ENQUIRIES REGARDING THIS PROGRAMME TO BE ADDRESSED TO 063-3487.

10. GUARDS PREPARING TRAIN LISTS AT THE COMMENCEMENT OF EACH TRAIN MUST PASS THESE, AMENDED AS NECESSARY, TO THEIR RELIEF.
    ON COMPLETION OF WORK, TRAIN LIST DETAILS SHOWING LOCATION AND CHANGE OF STATUS TO BE TELEPHONED TO AREA FREIGHT CENTRE. THIS TELEPHONE NUMBER IS SHOWN AT END OF EACH JOB.

SPECIAL ITEMS CONCERNING THIS ISSUE:— SEE NEXT PAGE

-13- SUNDAY 10 JUNE 1984

(17) E.P: DENBIGH HALL NORTH JN - HANSLOPE JN.

DOWN } SLOW {BY48 - RY9} BLOCKED 2300(SAT) - 1900(SUN).
UP }   {BY182 - BY47}

PERSON IN CHARGE OF POSSESSION
(RULE T.III 9.3)
INSPECTOR: 2300 - 0900 SALLAVAN
           0900 - 1900 MILLSA
RELIEF BY:

S.P. TAKEN AT: BLETCHLEY P.S.B 2300 - 1600.
WORK:(A) CLAY DIG & DN SLOW 54¾ - 55mp   SITE 1600 - 1900.
      + S&T WORK

TRAIN 9L59	DEPART NORTH AMPTON 2245 (SAT) RUN TO HANSLOPE AND SITE UP SLOW
2 X CLASS 25(MV8)	54¾mp STAND CLEAR SOUTH END UNTIL REQUIRED W.A.R O/C 0800
30 ZHVS	RUN TO BLETCHLEY AND STABLE. LOCO'S TO WORK 7L61.
30 ZBOS	NORTHAMPTON PKG BLETCHLEY RELIEF
10 PLAICE(SAND)	TOPS REPORT TO 061 2298
B&O	MAX LOAD = 1500 TONS
	LOCOS WORK 7L61
TRAIN 8L60	DEPART NORTHAMPTON 23.15 (SAT) RUN TO HANSLOPE AND SITE UP SLOW
1 X CLASS 31	54¾mp W.A.R O/C 1200 RUN TO BLETCHLEY AND STABLE
T.R M 78236	NORTHAMPTON PKG NORTHAMPTON 1ST RLF BLETCHLEY FINAL RLF
MESS VAN	TOPS REPORT TO 061 2298
20 MERMAIDS	LOCO STABLE BLETCHLEY
TRAIN 7L61	DEPART BLETCHLEY 1000 RUN DN SLOW TO SITE 54¾mp... W.A.R.
2 X CLASS 25(MV8)	O/C 1600 RUN TO NORTHAMPTON DN SIDE.
12 HOPPERS	BLETCHLEY PKG
PLOUGH BRAKE	TOPS REPORT TO 064 3229
	LOCO STABLE NORTHAMPTON
(B) 2300-1600	CONCRETE REPAIRS BRIDGE 175 52½ - 52½mp N.E.T.R PASS BALLAST TRAINS

in useful on occasions when the location of such points was disputed by one particular Signal & Telegraph Department representative. When these situations arose, I was fortunate in having the support of the meeting chairman who would put an end to any argument by stating, "If Jack says that this is the correct blockage point, then it is!"

One example of a task that our section carried out was the weekly production of what was known as a ballast programme. This was a programme of all the engineering work taking place within a particular area. The term 'ballast' came about because the majority of work involved relaying and re-ballasting the track. In line order, this consisted of details of the possessions, blockage times and details, together with any isolations that were required in conjunction with the work being carried out. This was followed by the details of the ballast trains themselves. Such details would be set out as follows: 'Train 9L22: two times Class 25s + brake van + 40 empty wagons + brake van. Train to depart Willesden Brent Sidings at 23.00 – run to site on the up slow at Kilburn. Work as required. At 08.00, engine to run round and train to run to Lidlington tip. First crew Stonebridge Park men book on at 22.30. Relief at 05.30 by Bletchley crew'.

With regards to the trains required, and crews to man them, the various motive power depots that were located near to where the works concerned were taking place would be advised of the requirements prior to publication. This was to ensure that both staff and locomotives were available. If the depots concerned could not cover the requirements then alternative arrangements would have to be made. Once the ballast programme had been completed, it would go for printing every Thursday, and distributed to all persons concerned on the Friday. Within our office, we had a list of operating inspectors who were eligible for covering the various track possessions. These possessions would be allocated to the relevant inspectors, provided the latter were available.

In addition to the weekend work, other tasks would be carried out during the course of a normal week. I can recall that, at this particular moment in time, these tasks included such things as bridge replacements, and work carried out in conjunction with the building and maintenance of the M1 Motorway close to the Midland main line at Mill Hill, Silkstream Junction and Hendon. Another unusual piece of work that was undertaken was the rafting over of the tunnel near to London Marylebone on the southern-most section of the former Great Central main line that ran underneath Lords Cricket Ground. The term 'rafting over' meant that concrete beams were placed over the track rather than building a separate bridge or tunnel. To cover all these various tasks, we had no fewer than four Operating Inspectors attached to our section.

It will be noted that all of the work mentioned so far was pre-planned and carried out at agreed times and locations. However, on other occasions, it was necessary to carry out things such as emergency track repairs. In situations such as these, permission had to be obtained beforehand from the Regional Control Offices at Crewe or Derby. (At this time Derby was still covering the Midland lines, a situation that changed in 1971 as Crewe took over these routes instead). This was especially necessary should temporary speed restrictions need to be applied. Once a programme had been agreed by the relevant parties, the details would then be wired to all depot booking on points, so that the train crews knew what was happening. Sometimes, if for example a derailment occurred or, as happened on one occasion near to Rugby where there was a bad bank landslip, we had to make arrangements for additional ballast trains at short notice, and find operating staff to oversee the work. In addition, site meetings were organised on these occasions, when we would discuss with the technical department what was required in detail, and how the work needed would best be carried out.

Although the job that I had was a clerical one, I was still allowed, after the regular inspectors had been allocated their weekend work, to cover other operating duties at weekends. This turn of events meant that I was still subject to my annual rules and regulations examinations. At times when there was an acute shortage of inspectors, senior relief signalmen would be called upon to cover minor engineering work. I remember that on one occasion, I became the subject of a complaint from one such signalman, who (through his trade union representative) inferred that I, as a clerk, was obtaining weekend work in preference to him. When his complaint was fully investigated by the local staff office, it was discovered that he had been working at signal boxes up and down the line during each weekend and would have, therefore, been unavailable for inspection work of the type mentioned above. On these grounds, his case was dismissed.

After two years working in this position I became restless with what I was doing. I found it somewhat mundane at times, even though the tasks involved took me to other locations on occasions. I had looked for alternative openings within the railway – however, as I could find nothing suitable, I decided to leave the railway industry and seek other work. It did not take me many weeks to realise that railways were my life, and I soon started back, this time working in the Euston Control Office. In railway terms, a control office was what would be best described as a kind of nerve centre. It kept in continual contact with all power box supervisors and signalmen within a given area. In addition, it would also be in contact with train crew supervisors, motive power depots, all operating departments and regional control. The control office would deal with and make decisions, covering all contingencies. It would keep up-to-date records of all train movements, and would be responsible for making and agreeing decisions regarding regulation of trains in the case of either disruption or late running. Another example of a task undertaken by a control office would be to introduce emergency running arrangements as and where necessary.

Once again, I found myself on my old Midland line section working on what was known as the Midland Records Desk. My job entailed recording details (which were phoned over to me from designated signal boxes) of all train movements between Sharnbrook and London St Pancras. It was similar to my days working as a signalman because it involved working on a three shift basis, with occasional weekend duties. I spent almost ten months based in this Control Office when, one day, I was called in to see our operating manager. He asked if I would be interested in going to Kensington Olympia in order to work as a station supervisor. Kensington Olympia had recently been taken over by the London Midland Region, and the Area Manager there was looking for a replacement for a previous supervisor, who had opted to move to the Western Region. I replied that I would be interested and, following on from our informal chat, an interview was quickly arranged.

My interview went well, and I was then examined on my knowledge of rules and regulations by the local Area Operating Assistant, who was a former Great Western Railway (GWR) employee. Against one of the questions that he asked me, I gave an answer which, it turned out, was one where the Midland's interpretation of the rule in question was different to that of the GWR. We agreed to differ on this one point and, as the rest of the exam had gone well, I was accepted for the supervisor role and began my training a couple of days later, this being in August 1971.

CHAPTER THIRTEEN

KENSINGTON OLYMPIA

**Picture 42** _Kensington Olympia seen during the early 1970s, showing the whole of the track layout, and looking towards Willesden (Author)._

When I began my period of time as station supervisor working at Kensington Olympia during the summer of 1971, this station (which had previously been known as Addison Road until 1946) was very much a hive of activity. Situated on the West London line from Willesden Junction (which was located on the London Midland Region) to Clapham Junction on the Southern Region, and also having a further main line connection in the form of the route to Old Oak Common, via North Pole Junction, on the Western Region, it oversaw a full complement of services. For example, a set of inward-bound milk trains were run – three coming from the West of England and one from Wales. Olympia also found itself the distribution point for three corresponding West of England-bound empty milk tank trains, together with a similar working going to Wales. Probably the most unusual workings were the 'Motorail' services, Olympia becoming the London terminal for these trains. Inter-regional parcel services were attached and detached here, and whenever events were taking place at the Olympia Exhibition Halls, a full Underground service was run to and from Kensington High Street, this station being on the latter system's District line.

Prior to beginning my new job, I was given a week's training on nights (which at Olympia was the busiest turn) and then a second week of training which was split between both early and late turns. Following this I was 'thrown in at the deep end', as they say. It was fortunate that my years working as a relief station master stood me in good stead. In my role as station supervisor, not only was I responsible for all the station workings on whatever shift I was on, but I was also required to carry out regular visits to all the signal boxes situated on the West London line. In location order (and starting from the east side of Kensington Olympia), these were as follows: North Pole Junction, Viaduct Junction, Kensington North, Kensington South, Lillie Bridge, Chelsea, and Latchmere Junction.

The station track layout was a somewhat complex one. It consisted of both up and down platform lines, together with up and down through lines. At the north end of the station there were no less than four bay platforms on the up side and two further bays on the down side. The southern end of Olympia featured two bay platforms on the down side, whilst the up side was the home of the previously mentioned District line shuttle service of the London Underground. Although Kensington Middle signal box had been closed on February 23rd 1958, the rail connections that it had previously overseen were still in use, but operated by the South box. This connection enabled incoming milk trains to have their formations re-marshalled for their final destinations within the London area.

The running of these milk trains was a very well organised operation. As all trains came to and from the Western Region (WR), the locomotives used were based within that area. Once the trains arrived, the milk tanks were re-marshalled in readiness for travelling to their final destinations. With the exception of the engine off the incoming Welsh service (which then worked a further milk tank train to West Ruislip), the WR machines would be detached and returned 'light engine' to Old Oak Common, whilst different locomotives would be attached for the final part of the journey, these being to Cricklewood (for which Midland engines would be used), Ilford (Eastern engines) or Vauxhall (which were Southern locomotives). In addition, our own diesel shunter would work milk trains bound for Wood Green Depot. I can recall that, on one occasion, a Southern Region-based crew were sent across who were not familiar with the procedure required at Clapham in order to get their train to its final destination at Vauxhall. I had, in the past, travelled out with this working, so, in order to help them out, offered to go with them. Rather than admit that they did not know the road, they agreed to me going with them!

Once these milk trains had arrived at Kensington, and the shunting and re-marshalling of their respective formations was taking place, no other trains were allowed to run within the immediate locality. One of the effects of this policy was that any down freight services not running to the booked timetable were held at Viaduct Junction, either in the loop or on the main line. At times, this caused friction between one set of signalmen, and frustration on my part. In railway regulations it states that if a train which has been offered to the next signal box on its route is not accepted, it should be offered again at short intervals. Unfortunately one particular signalman at Viaduct Junction kept doing this, although he was fully aware of the reason why the train at his box was being held. It was most unfortunate that the Viaduct signalman was a Nigerian and his counterpart at Kensington was a West Indian, and they did not get on with each other. As much as I tried to explain to the Viaduct signalman that a degree of common sense was required in this situation, he would not accept this.

The main day duties at Kensington were carried out in connection with the Motorail services. The name 'Motorail' was the brand name for all British Rail (BR) services that carried passenger's cars. The idea for what became Motorail had come about during 1955 when a named express train, which was known as 'The Car-Sleeper Limited', had originated, running between London and Perth. Destinations served by Motorail workings ranged from Penzance and Plymouth in the West of England, to Inverness and Fort William on the west side of Scotland. Many services were run in conjunction with sleeper trains, a variety of both open and closed wagons being used to transport the private vehicles. Motorail itself was started in 1966, a unique terminal being opened at Kensington which in turn became the hub of a national network of such trains. During its lifetime, it was run as part of the Inter-City sector of BR.

Despite the novelty of the service that was offered, and the obvious time savings to the customers, by the time that the national railway network was privatised in 1994, no Motorail services remained in situ, usage having declined by the start of the 1990s to a point where the trains were being run at a financial loss. In 1999, the First Great Western (FGW) train operating company launched a Motorail-type service as a part of their overnight sleeper train workings between London Paddington and the West Country – however, this was terminated during 2005. With the current swing back towards rail travel, and the need to take cars off the public highways in order to be 'nicer' to the environment, could 'Motorail' or a similar service make a return in the future? Food for thought for everyone concerned.

The Motorail trains that I dealt with had a variety of destinations, those on the Midland Region travelling to Perth (this being an overnight train) and Stirling, with a Carlisle portion. In addition there was also a combined day service to both Perth and Carlisle. Those trains traversing the Western Region ran to St Austell in Cornwall, with an additional Saturday-only working to Fishguard Harbour, on the west coast of Southern Wales. During the height of the summer season there was an additional Saturday night service to the West Country and, during my second year at Kensington, a weekend overnight service ran between Stirling and Dover. This latter train had an additional portion attached at Kensington on its north-bound journey and, in the opposite direction, a portion was detached. I recall that on many occasions, the overnight train coming in from Perth would arrive with a number of vehicles having had their windscreens broken. These breakages were caused by vandals in the Glasgow area throwing stones, and other missiles, at the trains. It was fortunate that we had a garage based near to Olympia that was able to replace the broken windscreens very quickly although, on a few occasions, the repair in question was delayed if the damaged vehicle was a foreign one. This was because the new windscreen would have to come from abroad. When this situation occurred, the railway would have to either arrange overnight accommodation for the said vehicle's owner, or make alternative arrangements for the owner to travel home without the car, which would then be collected once the repair had been completed.

On occasions, especially during the winter months, difficulty was experienced in starting up individual vehicles when they were being removed from the car-carrying trains. When this occurred they were pushed off the trains, and then jump-started. I remember that I had a most embarrassing experience on one such occasion when I went to drive a car off a train that had arrived from Scotland. I started the vehicle up, went to put it in gear, and the gear-stick came off in my hand! As you can probably imagine, the car's owner made a fuss when he found out what had happened – however, I remained convinced that he knew that a problem had existed during the time that he had driven around Scotland during his holiday. Another unusual incident occurred when an Irishman, who had arrived off the train from Fishguard, and who had had a few drinks, slipped off the side of the ramp connecting the car-carrying part of the train to the platform, and ended up with a hole through the floor of his car, underneath the driving seat. Our errant passenger then looked to make a claim against the railway for damage to his vehicle. However, on closer inspection, it became clear that the whole of the underside of the vehicle was rusty and, as a result, he had no grounds for a claim. It was pointed out to him that, if he wished to continue his line of thinking, the case would be referred to the British Transport Police. On hearing this unwelcome news, he soon shut up and drove off!

On a number of occasions, problems would occur with two or three car drivers, plus their vehicles, who wished to use the Saturday morning service from Kensington to St Austell. The departure time of this particular working was 01.00 on Saturday – however some people mistook this to be 01.00 on Sunday morning! Fortunately for them, there were always a couple of covered Motorail vehicles attached to the formation of the corresponding overnight sleeper train from Paddington to the West of England. We were able to arrange for both passengers and vehicles to use this train instead. I remember in particular one family that found themselves in this situation were so concerned that, even with the directions that I had given them, they would not be able to find Paddington and their substitute train service. As there were no railway movements for some three to four hours within the Olympia area, I agreed to go with them, in order to show them the way. They were so grateful that they gave me a substantial tip for my efforts. On my way back, I decided to use my unexpected windfall in a most positive way, by stopping at an overnight restaurant and having a most enjoyable meal!

The Motorail service to Dover, which I talked about previously, had sections of its formation coupled and uncoupled whilst waiting at Kensington. The two coaches which were detached at Kensington from the south-bound service were attached to the empty stock from the incoming arrival from Perth, the whole formation then travelling to Willesden Carriage Depot for servicing. (The same two carriages would then come back in the evening with the Perth stock, the coupling procedure then being reversed). Whilst this was taking place, our diesel shunter would also detach four car carrying flat wagons from the rear of the train and place them in the Motorail terminal. The train engine would be re-coupled, a brake test made, and the train was then sent on its way to Dover. All of this activity was completed within the ten minute time frame allowed by the timetable. When the same service was going north to Stirling, the train would arrive on the down through road and the same process would be carried out, but in reverse. The four car carrying flat wagons were waiting to be attached to the train's rear, whilst the train's engine would be uncoupled from the front, and crossed over to the down platform, where it would be attached to the two extra coaches. Both locomotive and carriages would then be re-coupled to the main train, a brake test made, and departure was then made, once again within the ten minute time scale.

I can recall, on one occasion, that the shunter at Kensington forgot to couple two empty coaches off the Stirling train that were bound for Willesden Carriage Sidings, with the result that they were left behind! This was not realised immediately, and an urgent phone call had to be made to the Train Crew Supervisor at Willesden, who arranged for a light engine and guard to be sent across to collect them.

The Motorail service was extremely popular with all sorts of people during its heyday. It was used by a number of VIPs and even minor members of the Royal Family. Once a year the Bentley Drivers Club would use the service to take their cars to Scotland for a rally. As you can imagine, this was quite a sight, with a large number of these classic vehicles all gathered together in one place.

CHAPTER FOURTEEN

KENSINGTON OLYMPIA
Part Two:
EXCURSIONS AND OTHER HAPPENINGS

During the period of time that I was working as station supervisor at Kensington Olympia, I found that there were many unusual trains of all kinds that would use the station in the course of their respective journeys. This was in addition to the Motorail services, milk workings and parcels trains mentioned in the previous chapter. During the course of the Easter holidays and the summer months, a large number of excursion trains called at Olympia, on their way from a miscellany of stations on the Midland, Eastern and Western Regions, to various seaside resorts on the south coast. The majority of these trains were supposedly booked a crew change – however, this didn't always apply. In practice such trains were routed onto one of the through roads, where (when required) not only the footplate crews, but also the train guard was changed as well. South-bound trains would arrive at Kensington, their drivers and second-men looking for relief by a Southern Region (SR) crew. It was then the job of the station staff to contact the Southern Control to find out where the relief crews were. It was generally the case that these crews would be waiting at Clapham Junction, this being because the Southern men did not have any route knowledge of the West London line between Clapham and Kensington. Occasionally we could persuade the incoming crews to take their train forward to Clapham. Sometimes, this was done on the understanding that I would go with them, in order to act as a conductor. This sequence of events also happened to trains coming in the opposite direction from the southern coast to the Western Region.

I can recall another problem that occurred on occasions with these special trains. This involved the routing from Latchmere Junction to the different Southern divisions. At the time, a number of these excursions were advertised as 'Mystery Trips', and it had become the norm for bets to be taken on these workings as to their final destinations. When these trains were listed in the Special Trains Notices publication, instead of a final

Picture 43 Former GWR 6000 'King George V' seen in the Motorail bay at Kensington Olympia in October 1971, during the series of special train workings that helped to overturn the ban on steam locomotives running on the national network (Author).

Picture 44 'Flying Scotsman' depicted at Kensington Olympia early in 1973 (Author).

destination being noted, the specials would be shown only as 'to SR'. This in turn caused problems for the signalmen at Latchmere Junction because, with three possible routes onto the SR, they were not always advised by the SR Control which route to set up. On one memorable occasion the signalman on duty tried all three routes, and still the excursion train remained stationary at his junction signal, the driver (like his signalman colleague) not being sure which way to go. Eventually, after a number of phone calls, the problem of which route to take was sorted out, but not before quite a considerable delay had been incurred.

When the annual 'World Travel Show' took place at Olympia, we would have four coaches from the train formation of the famous VSOE Orient Express stabled in the south end bay of the station. Willesden depot would provide a diesel locomotive to heat these vehicles, whilst the staff at Kensington would water and clean them. During their time in situ, they would be used as a reception for VIP type visitors, and also for publicity purposes. On most evenings, after the show itself had closed for the day, I was invited to join the train staff for a meal and a drink. Little did I realise then that, quite a few years later, my wife Pat and myself would travel on this train all the way to Venice. To my surprise, the train manager recognised me and we were both given VIP treatment during the journey to Folkestone!

At this moment in time, steam locomotives were beginning to reappear on the national network, following the end of the infamous 'steam ban', which had lasted from the end of regular steam working in August 1968 to October 1971. The first steam engine to be used on special excursions was former Great Western Railway 4-6-0 6000 *'King George V'*, and we were most honoured to have this illustrious visitor not only bring its special train into Olympia, but to be stabled in the terminal for two nights, before setting off for the West of England with another special working. Like the VSOE train, I got to know the staff working on the steam special and, as the day of the West Country trip was also my rest day, I was invited to travel as far as Didcot, working as a steward. My area manager was also invited to travel on the train as a special guest. Apart from 6000, we at Kensington also paid host to arguably the most famous steam locomotive of all, LNER 4472 *'Flying Scotsman'*, this being on a promotional visit not long after its return from its four year period of time running in North America.

In amongs all these excursions, Kensington did play host to some ordinary trains as well! These were in the form of a Monday to Friday morning commuter train service, which ran from Clapham, and which returned in the opposite direction each late afternoon. This was a train service that had originated during the Second World War, and which was run for the benefit of civil servants whose places of work were located around the area of Kensington station. I mentioned earlier that a shuttle service was run by the District line of London Underground (LU) between Kensington High Street and Kensington Olympia whenever a special event was taking place at the exhibition halls. When this service was operating, some of the clerks who normally worked in the Motorail office would cover duties in the booking office. Rather than having large sums of money kept on the station premises overnight, we would have a pass to the exhibition hall, and use the mobile bank in Olympia to deposit this cash. This enabled us to have a free look at such events as the 'Ideal Home Exhibition', the 'Fine Art Exhibition', the 'World Travel Fair' and even the 'Horse of the Year Show'.

Mention of the London Underground, and of London Transport (LT), reminds me that at this time we had a line connecting Kensington Olympia with the LT depot at Lillie Bridge. Most mornings saw a trip from this depot to exchange freight traffic with BR which, not so long before, would have been worked by one of LT's small fleet of steam locomotives, whose main role was to provide power for LT engineering trains. Unfortunately, by the time I came to Kensington, the steam workings had been taken over by an LT owned diesel locomotive.

On the freight train side of things, there was a considerable amount of both local and long distant trains, passing over our section of line, to and from the different regions. Until it closed in 1971, Chelsea Basin was the main coal distribution depot for the local area. For the coal trains to get into the yard, they had to negotiate a steep gradient to get over a bridge, which spanned a creek off the River Thames. In order for the coal trains to have a good 'run' at this gradient, the distant signal for the route (which under normal circumstances would be fixed at caution) was allowed to be cleared for the move into the yard. The drivers of these trains had to be very careful in bringing their charges to a stand in the yard, as on the other side of the buffer stops was the River Thames itself! Both Brompton Yard and Warwick Road Sidings were served by a local trip working from Willesden Brent Yard on an 'as required' basis, as was Lillie Bridge Sidings. None of these workings lasted too long into the 1970s.

Whilst I was at Kensington, we had a number of freight train derailments, and a lucky escape from what would have been a major disaster. The latter occasion took place one night when I got a phone call from the duty signalman at Latchmere Junction (Chelsea Box being closed during the night); he informed me that the driver of a train made up of loaded one hundred ton oil tanker wagons had reported a bad bump as he had passed over the LU lines at West Brompton. I made my way to the site in question and found a two foot section of rail that was broken! It was a miracle that the oil train had not become derailed. If it had done so, the wagons would have tipped down onto the Underground, and spilled thousands of gallons of oil everywhere. I immediately blocked the line and called the permanent way staff to replace the broken rail.

On another occasion at the same location, but on the opposite line early one Monday morning, a derailment did occur. The section of track in question had been reballasted and then relaid over the preceding weekend, and had been re-opened for traffic, but with a speed restriction in force. The first train to travel over the section was (you've guessed it) a formation of one hundred ton oil tanker wagons, but this time they were empty. However, the weight of the wagons was still enough to buckle the track, and the train became derailed. The emergency services had to be called in as there was a fear of a fire starting up. In the event, the fire service had to close West Brompton Underground station for no less than two days, whilst the rerailing of the errant train took place. Normal train services were allowed to pass through, but not stop, at West Brompton.

During my period of time at Kensington, there were also a further two major derailments that took place on this section of line, one of which was between Mitre Bridge and North Pole, and the second opposite Kensington North signal box. The former accident involved a mixed freight train, which had first left the rails on passing Mitre Bridge, and by the time that the train driver had realised the situation, the vehicles making up the train formation had not only torn down the track and signal wires, but were piled up three wagons high. The breakdown train from Willesden concentrated on clearing the line opposite to that from which the train had become derailed. The result was that we were able to run normal services on this line at 'caution' that same evening. Fortunately, the points controlling the line to Old Oak Common (Western Region) at North Pole were unaffected by what had happened, and I arranged with the Senior Officer on call to put two lots of single line working in (in this particular situation the Senior Officer on call would attend the site of a major incident, and would be in overall charge of the site). The down line was used for trains travelling to and from the Western Region, and the up line was used for services going in the Willesden direction. This meant that we were able to run the normal Motorail workings and a limited freight service.

The second accident was one that I actually witnessed. I was going off duty and had just crossed over the line footbridge, when I saw a big cloud of dust appear opposite the North signal box. I immediately dropped my briefcase and ran towards the train concerned, putting my hands up to draw the driver's attention. He had already realised that his train was off the track and soon brought it to a stop. One wagon, which had turned on its side, had completely demolished the home signal, and a second wagon had somehow buckled a rail, which was curved almost half round. Needless to say, I stayed on beyond the end of my shift to help sort the mess out, and to see what services we could run later that evening. To my surprise, when I finally went to collect my briefcase, which it will be remembered I had left at the bottom of the footbridge, I found that it had been stolen! The case was found up the line a couple of days later, minus its contents.

Whilst I was at Kensington, I attended a four week supervisory course at Webb House Crewe and, having passed the exam set at the end of the

NATIONAL EXAMINATIONS BOARD
IN SUPERVISORY STUDIES

NEBSS

THE CERTIFICATE IN SUPERVISORY STUDIES

This is to certify that
Jack Allardice Turner
has completed a course of instruction at
British Railways School of Transport
and passed the examination in the year
1973

Chairman
National Examinations Board

Chairman
Examinations Advisory Committee

Holder

Principal

Appendix 2 The NEBBS certificate awarded to the author early in 1973 (Author's Collection).

course, I then had to undertake a project to gain a National Examination Board of Supervisory Studies Certificate. Webb House was the London Midland Region's residential training centre at the time – it had been located there as far back as the days of the London and North Western Railway (LNWR). It was named after Francis William Webb, who as mentioned earlier in this story, was Chief Mechanical Engineer of the LNWR from 1871 to 1903. As my own area manager did not have a suitable project for me to carry out, it was arranged that I would take on a project for his opposite number at St Pancras. At that time, there was a need for an additional evening rush-hour commuter train between London St Pancras and Bedford, and my task was to make all the necessary arrangements to enable this train to run. This involved not only finding an appropriate path in the timetable to Bedford for the new service (together with the corresponding empty stock working to and from Cricklewood sidings), but also finding the rolling stock and train crews to work it. I had a fortnight to complete this project and to produce the necessary paperwork to support it. I am pleased to say that I managed to do so and, as a result, was presented with my NEBBS certificate by my Divisional Manager.

By the early part of 1973, I had worked at Kensington for almost two years, enjoying the work and the rich variety of trains that used the station. However, things change quickly on the railway. At this time it was decided to absorb Kensington into the Area Manager (Euston) organisation. Changes in rail traffic had also taken place prior to this. The milk and parcels traffic had ceased, whilst the Motorail workings had been scaled back. The latter group of trains had lost their Western Region services, whilst the London Midland workings were reduced to a single train that ran from London Euston to Perth. The Motorail office at Olympia was closed and the staff transferred to Euston, as were the car drivers. As a result of these alterations, the night supervisor turn at Kensington was withdrawn. There were three supervisors (including myself) still based at Olympia, and the original idea was that all of us would do in turn two weeks at Kensington, and then a third week carrying out various tasks for the Divisional Operating Office. Without going into detail as to what actually happened, one of the supervisors moved onto a new position on his original base on the Western Region, whilst the second supervisor was not interested in working at Euston every third week. This meant that I finished up working on a regular basis for the Divisional Operating Superintendent. To cover the remaining work at Kensington, a new supervisor was appointed.

The first job that I did, as part of this new working arrangement after leaving Kensington, was to spend a period of one month situated just south of Hendon as Operating Inspector on site, where the-then new M1 Motorway extension was being built. My duties involved being out in all weathers, twelve hours a day and seven days a week. It was hard work, but it was well paid. At the end of this task, I then undertook various jobs within the Euston area. As by this time I was officially redundant, I was once again looking for a new position. I discovered that a station manager position, based at Willesden Junction New Line (the term 'New Line' covering the third-rail suburban services between London Euston and Watford Junction) had appeared in the vacancy list. I applied for the job and was granted an interview. Whilst my interview went well, in the end the vacant post was given to a management trainee graduate who had recently finished his introductory six month intensive railway training course.

CHAPTER FIFTEEN

PROMOTION TO DISTRICT SIGNALMAN'S INSPECTOR WILLESDEN

(Author's note; a map of the Willesden area can be found in Appendix 9)

After the end of my period of time working at Kensington Olympia, I once again found myself redundant, and looking for a new occupation. Although I was unsuccessful in my application for the station manager's position at Willesden (New Line), a second suitable job appeared on the vacancy list not long afterwards. This was a signalman's inspector position, and the opening had come about as the result of the previous job holder unfortunately passing away. I applied for the job on offer and I was fortunate that this time my application was successful. After a very intensive rules and regulations examination (this being preceded by an interview undertaken by the local area manager), I was appointed to the post in October 1973.

The Willesden area at that time had no fewer than forty-seven manual signal boxes and one power box within its boundaries. Location-wise, these stretched from Bollo Lane (Acton), Kew East and Latchmere Junction in the west to Broad Street, Dalston East and Upper Holloway in the east. In addition, there were also the various Willesden-based freight yards and carriage sidings, together with the New Line from South Hampstead as far as Kenton, which was south of Harrow and Wealdstone. In my new position, I was responsible for organising the annual rules and regulations examinations for all the regular and relief signalmen within the Willesden area, these being no less than 170 in number. In addition, I also arranged rules and regulations exams for the guards employed at Willesden on the DC lines (as well as London Euston to Watford Junction; the former route ran between the now-closed Broad Street terminus and Richmond). Visits had to be carried out on a regular basis to all Willesden area signal boxes. A train register check had to be implemented on two occasions per annum, in connection with the annual safety audit (this audit was carried out by a representative of the Chief Operating Manager). The purpose was to ensure that regular visits of this type were carried out to all signal boxes and other operating centres. A record was maintained of each visit, of any discrepancy that came to light, and how each problem was subsequently dealt with. Records were also kept of any incident or derailment that occurred, together with any investigations undertaken and any required actions that had to be taken. In addition, I had other duties to carry out. These included dealing with any operating incidents, liaising with other technical departments, and attending resignalling and other engineering work meetings. As the reader will no doubt note, it was a very responsible job.

When I first started working at Willesden, the area manager gave me the task of shadowing the supervisors who were working in Camden Goods Yard. This involved working alongside them on a three shift basis. Over a period of years, the amount of freight traffic handled by the yard had dropped off considerably, and a scheme was in hand to close the depot. My task involved recording the actual traffic flows, and to give a considered opinion as to whether it was still necessary to have supervisors to oversee the remaining goods traffic. Once I had submitted my report and my suggestions, a combination of this, together with the downward fall in traffic, led to the supervisor posts being withdrawn and the yard itself being eventually closed.

The time that I spent earlier in my railway career working as a signalman and relief station master in the Bedford area was a great help when it came to learning the various duties that came with my new position. Getting to know and work the many manual boxes scattered across the Willesden sector came easily. However, the single power box (this being a signal box that was operated by electricity, as opposed to the old manual lever type) was something new to me, and this took a little longer to master, having an 'NX' panel. In a nutshell, this meant that to set a route for a train passing through the area controlled by the box, it was necessary to press the entrance (or 'N' button) on the panel – to leave the area, one had to operate the 'X' or exit button. I was also fortunate inasmuch as a number of the signalmen were people who had worked previously on either the London St Pancras to Bedford or the West London lines, and I had already got to know them in the course of my duties on both these routes. We had a mixture of nationalities employed as signalmen and, as in the incident referred to in the chapters covering my time working at Kensington Olympia, this could lead to friction between different parties. I recall that on one occasion, we had to separate two of them, one of which had left his signal box to sort his next-door neighbour out!

An unusual problem that I had to deal with concerned a lady signalperson. Although in the course of her work she got on well with most of her colleagues, she began receiving abusive phone calls from an unknown member of staff. The caller stated that signalling was a man's position and that she should not be doing her job. After a period of investigation, we found the culprit, who was another signalman. He was disciplined for what he had done and, prior to this, he was temporarily suspended from his duties. I must admit that this person (in my opinion) was the last individual that I would have suspected of carrying out this campaign of verbal abuse. To give him his due, he ended by apologising to his female colleague, and they got on okay after this had been done.

I was fortunate in that I got on very well with the majority of the signalmen that worked within the Willesden area. On my periodic visits to each box I was generally offered a cup of tea. One of these signalmen knew that I liked shortbread biscuits, and made sure that at least one was on hand any time that I called in – one of his colleagues got to know of my passion for chocolate biscuits, and I was treated to a few of these as well! Another signalman kept a 'best' set of a china teapot, with appropriate cups and saucers, for us to have our well-earned brew in.

As with other parts of the railway that I been involved with, old ways of working were being superseded by new ones, this being made possible by the introduction of new technology. As far as the signalling side of things was concerned, two of the most far-reaching changes involved the replacement of the traditional semaphore signalling by colour light signals, whilst the lever frames in the old-fashioned manual boxes were made redundant, and replaced by small panels, along the lines of those found in power boxes. Of course, this replacement programme meant that all regular and relief signalmen had to be trained to work the new systems and, as all power boxes were worked under the track circuit block regulations, they had to learn these new rules as well. Three of the level crossings situated within the Willesden area had their old style gates taken away (these having previously been operated by turning a large wheel found within the adjacent box itself) and replaced by barriers, which were opened and closed by hydraulic equipment controlled by a push-button panel that, once again, was found within the crossing's parent box. The training programme was enlarged to teach the signalmen concerned how to operate the new crossings both from within the box and on the ground, in case there was a failure.

On occasions, I would be called upon to operate one or another of the many signal boxes within our area, thus enabling me to 'keep my hand in', utilising the experience that I had gained earlier in my railway career. I can recall one such incident that happened on a New Years Eve. No doubt because of the ongoing festivities, a number of signalmen failed to turn out for their respective night shifts. Along with my area manager, I was called out to work the two carriage shed boxes at Willesden; this enabling trains of empty carriage stock to be serviced, thereby making them ready for use on the following morning's train service. To cut down on delays to departing services from Broad Street during the weekday evening rush hour, it was decided to open Dunloe Street signal box (which was situated between Broad Street and Dalston Station) during this period of time to shorten the block section. Outside of the evening rush hour the box was normally closed (or 'switched out') and the block section extended from Broad Street to Dalston station. As there were no spare signalmen available, either myself or a Divisional Signalman's Inspector would open and work the box during this period. After a number of months, the train service was revised, and there was no further need to open the box.

One box on my 'patch' was that at Kew East Junction. This particular establishment was somewhat unusual as it backed onto a cemetery, a fact which preyed on the minds of some of our West Indian and African staff who, during their training, came to realise that on occasions they would be working a night turn there by themselves. In addition, when passing out a relief signalman to work this box, we gave them a somewhat unusual instruction that any food that they took with them was to be kept out of sight and not on the table provided, if the windows were open. This was because various squirrels based in the immediate vicinity of the box would come and take it! I knew for a fact that one of the regular signalmen who worked there had encouraged these animals into the box, and had even trained them to beg! On one occasion, when I had cause to visit the box, a mother squirrel had brought along her group of youngsters for us all to see. In addition to the squirrels, the other form of wildlife to be found both here, and at nearby Bollo Lane, were foxes.

At this particular moment in time, the Southern Region (SR) was commissioning a new power box which was being built at Feltham. As the area of operation for the new box would extend as far as Kew East, I was invited by the resident SR signal inspector to visit the new box, which I also did on a number of subsequent occasions, the aim being to tie-up the working between the two signal boxes. The purpose of the tie-up was to ensure that all communication methods between the two boxes (for example, train describers, emergency bells and telephones) were all working correctly. The inspector also suggested that it would be a good idea if I was to learn how to operate the emergency panel (this also being known as a 'slade' panel) which was situated at Gunnersbury. This was where the District line of London Underground joined the North London line between Broad Street and Richmond. In normal circumstances, the junction would be worked from the signal box based at Richmond – if, for any reason, this link was broken, then the Gunnersbury slade panel could be used to operate the junction normally. Sometime later, when the Victoria power box was being brought into use at Clapham Junction, I paid a number of visits to this establishment as well, the idea being to tie-up the working of the West London line from here as far as Kensington South Box. The appearance of these new boxes and panels meant the end of the line for many of the old-fashioned manual signal boxes – in this area alone, Chelsea Yard box had already been closed, followed by that situated at Latchmere Junction, the work being taken over by the new Victoria power box.

New technology was appearing in other forms as well during this point in time. A new train describer system (TDS) was being brought into use on the West Coast main line (WCML). The purpose of the TDS was to determine the exact location of a train within the geographical area covered by the signal box in question. Each train was given a unique reporting (or identification) number, which was put into the signalling system at the train's originating point. Just prior to the train entering each signal box's designated area, this number would appear on the box's panel, and the signalmen would be able to chart its progress as it passed through their area.

I remember that when the technical staff who were responsible visited the power box at Willesden, they found that it was impossible to replace the TDS that was already located within the existing train panel. This was because the likelihood of damaging the signalling and power equipment was too great. The solution to the problem was to construct an entirely new signalling panel. It was fortunate that there was enough space behind the 'live' panel to build the new system in situ – in addition, the Signal & Telegraph (S & T) staff also set up a test bed in the box's relay room, this being to ensure that all functions had been thoroughly tested and found to meet all current safety standard requirements, prior to the weekend when the old panel was taken apart, and its successor commissioned. As well as this, a number of new interlocking features were brought into operation during this time, two of these that still easily spring to mind being known as 'Electronic Route Setting Equipment' (ERSE) and 'Solid State

Interlocking' or SSI. In a railway signalling context, the interlocking equipment would be used to ensure that once a route and signals had been set for a particular train, these could not be altered until the train in question had passed through the section. In addition, the equipment would not allow any conflicting train movement to be made.

In time, the whole of the West London line between Willesden Mitre Bridge, Kensington Olympia and Latchmere Junction (where the route joined the Southern Region) was resignalled and came under the control of Willesden power box. This meant that an additional train panel had to be fitted inside the box. It was constructed within the S & T workshop and transported by road to the box. In a skilled operation, the road that the box backed onto was closed overnight, the side of the box itself was removed, and the panel lifted in by a road crane. Following a period of being fitted out and fully tested, it was brought into full operation. Because of its position within the box, a new signalman was appointed.

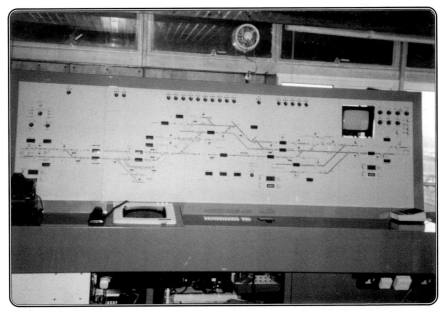

Picture 45 The new West London line panel, installed in Willesden power box (Author).

An establishment within the locality which is still very much in operation at the time of writing is the London Underground Limited (LUL) depot at Stonebridge Park, situated not too far from Willesden Junction on the DC line to Watford, which is responsible for looking after the fleet of tube trains that operate the Bakerloo line. This new depot was brought into service during April 1979. To control train movements into and out of the depot, a new route setting control panel was brought into use within Willesden (New Line) box, the purpose being to work the section of line that ran from the connection between BR and the Bakerloo line at Queens Park to the depot's own box. However, the manual signal levers were still retained for controlling local movements in the actual Willesden 'New Line' area. As with the main line power box at Willesden, both regular and relief signalmen had to be trained for working the new panel described above. As part of the new working arrangements, I was able to persuade the Senior Operating Manager that as a record had to be kept of all train movements, a train recorder would be required on each of the two day shifts.

The implementation of this scheme meant that I was involved in a number of meetings with the area LUL Operating Inspector. When this scheme was finally brought into use, and the depot became fully operational, my area manager and myself were invited to meet the Bakerloo line's Operating Manager, and to join him on a special train that travelled over all parts of the Bakerloo, together with a visit to the now-closed Aldwych branch. After a late lunch with the Operating Manager at a restaurant near to Baker Street station, my day was rounded off by a tour of the signal cabin at Finchley Road.

The New Line box at Willesden provided a fund of memorable stories, two contrasting examples still springing easily to my mind, even though more than thirty years have elapsed since they happened. The first of these was quite dramatic and concerned a gang of thieves who were intent on breaking into the cash office at Willesden Junction. Prior to doing this, and to ensure that they were not disturbed, they threatened and tied up both the New Line signalman and station foreman on duty at the time. Luckily, neither of these members of staff were seriously hurt, but obviously they were both badly shaken up by their nasty experience.

The second story is in a much more light-hearted vein. On a night turn, there was a gap of four hours between the last passenger train of the day and the first one of the next. As such, each signalman employed on this turn managed, as the saying goes, to 'get his head down', or in other words, to have a few hours sleep. On one particular occasion, after spending a late night dealing with an incident on the main line, the area manager concerned decided to pay an impromptu visit to the said box – imagine his surprise when he found the signalman on duty not only asleep, but dressed in his pyjamas!

CHAPTER SIXTEEN

FIRES AND DERAILMENTS

One of the most important (and arguably <u>the</u> most important) section of railway that came within the boundaries of the Willesden area was the line running between Broad Street and Richmond which, over a period of many years, became known as the North London line (NLL). The origins of this route can be traced back to August 1846 when a plan to build an eight mile railway from Chalk Farm, in North London, to Poplar was approved by Parliament. The original company was known as the East & West India Docks and Birmingham Junction Railway until 1853, when it changed its name to the North London Railway (NLR). Progress was slow with the building of the Chalk Farm–Poplar line, the whole route not being opened until January 1852. Despite this slow start, the NLR was already looking to expand the passenger train services on offer. One of its many connections was at Bow, and enabled NLR trains to access Fenchurch Street, via the tracks of a separate company, the London & Blackwall Railway. This arrangement lasted from 1850 until 1865, when the extension from Dalston Junction to Broad Street opened. The NLR also expanded its network in a westerly direction, beginning in August 1853 with the opening of a line from Camden Road (which was situated on the original Chalk Farm to Bow route) to Kew. This piece of railway was originally known as the North & South Western Junction Railway, and was a joint enterprise between the NLR, the London & North Western Railway (LNWR) and the London & South Western Railway. The final connection to Richmond was completed in 1858. During the period up to 1923, and the railway 'grouping', many of the small private railway companies were taken over by larger organisations. The NLR eventually became part of the LNWR in 1922, the latter railway having previously taken over the working of the NLR in 1909.

During my period of time working within the Willesden area, there were a number of incidents that took place, these ranging from serious fires to train derailments, and including other happenings, such as signals passed at danger, signalling irregularities of various kinds and collisions. Some incidents were more serious than others, and it was fortunate that I was able to draw on my by-now considerable knowledge of the railway industry to help me solve the problems presented.

I can recall that there were two major fires on the NLL, both involving signal boxes. The first of these took place on Christmas Eve 1975, during my second year at Willesden. I was at home on Christmas Day morning, looking forward to the day's festivities, when I received a telephone call from my area manager. In his dry humorous way he said, "You don't think that I am ringing you up to wish you a Happy Christmas?" He then went on to explain that the signal box located at Canonbury Junction had, unfortunately, been burnt down during the preceding night, and that I was required to be on site, early on Boxing Day morning, for a twelve hour shift, my main task being to supervise hand signalled movements, covering the Broad Street to Richmond local passenger service. So much for my Christmas break! In actual fact I ended up spending a number of weeks carrying out this vital duty. Things were made a little easier by the Signal & Telegraph (S & T) Department who installed temporary signalling instruments, although both myself and my staff found that we still had to hand signal all trains. In addition, the Works Department had provided a portacabin for our comfort and convenience, a great help at this somewhat chilly time of year. In time, the control of this junction to the Eastern Region was transferred to Canonbury Station signal box, and this brought an end to the need for the hand signalling system.

The second major signal box fire took place on a Sunday night at Gospel Oak. The saddest thing about this incident was that it resulted in the unfortunate death of the signalman on duty. The fire itself was caused by a short circuit of the DC power cables and, in a strange irony, despite the passing away of the signalman, little damage was caused to the equipment contained within the box. In my time working within the Willesden area, this was not the only incident that took place at Gospel Oak; on another occasion a passenger train was irregularly allowed into the section of line running towards Camden Road. This in turn led to a serious rear-end collision with a Kings Cross-bound cement train that had begun its journey at Cliffe, in Kent. The freight was being held at the signals located at Camden Road, and it was at this point where the collision occurred. The passenger train was a local suburban working between Richmond and Broad Street. As a result of the collision, thirteen of its occupants were taken to hospital, although thankfully there were no fatalities. The accident happened during the late evening of the day in question. Despite extensive damage to the front of the passenger working (which was formed of a Class 501 electric multiple unit that had become derailed), the breakdown crew worked extremely hard throughout the whole of the same night, and their efforts were rewarded when all services returned to normal for the start of the following day.

A similar signalling irregularity to that mentioned above also took place around this time, the location this time being between Dalston Station signal box and Broad Street, the train in question once again being a Richmond to Broad Street service. In this latter case, it was lucky that no collision took place. The Camden Road accident was fully investigated by the railway inspectorate and the findings reached were subsequently used to improve operating safety procedures.

Picture 46 The author keeping his hand in at Dalston West Junction box during 1974 (Author).

Dalston Western Junction became the scene of another unhappy incident, this being a major derailment of a Freightliner container train. The accident had the effect of closing the connecting route to the Eastern Region at Canonbury Junction (this leading to Finsbury Park) for no less than two days. A thorough investigation of the accident by all the departments concerned (these being S & T, Permanent Way, Operating and Carriage & Wagon) came to the conclusion that the signalman in Dalston Western Junction signal box was at fault, as he had replaced the trailing points under the rear of the train, before the wagons had cleared these points. This he vehemently denied. I personally felt that this signalman had been wrongly punished, my own gut feeling being that a combination of the train's speed through the junction, and a loose load in one of the train's containers, had combined to cause the derailment.

Moving to the western end of the North London line, Acton Central was the scene of a further derailment. This was one that, in my opinion, should never have happened. On the day in question, because of a problem that had previously occurred in the Gunnersbury area, all local passenger trains travelling from Broad Street to Richmond were being terminated at Acton Central; they then returned to Broad Street. After the arrival at Acton of one such train, it was signalled to cross over from the 'down' to the 'up' line – once this movement had been completed, it then reversed back into the platform to collect its passengers and to await its time of departure. At the Willesden end of Acton Central was a set of catch points, these being to stop any trains running backwards down a falling gradient. There was enough room to complete the reversing movement without fouling the catch points – however, in this particular case, instead of stopping over the crossover points, the driver of the train kept reversing, a move which was only arrested by the train's guard applying his brakes, and bringing the unit to a stand over the catch points. The guard, forgetting that the train was still situated on the catch points, told the driver to move the unit back into the station proper, the result being that the train's rear bogie became derailed! With such a busy service to run, it was imperative that the train be rerailed as quickly as possible. Once again a competent breakdown crew came to our rescue. When they arrived, they put a few blocks of wood under the derailed bogie, told the driver to move the train slowly forward, and, with no bother at all, the bogie rerailed itself.

Although to the reader it may seem somewhat alarming to read of these accidents, it should be remembered that in those days (as is still the case today) the North London line was extremely busy. As well as the local passenger trains between Broad Street and Richmond, which on a normal weekday would run every twenty minutes in both directions, there were many inter-regional trains, mostly carrying freight of one kind or another, that used the route to cross Greater London from one of the main trunk lines to another. In addition, there were also a large number of local interchange workings. This resulted in a very intensive train service, even by the standards of those lines serving various parts of the capital. Going in an east-bound direction, if these long distance workings came from the Southern Region, they would access the NLL via Kew, or the West London line. If they originated on the Western Region, the joining point was Acton Wells Junction, whilst the connection points with the Western division of the London Midland Region (LMR) were either Willesden or Camden Road. Travelling in the west-bound direction, those services from the Eastern Region would find their way onto the NLL at either Dalston Western Junction, Camden Road or Gospel Oak, those from the LMR joined the route only at Willesden, while the trains from my former Midland division accessed the link at Acton Wells Junction. During a normal working day, the usual service pattern was to fit two freight services in between each passenger train. Such an intensive timetable demanded great vigilance from all members of staff concerned with its running.

I mentioned earlier that, during my time working in the Willesden area, I had many dealings with those signalling inspectors who were based in the adjacent sections of line which were part of the Southern Region. As a result, I had built up a good working relationship with this group of people, which was used to our mutual benefit on a number of occasions. It was unfortunate that I did not have the same good relations with my opposite numbers on the Western Region (WR). In my experience, the WR men seemed to keep themselves to themselves. This unfortunate set of circumstances hindered my efforts to deal with a hold-up that occurred one day at Acton Wells. On this particular occasion, there were three freight trains on the down line between Willesden High Level and Acton Wells awaiting permission to gain the WR main line. The cause of the problem was because the WR were carrying out a programme of signal alterations in the Acton area, a programme of which neither we at Willesden (or the Euston Control office) had been advised of. Because of the work taking place, the arrangement was that WR-bound workings were being hand signalled off the section of line that joined the NLL to the WR. I found myself having to go to Acton Wells to investigate what was causing the hold-up, and it was only once I had arrived on site, and spoken to the people concerned, that I found out about the signalling work that was taking place. Almost unbelievably, the hold-up had come about because the hand signalmen concerned were working twelve hour shifts, and they had gone off for their lunch break! Taking the initiative, I had to make arrangements to shunt the offending trains into a set of sidings (these being known as Willesden Old Oak Sidings) which enabled the NLL to be cleared, and the local passenger service to begin running again. If the WR had been considerate enough to inform the London Midland Region in advance what was going on, a great deal of trouble and delay could have been avoided.

Acton Canal Wharf was a place where some interesting occurrences took place during my time working at Willesden. One such occasion concerned a redundant power station that was situated where this line crossed over the West Coast main line (WCML) from London Euston. It had been decided to demolish the power station's two cooling towers. As part of this work, both the main line and the route from Cricklewood to Acton Wells were blocked to all rail traffic for a period of some two hours, and the electric power was switched off, while the towers were destroyed. I was the Operating Inspector on site at this time, and the actual demolition was quite a spectacle to see.

The link off the connecting line from Willesden to the Southern Region (SR) was protected by trap points, so that any train over-running the protecting signal would not foul the branch line to Acton Wells. I can recall that one evening, the driver of a light engine returning to the SR mistook his signal, the result of which was that his locomotive ran through the trap points, off the railway line altogether, and ended up being buried up to its axles in the soft ground located at this point. It was fortunate that the errant machine did not foul the branch line after this accident. To rerail the engine, a breakdown crane was sent across from the SR. However, despite their best efforts, the Southern crew were unable to rescue the stranded machine. Therefore, arrangements were made to bring a second crane to the scene of the accident, this time from Old Oak Common on the WR. Between the two cranes, the engine was rerailed, and thus managed to regain terra firma.

In an operating context, Acton Canal Wharf played an important role in the diversion of the overnight sleeper train services running north from London Euston, whenever there was a blockage of the WCML south of Rugby. These trains were hauled by an electric locomotive as far as Willesden, where the engine was detached. A diesel was then coupled to the rear of the train and pulled it over the connecting line to Acton Canal Wharf. At this point, a second diesel, which had arrived light engine from Cricklewood Diesel Depot, was attached to the front of the sleeper, the locomotive at the rear uncoupled and the complete train then running over the branch line to Brent Junction (which was near to Cricklewood), which is where it would access the Midland main line. It would then run as far north as Wigston (which was located just south of Leicester) and then take the westward cross-country route to Nuneaton, where it would re-join the WCML. After supervising the movements that took place at Acton Canal Wharf, and having finished my shift, I would travel back to Bedford by using the last sleeper train of the evening, having previously made arrangements for this train to stop at Bedford to drop me off.

CHAPTER SEVENTEEN

WEST LONDON LINE

Within the Willesden area, a second railway that formed a useful cross-capital link was the West London line (WLL), which connected various routes on the north side of London with the Southern Region, the latter being accessed by way of my old stamping ground at Kensington Olympia, and via Clapham Junction. Between Willesden and Kensington could be found the junction where a spur off the North London line at High Level Junction joined up with the WLL, this location being known as Mitre Bridge.

Mitre Bridge was also the home of a scrap metal recycling plant which was owned and operated by a company known as the '600 Group'. The plant was accessed via a level crossing (which traversed the WLL, and which was worked from the Mitre Bridge signal box) and a road which ran alongside the railway line towards South West Sidings. As a safety measure, there were heavy steel loading gauges which were constructed each side of the level crossing barriers. During my time working at Willesden, we were always having problems with overloaded road vehicles crossing over the railway at this point, and under the overhead electric wires, which ran to a point just beyond the signal box. Some idiot drivers (you could not call them anything else) found that their loads of scrap metal were piled up so high that they would touch the height bar on the loading gauges. If this happened they would reverse their vehicles and take a second run, thus getting the load through by sheer brute force. Their loads, which were usually scrapped cars, would often touch the overhead electric wires. It was fortunate that the 25,000 volts of electricity running through these wires would go to earth through the lorry's tyres, in turn bringing the circuit breakers out. The same problem would occur with vehicles that had loose aerials; these would fly up and hit the overhead wires.

On one occasion when I was making a visit to Mitre Bridge signal box, an overloaded lorry arrived at the crossing, and I decided to speak with the driver, pointing out this fact. It was obvious that he came from a traveller's site and, once I had spoken with him, he told me to mind my own business! Undaunted, I pointed out the dangers, and showed him the official warning notices, but he remained adamant that he was going to drive over the crossing. I then stood in front of his vehicle, and stated that if he did so, he would have to drive over me first! Fortunately, at that moment, a second lorry came out of the recycling plant, travelling in the opposite direction. The driver of this vehicle, seeing the problem, came to my aid, and eventually persuaded his uncooperative colleague to turn back.

As can be imagined, you could never take chances with the 25,000 volt (or 25kV) electricity supply. One day I got a call to go to Mitre Bridge signal box to discover the cause of a small fire that had broken out in the corner of this box, where a gas stove was located. After some investigation, I eventually found out how the fire had come about. What had happened was that the aerial of a lorry using the crossing had touched one of the overhead wires. Instead of the power going to earth via the lorry's tyres, it had run along one of the rails towards the box, then going to earth via the earth wire that was attached to the gas pipe that was situated under the box itself. This in turn had set fire to the gas supply. Fortunately the signalman on duty at the time, after overcoming his (understandable) initial shock, had acted quickly and put the fire out.

On another occasion, I was reminded (if I needed any reminding) of the care that had to be taken when working alongside the overhead wires that carried the 25kV electric supply. The root cause of the problem with this particular incident was a freight train that had travelled up from Dover to Willesden (Brent Sidings). Once it had arrived at Mitre Bridge, it had to pass through what was known as the 'low level goods line', this route passing under the West Coast main line (WCML) by means of a bridge, en-route to Brent Sidings. Unfortunately, the freight train had become derailed just prior to passing under the bridge, and a refrigerated van containing carrots ended up leaning on an overhead line equipment (OLE) post. As was routine with incidents of this kind, the power supply was cut off by the Electric Control Room, but despite this, when a train utilising the down fast line on the WCML passed overhead, there was a flash and a bang on the food van, this being where the electric supply had jumped the gap in order to find an earth. Needless to say, the WCML fast line had to be blocked whilst additional earth poles were put up around the errant van.

In a large area such as Willesden that contained a vast number of sidings, derailments were a regular occurrence. Some were of a minor nature with small delays resulting, but others were much more serious, causing hold-ups and diversions. One of the latter type came about following the journey of a heavy stone train that had run up from Westbury, in Wiltshire, this being the first working of its type. This train was travelling through the group of lines collectively known as Old Oak Sidings, which it had accessed from Acton Wells Junction, en-route to its final destination on the Eastern Region. As can be imagined, the weight of the stone train was extremely heavy, and the track foundations on the through roads were made up mainly of ash and cinders – as a result the track was unable to support the weight of the freight train. Four or five of the wagons became derailed, tipping over and spilling the stone everywhere. It took some time for this mess to be cleared up.

The low level goods line, which was the scene of the derailment involving the refrigerated van, was also the setting for a second derailment; this time the train in question was made up of empty mineral wagons, and the derailment came about for what at first did not seem an obvious reason. I mentioned in the previous chapter how, on occasions such as these, an accident investigation would be carried out as a joint exercise by all the railway departments concerned. In this particular case, this is exactly what happened – however, despite all the effort expanded, the cause of the derailment remained unknown. It was at this point that the British Rail Research Department (who were located at Derby) were called in. After extensive tests, and taking track measurements, they found that a combination of a worn wheel tyre on one of the wagons involved, together with a slight track defect, was the cause of the derailment.

As a 'rule of thumb', when a derailment occurred that involved a set of points, and the derailed vehicle ended up going towards two railway lines (or 'roads'), if the mark indicating the first point of derailment was eight sleepers from the blade of the points, then the cause of the derailment was an error on the part of the signalman controlling the section of line in question. If the same set of circumstances took place at a set of hand-points (these being points that were worked by a hand lever rather than from either a signal box or a ground frame – as such having no detection), this would have been an error on the part of the shunter having moved the points under the railway vehicle. Another cause of derailments where sets of points were involved was when a train driver would accidently pass a signal that was set at danger. In addition, a mixture of derailments and collisions that occurred within the freight yards that I was involved with came about as the result of wagons that were standing 'foul' (or obstructing) adjoining lines. When accidents occurred, the incident in question was dealt with by the Freight Yard Supervisor (for goods sidings) or the Senior Carriage Siding Supervisor (SCSS) for those happenings involving coaching stock. If a serious incident took place within the carriage sidings at Willesden (a 'serious' incident being one that would delay a working of empty carriage stock into London Euston for a timetabled service), then I would have to attend. This would release the SCSS to oversee the re-routing of the coaching stock at the Wembley end of the Willesden sidings, via the up slow line platform.

One or two derailments around this period of time, that were caused by signals being passed that were at danger, come to mind. One occasion, which took place a couple of days before Christmas Day 1977, occurred during a time when the London Fire Brigade were on strike, and the military forces were providing cover with their famous Bedford 'Green Goddess' fire engines. A Freightliner (FL) train had departed from the terminal, and had crossed onto the up slow line just north of Kensal Green tunnel. This train should have come to a stand at a red signal in order to allow a light electric locomotive, which was travelling on the down slow line, to cross in front of the freight, in order to access the Traction Maintenance Depot (TMD) at Willesden itself. Unfortunately, the driver of the FL train misread his signal, and continued along the up slow, colliding almost head on with the light engine. Both locomotives and the first two FL vehicles were derailed, and a small fire broke out. When I arrived at the scene of the accident, I went to the TMD Supervisors Office to see if any of the train crews involved had been injured. Not only did I discover the FL driver sitting in the office in a shaken-up frame of mind (he had jumped off his train prior to the collision), but he was also being questioned by a member of the local civilian police CID. I informed this officer that he had no right to be on railway premises carrying out a questioning exercise – the only people who had the right to do this were our own British Transport Police (BTP). Having established this point, I then spoke with the driver, and asked the supervisor on duty to arrange for this man to be taken to a local hospital for a check-up. Following this, I made my way to the nearby power box. Here, once again, I found a member of the civilian police CID trying to question the signalmen as to what had happened. As with his colleague in the TMD, I informed him that he had no right to be there, and that his questioning was interfering with the work of the signalmen, which could cause them to make a mistake. I then requested that he leave the box, which thankfully he did.

At times, it seemed to me that the Willesden area seemed to be a magnet for mishaps of one kind or another. On a separate occasion, on the adjoining DC lines between Watford Junction and Queens Park, a Bakerloo line tube train ran into the rear of a stationary passenger train that had been travelling between Watford and London Euston. The only good things about this unfortunate accident were that not too much damage was caused to either train, neither were there any passenger injuries.

The problem of accidents of one kind or another caused by trains overrunning signals that were set at danger (or SPDs in railway speak) was one that reoccurred on a number of occasions during the time that I was based at Willesden. One evening, a local train from London Euston to Bletchley, which was travelling on the down slow line, passed a signal situated just north of Kensal Green tunnel that was set at danger, the train coming to a stand some 200 yards beyond it. When I went to interview the driver, I had something of a shock, as he was a former footplate colleague of mine. In 1948, when I had become a passed cleaner at Bletchley, I had, on a number of occasions, fired to him. Once I had spoken with him, he admitted his mistake, and I then had to arrange for him to be relieved from his duties and to travel home as a passenger. Subsequently, I learnt that this was not the first SPD that he had passed in recent times – as a result, the unfortunate driver had to be taken off main line duties completely.

A further incident of this kind that could have had very serious consequences took place on a Friday morning, at a moment in time when I was on one of my regular visits to Willesden power box. Whilst I was in the box, the London-bound 'Manchester Pullman' express train passed the protecting signal for the junction that crossed from the West London line to the down slow, and then onto the section of railway that led to the adjacent carriage sidings. (A protecting signal was a stop signal that, when set at danger, protected a train that was fouling another route. Such a signal could be found at a number of locations, for example coming out of a loop or siding, at a junction, or even in the form of a ground signal controlling a crossover). At this period in time, the 'Manchester Pullman' was still formed of coaches that were vacuum-braked, these being fitted with a special type of brake block which had to be changed regularly, on each and every weekend. This was because of the wear on them. Newer carriages possessed air brakes, one advantage being that they could be brought to a stop in a shorter distance than those with vacuum brakes. When this SPD was investigated, it was discovered that the Pullman train's driver had worked only on air braked trains for the whole of the week leading up to the incident mentioned. As a result, he had under-estimated the braking distance required with the older rolling stock and therefore was not able to stop at the danger signal. Normally this prestigious train would have been given precedence over most other workings. However, as it was always difficult to find a path across the main line at this time of the morning, and as the express was running early, the signalman concerned had decided to give an empty stock movement priority. It was halfway across the junction when the Pullman train passed the danger signal; the express came to a stand a mere one hundred yards short of the empty train.

I immediately went and found the Pullman train's driver in order to conduct an interview. In an interesting co-incidence, the London Midland Region Safety Officer was travelling in the cab with him. The driver should have been taken off his duties straight away, but there was no spare driver immediately available. In order to minimize the delay to this most important train, and after consultation with both the Regional Control Officer and the Regional Motive Power Superintendent, it was agreed that I would accompany the driver in the cab for the remainder of the train's journey into London Euston, but running at a reduced speed. Needless to say, on arrival at Euston, he was met and taken off by a footplate inspector.

I also had my share of fatalities, and one particular incident of this type sticks out in my mind more than others. In a very sad occurrence, a young man threw himself in front of a north-bound express that was passing Kilburn. I was detailed to investigate this accident and, as a start, Willesden power box had blocked all four running lines. The railway station at Kilburn was located very close to the local police station. When I arrived on site, I found not only a police sergeant, but four new police cadets. As can be imagined, the body of the dead man had been badly cut up. The sergeant had given each cadet a plastic bag and told them to collect the remains – in his opinion this was, "Cruel, but good training." One of the cadets was a young lady, and I ended up having to console her as she was in such a tearful state over what had happened.

On a brighter note, I enjoyed some interesting experiences, which came about during the course of my work. One of these concerned a Pullman special that ran between London Victoria and Ascot, during 'Ascot Race' week. During the course of its journey, this very luxurious working was routed over the West London line, and then through both South West and Old Oak Sidings (these being situated adjacent to the down fast line between West London Junction and Willesden Freightliner Terminal), Acton Wells and Kew, following which the train accessed the south-western section of the Southern Region (SR). To enable the train to pass through South West Sidings, all the points had to be clipped, padlocked and a hand signalman appointed. In addition, as the SR inspector in charge of the train was not familiar with the route through these sidings, the Willesden Inspector would accompany the train as it ran between Mitre Bridge and Acton Wells. On occasions, this task was my responsibility. I can recall that, on one particular occasion, as the SR were unable to supply an inspector from Victoria, I was asked to take his place and accompany the train from there to Kew. It was quite a spectacle on the platform at Victoria, with all the ladies' outfits and the gentlemen in their hired suits and top hats; in addition there was, even at this early hour, plenty of champagne flowing.

From time to time a shortage of qualified inspectors meant that I took on extra duties, some of which were very different from the norm. One evening, I found myself looking after the empty coaching stock of the Royal Train on a journey from Mitre Bridge to Clapham Junction. This situation had come about because there was no available SR inspector to take over from a colleague belonging to the London Midland Region who had come with the train from Wolverton, and who was already working an excessive amount of overtime.

On November 26th 1980, I found myself as part of a group of railway staff being used as guinea pigs in the trials of one of the prototype Advanced Passenger Trains (APT), this particular working taking place between London Euston and Preston. The idea of the trials was to give the train crew (including the dining car staff) experience of working on the APT with a full complement of passengers. For our part, we were asked to give our opinion as to how the train rode, and what we thought of the aircraft style seating layout. We found, in the course of our journey, that we could not find fault with either the food or the service provided by the crew on board, but we were not too impressed with the seating, either in the first or standard class parts of the train. In fact, we much preferred the more orthodox first class corridor compartment train that returned us from Preston (this latter service having commenced its journey at Glasgow Central) back to London!

The APT project had originally begun in the late 1960s when British Rail were looking to speed up inter-city services on the national network, in particular on the West Coast main line (WCML). This route, between London Euston and Glasgow, included many curves, and it was decided to build a train with a tilting mechanism which could traverse these curves at higher speeds than conventional trains, thereby cutting journey times. In 1972 the APT-E (for 'Experimental'), a four car train powered by gas-turbine engines, was built and sent on an exhaustive test programme to prove the tilting theories. This having been successfully completed, a trio of fourteen car trains known as APT-P (for 'Prototype') were then built, these being electrically powered. These three trains were brought into service in 1981 at a time when many technical problems were still being resolved. There was pressure from both managerial and political areas to show positive results, and unfortunately problems with both the tilt mechanism and the brakes (although the latter was due to the very cold weather of the time) caused the premature withdrawal of all three APT-Ps from service. In mid-1984, the trains returned to service, the problems having been corrected, but the will to carry on with the project had evaporated, and the planned production APTs were never built.

The APT-E is now in the custody of the National Railway Museum (NRM), and can be found at the NRM's Shildon base in County Durham. One of the three APT-P sets has been preserved at the Crewe Heritage Centre. In a strange twist to the APT story, once the project was abandoned by BR, the design of the powered tilt carriages was sold to the Fiat Ferroviaria company of Italy, who used it in their 'Pendolino' trains, a fleet of which are today hard at work on the WCML! So, it can be argued that the APT project was not a complete failure, in the way that it was ruthlessly portrayed as such by certain sections of the media, some thirty-odd years ago.

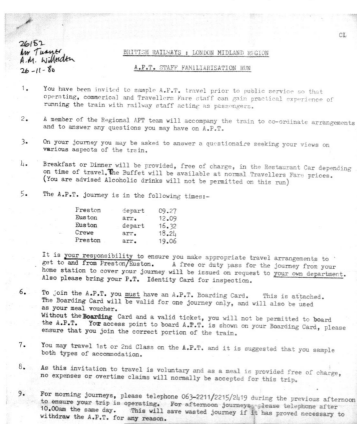

*Appendix 3
The itinerary and train ticket for the APT staff familiarisation run of 26.11.1980 (Author's Collection).*

CHAPTER EIGHTEEN

SPECIAL PROJECTS AND SPORTING EVENTS

As the reader will no doubt have gathered, my position as an Area Signalling Inspector at Willesden was one that contained many different roles and responsibilities, not unlike my time working as a Relief Station Master, where you would be expected to turn your hand to all manner of tasks, often at very short notice. I enjoyed the variety in my day-to-day routine, added to which, covering a wide cross section of jobs would enable me to add to my all round railway knowledge, which in turn would be useful when looking for suitable promotion opportunities.

Over a period of many years, much criticism has been levelled at the national railway network, and those who run them, about delays to services caused by bad weather conditions. Even during my time working at Willesden, people would laugh when it was reported (for example) that the 'wrong type of snow' had caused disruptions of this kind. As far as operational railway staff were concerned, extreme types of weather did cause major delays to train services. In some cases, should bad weather be forecast, there were things that could be done to offset the problems that would occur. For example, in the case of high temperatures, heat patrols would be provided by the local permanent way (or 'Pway') department. (A heat patrol meant that a group of Pway staff would patrol their section of line, looking for any signs of distortion or other irregularities in the track, and take immediate remedial action to avoid any problems). There was a particular type of point in use that was known as a 'switch diamond' (this being the name given to two sets of point blades facing and closing together, which operated simultaneously) which would cause no end of trouble during periods of hot weather. What would happen was that the heat would expand the point blades, which would then fail to fit up securely and, as a result, would prevent the lock which ensured that they were fitting up correctly to lock into place. Unless it was essential to use points of this type, they were secured in their normal position for the straight 'up and down' running of services, and trains needing to take a diversionary route would do so at an earlier location. If they had to be used, then a point clip would be fitted and padlocked – trains would be allowed to travel over them, but at a reduced speed. When the appropriate repairs to the points in question were carried out by the Pway department, the Signal & Telegraph section would also be involved, as would an Operating Inspector, his specific responsibility being to liaise with the local power box. Even straight sections of track were not immune to problems of this type. In areas where 'sixty foot' type rails were in situ, having recently been laid after replacing older rails, if the track had not fully settled in, the rails could buckle. It would be necessary for one to have to wait until the temperature dropped before the rail could be straightened. Hot weather could also play havoc with newer long welded rails; the heat could cause the expansion joint to 'creep' too far, and a small length had to be cut off.

In the case of heavy snow being forecast, it was the normal practice for the technical departments and the operating staff to be put on twelve hour shifts in order to keep points free of snow and ice. As can be imagined, this was not an easy task – even with the reduced train services that were operating. At junctions, a balance had to be kept between keeping the points moving, so that they would not freeze up but, at the same time, not to move them too much that falling snow became wedged in between the blades of the points, thus preventing them from operating properly. One of the major problems that occurred with this work was that as soon as a set of points had been cleared of both snow and ice, and anti-freeze added, a train would pass by on an adjacent line, and blow a quantity of loose snow back in the points again! With so many routes in the Willesden area, it was a never-ending job trying to keep the lines open.

Heavy rain was another form of extreme weather that could play havoc with railway operations. On a number of occasions major problems occurred when, during the course of heavy thunderstorms, bolts of lightning would strike one or another of the Signal and Telegraph (S & T) Department's location cabinets within our area, the result of which would be that all signals in the immediate vicinity would be put out of action. This meant that hand signalmen had to be used to cover all train movements until the necessary repairs could be carried out. As one can imagine this was a most unpleasant job, standing out in pouring rain. In addition to heavy rain, we had problems with flooding. There were times when, after a heavy downpour, the floodwater would come over the electrified third rail on the DC routes between London Euston and Watford, the water 'shorting' out the current. I well remember on one occasion, when I was visiting Kensington South box during the course of an evening shift, getting a call to go across to Kilburn. When I arrived, I found that the floodwater had already risen to a level above the running rails on the main line. At this location, the electrified DC lines were laid at a higher level than the main line; however the rain water had already flooded the tunnels at Primrose Hill, and was almost at rail level, this meaning that the London-bound DC services were being reversed at Kilburn. My own journey from Kensington to Kilburn was also badly affected by the rainy weather. Much of the tube network was out of action for this reason, and I got to my destination in a roundabout way, which involved using two bus services. On arrival, one of my tasks was to help clear debris from the running lines, so that the train services could continue to run, although at a reduced speed. Even though I was wearing a good mackintosh, and other appropriate wet-weather clothing, by the time that things returned to a more-or-less even keel I was soaked to the skin, especially around my feet and legs!

As I mentioned at the start of this chapter, part of my responsibility was the ability to take on additional work at very short notice. During the middle part of the eleven year period of time that I was working at Willesden, I was approached by my area manager and asked if I would cover one of the Willesden power box supervisors, during a period of extended leave. The supervisor in question was taking a total of eight weeks leave, this being to visit his family, who were living in Australia. The role was a time-consuming one, entailing three shifts (these being early, late and night turns), and would also involve being on duty for two out of every three Sundays, the shifts concerned being long ones. On a positive note, I was allowed to retain my own rate of salary, together with my on-call allowances, these being an additional payment over and above my normal wages for the inconvenience of carrying out on-call duties outside of normal working hours. I was not used to working in positions of this type in indoor locations, but as it was for a short period of time, I agreed to do it.

The job entailed being responsible for the regulation of all the various train services throughout the area covered by the power box. It also involved keeping Control and neighbouring boxes advised of any late running, together with notification of any incidents that had occurred which would affect the running of the timetabled service. In addition, when problems did crop up, it was the supervisor's responsibility to liaise with the various technical departments, and contacting 'on-call' members of staff, who could sort out these problems. You were, of course, also responsible for the signalmen within the box working under your command. During my time in this role I found that, while on some days everything would run smoothly, at other times you had your work cut out, especially if there were major disruptions on one line or another.

From time to time major building and civil engineering projects were carried out within the Willesden area. For example, during the mid-1970s, the bridges which carried the lines from Broad Street to Richmond over the north-bound route from London Euston had to be renewed. As can be imagined, this was a major operation, and one which took considerable planning, taking into account the fact that, quite apart from the bridge renewal work involved, blockages and diversions on the railway lines affected needed to be organised. I can recall that, because of the size and weight of some of the sections that made up the new bridge, a special five hundred ton crane had to be hired from a company in Germany. To take the weight of this crane, a large concrete platform had to be laid between the fast and slow lines of the north-bound route from Euston. It was fortunate that, to enable the mighty crane to reach the point where it was required, a sleeper crossing was available that linked the concrete platform with an adjacent road, that led to the Traction Maintenance Depot. Two portacabins were built alongside the platform – one cabin was to be the temporary Operating Engineering Office and the other was to be a type of messroom for the staff working on site. There were two reasons for the construction of these temporary dwellings, the first being that there was a lot of preparation work that had to be carried out before the arrival of the crane itself. The second was that the blockades of the railway lines in

Picture 47 Lifting a section of 'Bridge Five' at Willesden Junction. This structure carried the North London route across the West Coast main line (Author).

question were done at very short notice. In addition, arrangements were made for one of the newspaper trains that still ran from Euston at this time to stop alongside the site and drop some reading material off.

When the crane arrived, it needed the help of a smaller crane to build it and put it in position. As part of this stage of the plan, the overhead wires on the Euston line had to be temporarily removed. All went well when the new bridge was placed in position, but when we came to run the first train from Richmond to Broad Street, an unexpected problem was found. The small raised walkway alongside the railway line just fouled the side of the train. In order to solve this hiccup, a special steel circular cutting saw had to be used to remove a couple of inches from the side of the walkway. This enabled the local train to make its way across the bridge.

At the start of the operation to remove the bridge that traversed the Euston to Watford DC lines, the steam cranes belonging to Willesden and Hornsey depots were used. For a while, everything ran smoothly, with the dismantled sections of bridge being transferred to a special goods train that would take these items away. However, the operation was delayed, and the train crews eventually reached the end of their shift and thus were unable to move the freight. As a replacement crew would not be available for quite a while, it seemed as though the work would not be able to be completed within the allocated time-frame. It was fortunate for those of us in charge that there was a Management Trainee traction fitter observing all that was going on. This individual offered to move the train involved as he had previously trained on the type of diesel locomotive that was hauling the freight. This was unofficial, and against all regulations and, had any train driver found out what was happening, we would have ended up with a strike on our hands. As it was, the movement was only two wagons in length and, as a result, we managed to get away with it.

I was involved in another bridge replacement scheme during this same period of time. This was at West Hampstead, where the North London line crossed the Midland main line from London St Pancras, and was in connection with the electrification of the Midland line to Bedford. When the new bridge was positioned, a picture of the event was taken by the official London Midland Region photographer. I was standing on the bridge at the time, but was unaware that I was about to be immortalised in the photographic form. The resulting picture was then displayed in the entrance lobby of the General Manager Offices in Euston House. Quite a number of people recognised me and pulled my leg about it!

On certain occasions I found myself carrying out duties of a somewhat more laid-back nature, and quite some way removed from my normal day-to-day routines. One such occasion came about as the result of an enquiry made to the area manager at Willesden from the BR Public Relations Office. The question was asked whether it would be possible for an inspector to accompany a BBC film crew, who were filming a wildlife documentary. I was asked to take on this particular task, which involved escorting the film crew whilst they filmed from a train, and worked at various locations along both the North London line from Willesden to Kew, and the DC suburban route between Willesden and Watford. The documentary was a follow-up to a book entitled 'The Unofficial Countryside', written by Richard Mabey. Mr Mabey himself also travelled with the film crew and provided the commentary. The wildlife seen on the railway banks included squirrels, a vixen with her young cubs and a number of birds of prey. Not only was the wildlife filmed, but also some semi-rare flowers. To explain how seeds were scattered, the film crew laid down as near to a railway line in Kenton Yard as I would allow. They filmed the scattering of the fluffy seeds of the Oxford ragwort, as a train passed by.

On another occasion, I had a phone call from the Operations Manager at Crewe, asking me to meet Ralph Montague (who was the son of Lord Montague) and conduct him round all the signal boxes situated in Willesden Yard and Carriage Sidings, as he wanted to take photographs of them for his personal collection before they were closed. Mr Montague came on two occasions and he was kind enough to send me copies of all the pictures that he took. I also (unofficially) took Richard Foster (the author of a railway book entitled 'LNWR Signalling') and a friend of his (who was a prison governor) around many of the old manual signal boxes in our area, before they too were closed.

The reader will recall that in chapter eleven, whilst in my role as a relief station master, I briefly spoke about when I would assist at Wembley Central, when special events were happening at the old Wembley Stadium. However, it was not until I started working at Willesden that I realised the amount of planning and organising that had to be done beforehand to ensure that everything went according to plan, both on the days leading up to, and on the day of the main event itself. The planning process would get under way when the Special Timing Section at Crewe would issue what was known as a 'Special Traffic Notice', this internal publication listing both the timings of all the special trains for the various supporters and the alterations to the ordinary train service to accommodate them. The normal procedure was to run the specials over the slow lines to and from Wembley

Central, with plenty of recovery time built into their respective schedules, in case of any unforeseen delay. All local trains, along with a Watford Junction to London Euston shuttle service, would be booked to use the fast lines, and all would call at Wembley Central both before and after the main event. On the Thursday prior to the weekend of the event in question, I would meet up with a ganger from the Pway Department and a technician from the Signal and Telegraph Section, our combined job being to test and oil the ground frame that was situated at the north end of the slow line platforms at Wembley Central, this being to make the frame ready for use on the following weekend.

It was the job of the train crew managers to book the necessary crews required to work all the specials. They would also advise the Train Crew Supervisor, who was located at Stonebridge Park (Willesden), of any relief crews that would be required to take over from those train crews arriving at Wembley, or whether any conductors would be needed to accompany any of these crews to the carriage sidings. Usually this did not cause any problems, but on occasions a train would arrive at Wembley, and the crews would insist on having a relief set of men take over. To cover a happening of this kind, there were usually a couple of extra Stonebridge Park members of staff booked on specifically for this purpose. I knew that on some occasions, even crews who knew the route into the sidings wanted relief. The reason for this was that they had managed to pick up tickets for the event in question from supporters on the special train – and who could blame them?

It was nothing unusual to have around twenty trains of supporters arrive at Wembley Central between the hours of 10.30 and 14.00, these being mainly from the north of the country. The passengers would alight, and then the coaches would be taken to the adjacent carriage or freight yard sidings for cleaning and servicing; this would, of course, have to be completed in time for their respective return journeys. At times, there was a surplus of coaches arriving in this way. In my Relief Station Master (RSM) days, I can recall that some carriages that needed cleaning were sent to Neasden on the Marylebone route, travelling via Acton Canal Wharf and Neasden Junction. Camden Goods Yard was also utilised in this way and, when special trains arrived from either the west of England, southern England or East Anglia, some of the servicing would be done at Watford Junction, special authority being given for these vehicles to be lined up on the up slow line between Kenton and Wembley Central to await their return workings.

Wembley Central had one important drawback when handling special trains of the type described – the slow line platforms could only hold a formation of eight carriages in length, the platforms being tailored to look after the local electric trains, which were of either three, four, six or eight cars in length, each car being shorter than the equivalent locomotive hauled coach. As most specials arriving at Wembley had more than eight coaches, the normal procedure was to stop the train with its rear off the platform. The next step was that one of the station supervisors would enter the last carriage still on the platform, and stop the supporters sitting in the coaches beyond this point walking forward. Then, as soon as the platformed passengers had alighted from the train, the train itself was drawn forward, so that the remaining supporters could get off. As regards the return workings, our hard work carried on long after the event in question had finished. You could always guarantee that, after all the special trains had departed, there would be a few stragglers turn up at the station, looking for a train to head home. It was quite a normal procedure to make arrangements for one or two north-bound expresses to stop 'out of course' at Wembley to pick these unfortunate individuals up.

In my earlier role as an RSM helping out at Wembley Central, I realised that although the station announcer would tell all arriving supporters which platform they would need to access to board their returning train (this being either platforms five or six), there was no indication or notices on either of these platforms telling passengers which was which! I pointed this out to the senior officer on duty, who admitted that no-one working in the locality had noticed this somewhat basic omission. Needless to say, it was put right before the next major event.

I mentioned earlier the easy timings of the special trains, and one 'stand out' incident comes to mind. On this particular occasion, Manchester United were playing in the Football Association (FA) Cup Final, and the directors of the club had hired no less a train than the 'Manchester Pullman', complete with all its dining facilities. As a result of its very easy schedule, the Pullman arrived at Wembley Central an hour early and, as such, the directors were only halfway through their lunch! Because of the many other special trains due, there was no way the Pullman could remain in the platform at Wembley until lunch was finished. Quick thinking on my part, combined with co-operation from the local train crew manager, alongside full support from our own Control and that of the Southern Region, enabled the Pullman to be sent forward over the West London line to Clapham Junction, then onto Kew and back to Wembley Central, via Acton Canal Wharf and the connecting line between there and Willesden Junction. This enabled the train's occupants to finish their lunch!

CHAPTER NINETEEN

A MOVE TO EUSTON

(Author's note: a map of the Euston area can be found in Appendix 8)

In 1984, having spent a number of years working in my position as an Area Signalling Inspector at Willesden, I then became a victim of another railway re-organisation, as a result of which I was made redundant. In this particular case the area covered by Willesden was merged with that of Euston – at the same time the Watford area was combined with its neighbour at Bletchley. As a result of these changes, two vacancies for positions similar to what I had been doing became available. The first of these was located at Bletchley and the second at Euston. I was asked to attend an interview for the former vacancy which, if I had been successful, would have meant that I would be working only fifteen miles from where I lived. It would also have been the completion of a 'full circle', career-wise, as I had joined the footplate department at Bletchley way back in 1948. Unfortunately, it became quite clear at my interview that I was not going to get the job on offer, which I was very annoyed about, given my experience and seniority.

However, there was an unusual outcome to my interview. About a week after it had taken place, I had a phone call one evening from the area manager at Euston, asking me to go and see him. I actually knew him, as he had previously held a position as area manager at St Pancras. It will be remembered in chapter fourteen of this story that during my time working as a station supervisor at Kensington Olympia, I had to undertake a project to obtain a National Examination Board of Supervisory Studies Certificate. It was the area manager at St Pancras who had decided what the subject of my project should be. On the occasion of our latest meeting, he offered me a cup of tea and asked me to sit down. Once I was settled, he began by saying, "Jack, I know you are upset about not getting the Bletchley job, but I need you here at Euston, as there is no-one else who knows the Willesden area like you do, and with a lot of work scheduled there over the next few years, I can't do without you. Equally, you already have a good knowledge of the Euston area so, no ifs or buts, you will be joining me at Euston."

Having now heard what he had to say, I felt quite happy to take the position of Area Signalling Inspector at Euston. During my period of time working at Willesden, I had on occasions been used to assist with hand signalling in the station area at Euston itself, these duties coming about as the result of various derailments. In addition, I had also acted as Operating Inspector, supervising engineering work that was being carried out, once again in the station area at Euston. Within the new Euston area setup, I was to join the-then current Operating Inspector, who I had known whilst working at Willesden. We would share roles and responsibilities within the new combined area, although in practice, I found myself spending more time back in my old Willesden haunts.

The Euston area extended only for a couple of miles, as far as South Hampstead. However, as can be imagined, this small area included Euston terminus itself. At that time the station consisted of no less than nineteen platforms, two of which (platforms nine and ten) were electrified on the DC third rail system, these being used exclusively by the Euston to Watford all station suburban services, which travelled via such places as Queens Park, Willesden Junction and Wembley Central, as opposed to the fast services on the AC lines that for the most part only called at Harrow and Wealdstone, together with Bushey. Outside the station itself was the down side carriage shed and the up side stabling sidings, the latter including a short loco holding siding. In addition, there were also sidings at Camden, where parcel vans were held and, outside of the rush hours, where electric multiple units (EMUs) were stabled.

As far as staff matters were concerned, we were responsible for the signal box supervisors, signalmen, shunters and coupler/tankers. The last-named were people whose job was to couple and uncouple locomotives to their various trains – in addition, they were responsible for watering the coaches, which was carried out using water bowsers. The work carried out by the coupler/tankers was of a heavy and dirty nature, and as time went on I discovered that this role had a high turnover of staff, more than other jobs located within our area. I shared the training of the coupler/tankers, both in the classroom and also the practical training, which was carried out in the carriage sidings situated at Camden, and which was where the former motive power depot had been. It was here that the trainee coupler/tankers were first introduced to the heavy buckeye couplings, and where a number of them decided that this particular role was not for them. Surprisingly, we had a young lady trainee on one of our courses, who was clever enough to get the 'knack' of lifting the buckeyes up correctly. At the end of the course she was able to pass the relevant exam with flying colours. As far as the water bowsers were concerned, the trainees were supervised by representatives of the Plant and Machinery Department; once the trainees had passed the required test they were issued with a certificate, which enabled them to drive the bowser. In addition to our work training the coupler/tankers, we carried out a similar function for new entrants to work as signalmen, the idea being to cover forthcoming vacancies. We also sent some of our trainee signalmen over to another school at Waterloo, on the Southern Region, to attend courses held there.

Picture 48 The visit of Mrs Gough to Euston power box (Author's collection).

As part of the extensive rebuilding of Euston station during the 1960s, a new signal box (or 'power box') was constructed. This impressive structure was one that I became very familiar with during this period of time, and I found myself conducting various interested parties around its large interior. A number of overseas-based groups of railway personnel came to visit including, as I recall, a couple from Germany and Malaysia respectively. Nearer to home, we were honoured to host a group from the Cambridge University Railway Club. As a result of their visit, I was asked to go to Cambridge University, to give a talk to the members about my railway career. This was quite an experience for me, especially dining in Jesus College! On another memorable occasion we had cameramen from the BBC filming for children's television. The subject of the filming was a young boy who had asked if he could announce the train departures from Euston station. One of the trains that he announced was the 10.15 express departure to Holyhead. One of this working's stops was Llanfair PG, the station with the longest name in Britain (in its entirety, the full name being Llanfairpwllgwyngyllgogerychwyrndrobwllllantysiliogogogoch). To his great credit, our newest announcer managed to pronounce the entire name correctly!

On a more humbling note, another visitor to Euston power box was a lady who at that time was working in the BR legal department. It was a happy coincidence that her visit took place at the same time that the Royal Train was working into Euston station. Our guest was invited, under the supervision of one of the signalmen, to set the route into platform one, which is where the Royal Train was scheduled to arrive. She felt very honoured and delighted to carry out this important duty. It was, therefore, something of a shock to us when, before leaving the box, she told us that she had been diagnosed with cancer only the previous day. Sadly, we heard only a few weeks later that she had passed away. At the same time, we also discovered that her husband was a railway author, Mr John Gough. Over a period of years, Mr Gough has written a number of railway books, one of which was entitled 'British Rail at Work: East Midlands'. To this day I possess a copy of this particular book, signed by Mr Gough, and thanking me for the kindness shown to his wife.

Picture 49 An early 1980s view of the panel inside Euston power box (Author).

I mentioned earlier in this chapter about the various training programmes that I became involved in. On the railway at that particular moment in time, would-be engine drivers were known as 'traction trainees'. As part of their intensive learning programme, both myself and my inspector colleague would arrange for groups of these trainees to visit either Euston or Willesden power boxes, the aim being for our apprentices to get a better understanding of how a power box functioned and how, for example, why they would not always get clear signals. I did try, on numerous occasions, to arrange for our signalmen to have trips in the cabs of various locomotives; however, I was unsuccessful in my attempts to do so – a great pity, for it would have enabled the signalmen to see how the railway operated from a different angle.

As the reader may have gathered, the railway was an ever-changing place during my career, with many re-organisations both large and small. One of the biggest changes came in the 1985/86 period of time, which was when BR changed from being a single nationalised industry to being divided up into a series of what became known as 'vertical franchises', these being companies who owned all the infrastructure and rolling stock, and operated all the services, either within a certain business section of the former BR, or a particular geographical area. In the Euston zone, two new companies appeared, these being Inter-City and Network South-East. One result of these changes was that my Area Signalling Inspector colleague moved to a new post, that of a Freight Manager based at Willesden, which for him was a promotion. This in turn meant advertising for a replacement, and from the applications received for the position, two people were shortlisted for interviews. At one of these interviews, the candidate involved admitted that he had not bothered to do any homework as to what the job involved, neither had he taken the time to look at the geographical area of work that might have been his new 'beat'. He went onto say that he had only applied for the position to enable him to take a day off from his current work! Quite naturally my immediate supervisor, who was conducting the interview, was absolutely furious with him. It was fortunate that the second candidate, who had worked for me as a signalman at Willesden before being appointed to the position of Area Signalling Inspector at Marylebone, proved ideal for the vacancy, one reason being that he had 'done his homework' and had found out about the area covered by the vacancy, prior to attending the interview.

CHAPTER TWENTY

BOMBS AND BAD WEATHER

During my period of time working as Area Signalling Inspector at Euston, as well as the changes caused by the birth of the Inter-City and Network South-East sectors of the former BR industry, the normal day-to-day routine of running the railway was seriously affected by IRA bomb scares, which unfortunately occurred on a regular basis. They were an absolute nightmare and involved all passengers being evacuated from Euston station, as well as any railway staff who were working on the premises. Whenever one of these incidents occurred, my role was to act as a liaison officer between the police and the station manager, or his representative. Perhaps the only 'perk' of having to carry out this role was the fact that I would be based in the warm and cosy police office, which was located on the west side of Euston station! As a result I would not have to stand outside in wet and cold weather. One duty, which fortunately I only had to carry out over the course of three to four weekends, along with other senior operating staff and members of the British Transport Police (BTP), was to come out especially at midnight to check all trains for hidden explosive devices. Once these checks had been completed, I then carried on with my normal day turn of duty. These thorough checks also had to be carried out in all the buildings on the station – it was indeed fortunate that we never found anything suspicious.

In a similar vein, something that I found very interesting was to take part in a series of table-top exercises simulating a major disaster, which the BTP arranged with our help from the operating side of the railway. As well as a cross-section of operating people, all the various emergency services were represented, and there was even an individual from the national press. The locations of these exercises were many and varied, being mostly held in hired halls, but we also used a major hospital situated in North London, and even the Police Training School at nearby Hendon, each of these on a single occasion. The exercise itself had as its focal point an 'OO' gauge model railway layout, upon which had been built a major railway installation such as a station, which often featured a bridge of some kind. A derailed train would be the centrepiece of the layout, this representing the accident that had occurred. Each of the emergency departments would then use model vehicles (such as police cars, fire engines and ambulances) to establish where they thought these vehicles should be located in order to deal with the accident and the clearance of any casualties. When they had done this to their satisfaction, a discussion would then take place amongst the various bodies to form an overall opinion as to whether it was generally agreed that their vehicles were indeed in the right place. To conclude the discussions, the BTP representative would then suggest where he would expect them to place themselves. Usually at some stage the Press Office representative would give a talk on how the liaison between the media and the Site Officer would be set up. The Site Officer's role would be to act as a co-ordinator between all railway departments and the appointed spokesperson. This officer would also keep the railway HQ informed, as well as the national press and the television stations. During my time working at Euston I was also involved on a single occasion with another table-top disaster scenario, this time organised by London Transport (LT). Various tube routes ran directly underneath the main line station at Euston, and this was how I became involved with our LT colleagues. The layout itself was built to 'N' gauge scale, this being around half the size of the more common 'OO'.

I mentioned previously that I had taken part in an exercise at the Hendon Police College. After the exercise had finished I was asked, together with a colleague of mine, to collect the model layout. As there were many IRA bomb alerts taking place at the time, we approached the police security hut there with some trepidation, although we had been given written identification of who we were to present to the officers on duty. To our total disbelief, we arrived at the hut, explained that we had come to collect a model railway and the security staff waved us through with no checks whatsoever! So much for security!

One horrific incident which I can still recall clearly all these years later concerned the finding of the dead body of a man in his early teens, this gruesome sight being located in Park Street Tunnel, which was less than a mile out of Euston, the body being situated in the carriage lines section of the tunnel. It was quite obvious that he had been hit by a train, although we had not received any reports from any of our train crews of anything untoward happening. The body was examined by a pathologist, who was able to ascertain an approximate time of death. Having established this piece of information, I then spent a number of hours going through the recording tapes in Euston power box to try and find out which train movement was responsible for this dreadful tragedy. Despite much effort on my part, I never did get to the bottom of this mystery, although I was subsequently called as a witness during the Coroner's Inquest and I was congratulated on the clarity of my evidence.

The area into and out of Euston was one that was fairly confined and this, combined with the large amount of scheduled train services, meant that any problem with either point or signal failures could cause congestion within a very short space of time. I was one of a number of senior members of the operating staff who were issued with pagers, the idea being that we could be contacted easily, and we could get to the scene of an incident very quickly. If the location of a hold-up was (for example) a set of points, we would attempt to rectify the problem ourselves. It could be something as simple as a small piece of rubbish or a stone that had caused the points to malfunction. If however we could not resolve the problem, we would clip the points so that trains could pass over them safely, this being a temporary measure until the Signal & Telegraph Department representatives would arrive to carry out a full repair. In the backs of our minds, we were always well aware of the fact that the train service had to be kept moving with as few delays as possible.

There were other, much more serious incidents which could (and did) cause massive delays to the train service. I well recall one occasion when, due to a power failure, Euston station was at a total standstill. At the time this happened I was visiting some of the outlying signal boxes within the area with a colleague of mine, utilising a car that belonged to BR. We were called back to Euston and, as we approached the station along Euston Road, we saw that there was something of a traffic hold-up. To speed things up we bypassed this obstruction by moving into a 'bus-only' lane, and entered the station forecourt via the 'bus-only' entrance. We traversed the full length of the station in our vehicle, and then turned sharp left under the station itself, which was where a service road was situated.

When we stopped and got out, we were apprehended by a police vehicle which, unbeknown to us, had been following our car, and had then pulled up alongside us. Two policemen got out and demanded to know what we had been doing. We replied by telling them that there was an emergency on, and to check our story with the BTP to confirm that it was true. They went to our railway police colleagues, and they must have been satisfied with the explanation that they received, because we never heard another word about the incident. It was sometime before the power failure itself was sorted out, and both my assistant and myself were utilised on the running tracks, hand signalling trains for a couple of hours.

Other incidents that spring to mind include those that were caused by derailments in a clutch of sidings located adjacent to Euston station which were known as the 'backing out' roads. I do not know the actual origin of this somewhat curious name, but my guess is it was because empty rolling stock would 'back out' into these sidings, on their way from the down side shed to the station (or vice-versa). The derailments involved coaching stock that was being drawn out of the down side shed into one of two 'long neck' sidings (these were two dead end sidings where trains exiting the down side shed would be drawn into, before being propelled onto the backing out roads). The empty coaching stock (ECS) would be pulled out of the down side shed by the same locomotive that would also be hauling the train once it had taken up its booked duty. This engine would then draw the train up one of the two long necks, following which it would then be propelled via the backing out roads into Euston station itself. At the end of each road were trap points which guarded against conflicting train movements. Unfortunately, on certain occasions, some of the shunters who rode in the brake vans of the stock being marshalled in order to control the brake itself misjudged the stopping point, the result being that the train itself became derailed at these trap points. In addition, because of limited clearance between each road, when a derailment happened, the vehicle concerned would demolish the ground signals that were protecting that particular movement.

Sometimes, the sources of problems that played havoc with the simple everyday business of running the railway were unexpected as much as unwelcomed. During my time at Euston, on no fewer than three separate occasions, we were affected by flooding that had been caused, not by bad or adverse weather conditions, but by burst water mains which were situated just outside the station. The first of these incidents caused flooding to a depth of no less than two feet in platform nineteen and the adjacent small loading dock. The second was initiated by a burst main that, unluckily, was located right above the previously mentioned Park Street Tunnel. The result was that a great mass of water poured into the tunnel itself. The overhead electric wires in the tunnel had to be isolated as a result of what had happened; in addition, after the water had been cleared, a thorough inspection of the whole tunnel had to be carried out in order to confirm that there was no lasting structural damage. However, the last of this sad series of incidents was also the most destructive, as the water involved flooded the station's underground car park. At the time, the car park was full and the water came up over the bonnets of the vehicles concerned. It took no less than two to three days before the water dropped to a more manageable level, but as a result, petrol had escaped from the tanks of many of the cars, and in the confined space the fumes created were overpowering. When the water had completely subsided I, along with an operating staff colleague, were asked if we would be prepared to go down into the car park and take details of all the vehicles that had been damaged by what had gone on – a grim task we reluctantly agreed to. What on the face of things was a fairly straightforward job took us the whole of one day to complete, as we had to stop to get some fresh air every fifteen minutes. As can be expected, there were many different makes of cars involved, ranging from humble Minis to more upmarket BMWs and Jaguars. All these vehicles were write-offs, and it must have cost the local water board a fortune in settling insurance claims.

Away from Euston itself, another area which became flooded from time to time was nearby Primrose Hill Tunnel, which was situated on the local DC passenger service route to Watford. Here the root cause of our problems would be a combination of heavy rain and blocked drains. When this occurred the DC service had to be suspended, because the flood water would cover the electric third rail, which in turn would cause the power to short-circuit. When the flood water came up to the underside of this particular rail it began to literally boil, and if you were in the vicinity you could see the steam created escape through the ventilation shafts!

Snow and ice caused problems on a number of occasions, memorable, but for all the wrong reasons. One occasion in particular that I well remember came about as the result of a scheme which had been put together to heat all the points, prior to the advent of that year's winter weather. I was responsible for arranging with the relevant technical departments possessions of the sections of lines involved, the actual installation being carried out by a private contractor. Although the original plan was that this work was to be completed during the autumn of the year in question (the scheme taking place during the late 1980s), due to various delays, it was still being carried out the following February! One reason for the time schedule being upset in this way was that, although the possession of the track had been organised and given, the private contractors had failed to turn up and, as a result, no actual work was done.

It was unfortunate that my good name was called into question around this time. I had booked a few days leave and had decided to go on a short holiday to York with Pat, my wife. When our holiday had finished and we set out to return home, our journey south was delayed by heavy snow, which also affected Euston, decimating the planned train service. As the contractors had not completed the installation of the point heaters, many unmodified points were frozen up. Somewhere along the line, someone had stated that the reason why the work required had not been completed was because I had refused to give the necessary possessions for the work required. This nameless individual had clearly not checked his facts correctly because, on those occasions where the contractors had not appeared, I had advised my immediate supervisor in writing of what had (or in this case, had not) happened. As you can imagine, because of this misunderstanding, my name was mud! Therefore when I returned to work, I was told to report to the Area Manager and, through him, explain to the General Manager at Crewe why I had not given the required possessions. It was fortunate that because I had already given an account of what had actually happened, I was able to clear my name.

Whilst on the subject of possessions, when any work was taking place within the vicinity of the station area of Euston, and because the signals that controlled the entrances to the different platforms covered multiple routes, it was necessary to keep those signals that we were still running trains past working. To ensure that these particular signals could not be cleared accidently, or a route set into where a blockage had been located, we had to issue a written request to the Signal & Telegraph Department to remove the links which controlled the circuitry covering the blockage, and retain those to the other lines. The same situation applied if there had been a derailment, once again so that we could still signal trains into the station around the blockage.

CHAPTER TWENTY-ONE

NEW PLANS AND PROJECTS

From the mid-1980s, more changes took place in the London Midland Region as the newly formed Inter-City sector started to expand and find its feet. As far as people like myself, who were working on the operational side of the rail network were concerned, the most immediate of these changes concerned the transfer of much responsibility from the various divisions that we had known in the past to the equivalent area manager's organisations. In addition, by this moment in time, a number of the Divisional Signalling Inspectors that I had worked with, either at Willesden or Euston, had either retired from the railways or, in some cases, had sadly passed away. I therefore found myself recruiting a number of additional inspectors to this particular role. These new inspectors would, in due course, find themselves covering various signalling and engineering projects, which were planned to take place in and around the Willesden area during this period of time.

Special train workings took place from time to time, providing an additional source of interest to my work. One such occasion took place on Wednesday November 11th 1987. The train in question was the first of a new electrically hauled 'Speedlink' freight service between Willesden and Peterborough. In the course of its journey, this working utilised a recently electrified section of track from the West Coast main line (WCML), via Primrose Hill and Camden Road, and then joining the East Coast route heading north from London at a location known as Freight Terminal Junction, this being situated approximately half a mile out of Kings Cross. The train began its travels at London Euston and, being the inaugural journey of its type, was initially formed of two Pullman coaches, the elegant duo being hauled by an AC electric locomotive, 85 011, which was driven by a crew based at Stonebridge Park. The coaches were to convey a cross-section of VIPs from various parts of both commerce and industry. I joined the train at Willesden, where 85 011 had been detached from the original stock formation, and had then attached a series of the latest container wagons, before being attached to the opposite end of the train and recommencing its journey. The original plan was that I would accompany

<u>*Appendix 4*</u> *The log of the inaugural run of the new Speedlink electrically-operated service between Willesden and Peterborough on November 11th 1987 (Author's Collection).*

the train as far as Freight Terminal Junction before an Eastern Region inspector would take over for the remainder of the journey. However, on arrival at my planned destination, nobody was on hand so, with the agreement of the train guard (who also was from the Eastern Region), I was allowed to stay with the special all the way to Peterborough.

As can be imagined, working for the railway over many years, I made lots of friends and on occasions I would meet ex-colleagues in the course of my work. One such occasion was about to present itself, unbeknown to me. When the special arrived at Peterborough, the plan was that it would stop in the station proper, before terminating its journey in the adjacent freight yard, this being arranged as so to pick up the resident Freight Manager. When this gentleman boarded the train, I discovered that it was none other than my former Operations Manager, this from the time when I began working at Willesden during the mid-1970s! Once the train had safely arrived in the freight terminal, I was able to leave it and join the VIPs in looking at demonstrations of Mini, Maxi Link and Trailer Train Road-Rail transfer systems that had been arranged. When this was finished, I then had to get back to my starting point at Willesden – the only problem being that I had no train ticket! It was fortunate that I still had all the paperwork relating to the 'Speedlink' working, which I was able to show to the ticket collector on the London-bound express that I boarded.

The late 1980s were a period of time when a considerable amount of engineering-type projects were taking place. One such undertaking, which took almost four years to complete, was the rebuilding of the six bridges which took not only the WCML but also the DC local lines, together with the freight and carriage yards, over the busy North Circular Road which was being widened. The actual work involved replacing some of these bridges completely and adding an extension onto the others. As can be imagined, such a project took a considerable amount of pre-planning. Prior to the physical work commencing, there were quite a number of meetings between the various local technical, operating and commercial departments, each of which were chaired by a Project Manager. Also in attendance were representatives of the timetable planning section, who were normally based at Crewe. On those occasions where the blockages of the railway lines involved the diversion of scheduled freight services, the representative from the diversionary route would also have to be present. To digress a little, at one of these meetings that involved diversions over the Eastern Region, a representative from York attended in his technical capacity. Imagine my surprise when I saw and recognised the Eastern Region representative. We had previously lived in the next street to one another, and had both attended the same school in Aylesbury. It had been almost forty years since we last met!

Before a start could be made on the replacing and rebuilding of the bridges themselves, a roadway had to be built, connecting the North Circular itself to an area of land adjacent to the bridges, where the required construction materials could be delivered. Once the work proper commenced, many complex operations had to be carried out whilst working on each bridge or its replacement. As an example, when the bridge carrying the DC local lines was being replaced, prior to the weekend of that particular operation, the power cables, along with those cables belonging to the Signal & Telegraph Department, had to be moved clear of the bridge. During the weekend itself, after the possession of the lines involved had been taken over by the site engineers, the first job would be to remove the track by hand and then a machine was brought in to remove the ballast and the waterproofing material. To finish this part of the work, the girders would be removed by a crane and the remaining brickwork broken up and removed. The new bridge (which had already been assembled) was then placed in position, the waterproofing, ballasting and the track all replaced, and the previously mentioned cables re-connected. It is astounding to recall that, despite the complexities of the work involved, all of the above would be completed within the course of a single long weekend possession, the duration being from 23.00 hours on the Friday night to 05.00 on the following Monday morning. Until the track was bedded in a speed restriction would be imposed over the new bridge.

Occasionally, things did not go to plan. On one occasion, when work was being undertaken to dig out the foundations for one of the WCML bridges that was being extended, it was found that water kept flooding the hole that was being dug. Despite many efforts to pump the foundations dry, the water kept pouring in and delays were being incurred. I was visiting the site one day and discovered this unhappy situation. I suggested to the engineers involved that, in all probability, they had come across the course of the River Brent, which used to flow in that direction many years previously. To confirm what I had told them, the engineers then decided to look at old maps of the area, which indicated the presence of the former river, following which they managed to divert the water away from where the digging operations were being carried out.

Around this time, I was finding more and more of my working days being taken up by project meetings of one kind or another. I ended up by leaving the more everyday tasks and duties to either my assistant or one or another of the engineering inspectors. However, I did find that I would be compelled to get involved with incidents that took place outside normal working hours. Living as I did, near to Bedford, I would find myself more or less permanently 'on call'. When I was summoned in this way, I would drive to Bletchley, make arrangements with the power box there to stop the next passenger or parcels train that was travelling up to London and utilise this to get to where the incident in question was. However, on other occasions, if for example the running lines had been blocked, or if there had been a major signal failure, I would drive straight to the scene of the happening. One such incident, which I can easily recall, did not in fact take place within my Euston/Willesden area, but just 'over the border' in the Watford zone.

On this particular occasion, which was on a Sunday evening, I was just about to go home, having been supervising some major engineering work that had taken place in the vicinity of Willesden power box. I got an urgent message from Control, asking me to go to South Kenton (this being just south of Harrow & Wealdstone) where a locomotive that had been hauling a north-bound express train had developed a major fault with its overhead equipment. In turn this fault had caused the overhead power cables to come down. My job was to report back to Control on what was happening. On arrival, I found a sight which I had never seen before – with the intense heat from the cables, the Class 82 electric locomotive involved had welded itself to the running rails! It was fortunate that the slow lines (those over which the local passenger and freight trains would normally travel) were not affected by what had happened, so at least we were able to keep the scheduled services running.

Once the overhead line engineering gang had arrived at the scene of the incident, and got the wire untangled from the train itself, I arranged with Control to bring a DC local train alongside the stranded coaches of the errant express in order to transfer the passengers. As well as myself, help was provided by the station supervisor from Harrow & Wealdstone and both train crews, ladders being supplied to enable the transfer to take place. The local train then took the passengers to Wembley Central (their luggage following on the next service), where a later north-bound Inter-City train was stopped 'out of course' to pick these people up and enable them to proceed on their way. It wasn't until all of this had taken place (which took just over two hours) that the Watford 'On Call' Inspector finally arrived on the scene and I was then able to go home.

On another memorable occasion, I was called out on a Sunday night to go and work at Euston power box as one of the two rostered signalmen had gone sick and there was no cover available. When I arrived at the box, I found that the cover was needed on what was known at Euston as the 'station end' (the staff at Euston had come up with this nickname – the other section being christened the 'country end'), this being the more complex of the two parts to work, and it was an area that I was not too familiar with. To add to my problems, I had had to discipline the signalman who was working with me only a couple of days previously. In my mind, I was thinking that my colleague was going to enjoy watching me struggling with my side of things. How wrong I was! In an act of great generosity, he offered to swap ends, thus easing my burden greatly. If, however, I thought that things would settle down for a quiet night's shift, I was sadly mistaken. About 04.30, the flood alarm went off for the DC line tunnel. I ended up having to sort out this latest incident after finishing my turn of duty in the box.

Amongst my other duties were those of a personnel-type nature. For example, I had to undertake disciplinary interviews with both shunting staff and signalmen, in addition to which I was required to hold enquiries into minor mishaps which did not need to be reported to the Railway Inspectorate. I also had the job of interviewing prospective new members of staff for our section, this being done with a member of the personnel department. On one occasion I made what could have been a serious error of judgement. I cannot recall the year in question, but it was during one autumn that I was carrying out interviews for the position of train announcer in Euston power box. My personnel colleague was a lady, as was the interviewee, the latter being very smartly dressed, living in Lincoln and had previously worked as a holiday rep in (if my memory serves me correctly) the Canary Islands. During the course of the interview, I pointed out to her that to arrive at the box in time for the early shift, she would have to catch a London-bound train by 04.00 at the latest! I then went onto say that she would have to walk across from Kings Cross in all weathers. She replied by stating that this would not be a problem to her, to which I replied, "I don't believe you." I went on to say that if the truth be known, once the spring came round, she would leave and return to her former position. I concluded by apologising, but pointed out that there was no way that I would employ her in the vacant position. Once the interview was finished, I then found myself being severely lectured by my personnel colleague. She complained about the way that I had dealt with the interviewee, saying that I was wrong in what I had said and that I was discriminating against her. She concluded by saying that she was going to report me to her immediate manager, who was also a woman. However, this outburst was the last that I heard of the matter.

In spite of my delegating various tasks, I was having to attend more project meetings. Many new schemes were coming to fruition, not least of which was the remodelling of Brent Freight Yard, this being done in anticipation of the traffic that was expected to come through the forthcoming Channel Tunnel. In addition, a new junction was to be laid in at North Wembley, whilst alterations were to take place at Sudbury. Additional Channel Tunnel-related projects that were in the planning stage included the major resignalling programmes to be carried out at Willesden South Junction, and also at South West Sidings. The project meetings in question were held either in London, Crewe or Birmingham. Sometimes these meetings could become somewhat fraught and, on one or two occasions, I myself clashed with the attending project manager over how the work in question could be carried out, where the safety of a particular section of line was concerned. It was fortunate that I had the full backing of the Regional Operating Management team at Crewe to confirm what I was saying. I also remember another such gathering, which was held on the Southern Region (SR) at

East Croydon and which had as its main topic, work which was to be carried out on the West London line. The SR people present wanted to put in a particular method of working on the line whilst the work in question was being undertaken, a method which I completely disagreed with as I felt that it was unsafe. Things got heated, and the chairman of the meeting, who was a senior operating officer, called for a break to calm things down. He then contacted the Operating Manager's Office (OMO) at Crewe for their views on the matter. The OMO agreed with what I had said, the follow-up to which was that I was asked for my opinion on how I would tackle the job in hand. Not only did I suggest an alternative (and safer) method of working, but I offered to assist them in finding the additional staff that would be required. I was afraid that at times I could be rather stubborn, especially if I felt that I was in the right!

Another of these meetings, this time in Birmingham, was a much happier occasion. It was a meeting organised by the line General Manager for senior staff which included my Operations Manager. However, at almost the last moment, he opted out and he sent me in his place! I mentioned earlier in this chapter that I kept meeting old colleagues in the most unlikely of circumstances, and on arrival I discovered that the Assistant General Manager, who was chairing the meeting, was someone who I had trained when he had first started working on the railway as a Traffic Apprentice (which, in railway terms, was a management trainee who worked within the Operating (or Traffic) Department). Before the meeting started, coffee and doughnuts were served by his secretary. He explained that the reason for having the doughnuts was that during the period of time that he was being trained by me at Willesden, at the morning get-together with the Operating Manager, it became a kind of tradition that doughnuts were served along with our hot drinks! He added that he thought it quite appropriate on this particular occasion!

CHAPTER TWENTY-TWO

NEW UPGRADES AND THE COMING OF THE CHANNEL TUNNEL

As I mentioned in the previous chapter, a considerable amount of both engineering and re-signalling work was taking place within the Willesden area during the period of time covering the late 1980s and early 1990s. Much of this work was being done in preparation for the forthcoming completion of the Channel Tunnel. This had a big impact on my area in a number of ways, not least of which was the construction of the North Pole Maintenance Depot, this being located on the opposite side of the Western Region (WR) main line to the existing facilities at Old Oak Common. It also meant that the empty 'Eurostar' rolling stock had to be worked to and from the original London terminus for these trains which, of course, was at Waterloo. The normal route for this empty carriage stock (ECS) working would have been to access the West London line at Clapham Junction, and then join the WR at North Pole Junction. However, when the building of North Pole Depot commenced, it was decided to construct an access road which, in the course of its journey, had to be built over the line between North Pole and Old Oak Junction, the latter being situated on the WR main line from Paddington, at the point where the connection from North Pole joined it. This in turn meant that the empty stock workings of the Eurostars had to continue their respective journeys past the connection with the WR main line, onto Willesden, and then travel through both South West and Old Oak Sidings to Acton Wells Junction. From this latter point they would travel to Acton Yard, finally accessing North Pole Depot by means of a reversal.

As one can imagine, much work and many modifications to the infrastructure had to be carried out to bring this section of railway up to the high standards required to accommodate these prestigious trains. Preliminary work took place over many weekends and involved signal alterations at Acton Wells Junction, the complete relaying of the through roads in both South West and Old Oak Sidings and the laying of cables for the new signalling. Obviously, new signals would have to be installed, and the position of each signal was agreed upon by a group known as the Signal Sighting Committee. This body was made up of one representative from each of the following areas: motive power staff, operating department and the Signal and Telegraph (S & T) Department. As part of the general plan, alterations were also made to the S & T relay rooms in the locality.

The largest part of this scheme (and which was the biggest and final part of the complete jigsaw) took place during October 1990. This involved the signals over a two mile area of the West Coast main line at Willesden being taken out of service for a whole week. In addition, the relay room at Willesden South was almost life expired, therefore it was decided to replace all of the equipment contained therein as part of the bigger plan. A relay room was where the S & T equipment, which operated both the points and signals in a particular area, was located. The required instructions to both the signals and points would be initiated in the 'parent' signal box, transmitted by cable to the relay room, acted on by the equipment contained within and then indicated back in the signal box, all in a matter of seconds.

When the main line signals were temporarily withdrawn from service, a replacement signalling system was brought into use, this being known as 'ticket working'. I will explain the full meaning of this system in a short while. However, before I do so, I will give some idea of the arrangements that had to be put into operation to maintain a service of trains into and out of London Euston during this period. It was first established by the operations department (in conjunction with the timing section) that only four trains per hour could be accommodated over each line (up and down slow, up and down fast). This was based on normal running time, plus allowances for stopping to obtain a ticket, running through the section at forty mph and finally stopping to hand the ticket over at the end of the section. Meetings were held with the other railway regions to agree diversions of certain services, in particular the important freight workings to the Eastern, Southern and Western Regions. In addition, agreement had to be reached with both Inter-City and Network South-East over their respective revised services. Once these had been concluded, the timetabling departments of the different regions concerned then had to produce temporary timetables, which in the case of the passenger services involved would then be published for the benefit of the travelling public. As far as the operations side of the system was concerned, possession details and timings had to be agreed whilst special traffic notices were drawn up and issued, these being given to train crews and other operating staff who were involved.

I had the important task of finding staff – not only additional signalmen to carry out extra duties in Willesden power box, but also other people to work out on the track within the affected section, these extra persons being used to implement the ticket working. Those for the box were recruited without too many problems. However, for the trackside tasks, I needed no less than twenty-four people! I ended up borrowing a whole miscellany of operating staff from all areas – Birmingham, Crewe, some supervisors from Euston and people from a number of places on the St Pancras line. In addition (and I can't quite remember how I did it), I managed to gain the services of a group of Senior Relief Signalmen from the Western Region. Once I had gathered them all together, they were accommodated in a hotel near to Euston. Arrangements were made with the staff canteen at Euston to supply them with food and drink whilst they were on duty.

Before these people took up their duties, I spent the greater part of two days with them in a classroom explaining exactly what was required. For those members of staff who had not been working in areas with overhead line equipment (OLE) or third rail electric lines, I went through all the essential rules required for working in these specialised sections. During the second day we visited the work site to gain a greater understanding of what was to be done. Later that same day, I examined them all on their knowledge of third rail railways and OLE, before allocating each member of the team to their respective posts.

Picture 50 *A temporary signal panel, seen in use at Willesden power box during a period of major resignalling work. The author is seen standing to the right of the picture, whilst seated is signalman Richard Dent (Author's collection).*

I mentioned earlier in this chapter a method of signal substitution known as ticket working. I would now like to explain what this means in what I hope are simple terms. To begin with, in the normal course of events, all trains passing through the area of railway covered by a particular power box would be worked under the track circuit block regulations. Under this method, a signalman would set up a route for the train in question on his panel – this being done by pressing the relevant entrance and exit buttons.

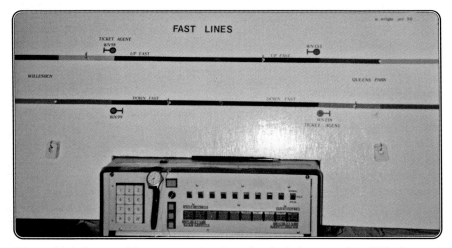

Picture 51 *A close-up of the temporary signal panel and telephone console at Willesden (Author's collection).*

Provided the section of chosen railway was clear and all the points contained within it were set correctly at each junction (and each signal was set at 'clear'), when the train concerned passed each signal, that signal would turn to 'danger'. Unless the piece of line in question was an automatic section (this being a section of fully circuited line where the signals would normally be set by the signalman to operate by the passage of the trains), the signalman would then set up the route again, in the same way, ready for the next train.

In the case of the work being undertaken at Willesden, new interlocking was required as part of the overall plan. This was the reason why the signals had to be disconnected. Each signal which was located immediately outside the area affected was maintained at danger. All drivers of each and every train that was brought to a stop at one or other of these signals were issued with a notice (or ticket) by a member of staff known as a signalman's agent, the ticket advising the driver that all intermediate signals between his current location and the first signal situated at the far end of the area of work were disconnected, and that any aspect that any of the signals within the affected area may show could be ignored. The ticket also advised the driver in question that the speed throughout the section covered by the work must not exceed forty mph, and that the ticket should be given up to a second signalman's agent, based at the far end of the work area. Each ticket would be numbered, and would show the date and time of issue on it.

In Willesden power box itself, temporary working diagrams for both the fast and slow lines showing the complete area covered by the ticket working system were produced by my Assistant Operating Inspector at Euston.

To:	Jack Turner, Chief Movements Inspector, EUSTON.	From:	InterCity Marketing, Room 900G, Stanier House, BIRMINGHAM.
	Copy to:-		
	Keith Winder Esq.	Tel :	050-4352
		Fax :	050-4625
		Date:	12th April, 1991

INTERCITY SERVICE EXCELLENCE AWARDS ANNUAL LUNCH

As a recent recipient of an InterCity Service Excellence Award I am delighted to invite you and your partner to the InterCity Service Excellence Awards Annual Lunch to be held in London on Monday 24th June. The event will take the form of a boat trip on the River Thames. This will commence at 12 noon and finish at approximately 16.00 during which lunch will be served.

I have asked your Area Manager to release you from duty for this day and to provide you with First Class travel facilities to London for you and your partner.

Please complete and return the slip below as soon as possible, indicating whether or not you intend to come. Further information will be sent to you nearer the time.

I look forward to seeing you in London on 24th June.

Peter Strachan,
INTERCITY MANAGER.

Appendix 5 The luncheon invitation letter from Mr Peter Strachen to the author, dated April 1991 (Author's collection).

These were then utilised by two of the extra signalmen that I had drafted into the box on twelve hour shift turns. Their specific task was to be fully responsible for authorising the various signalman's agents to allow trains through the affected section, this after confirmation from the agent concerned that the preceding train had cleared the section in its entirety, complete with tail lamp. To conclude this activity, the ticket number, the time that the train in question was given authority to proceed and the time that it left the section, were all recorded by one or another of the extra signalmen in a specific train register.

To cover the supervision of the ticket working, and to deal with any problems that might arise, one of the divisional signalling inspectors that had come from Crewe shared these duties with myself. I looked after the twelve hour day shift whilst he covered the corresponding night shift. The only change to this pattern of working was when one of my signalling inspector colleagues covered one of my day shifts. During the duration of the scheme, he was also responsible for organising short breaks for the hard-working signalman's agents, arranging for food and drink to be supplied to them during their respective turns of duty.

The entire South West Sidings remodelling programme was brought to a successful conclusion. This, in turn, led to two unexpected bonuses for me. The first of these arose as the result of an initiative from the Chief Operating Manager (COM), who was based at Crewe. As a 'thank you' to all the operating staff who took part in the whole of the upgrading scheme, the COM asked me to arrange a social event in a suitable public house. I chose one in Jefreys Street, Camden, where I knew the landlady, and also that her establishment had a private room for functions. The COM agreed to come along with his wife. As part of the evening's entertainment, a food buffet was laid on, the bill for the whole event being met by BR. Unfortunately this led to a very embarrassing situation for me. Prior to the evening beginning, it had been agreed between the pub's landlady and myself that she would work out the final cost at the end of the night and I would pay off the bill on the following morning. As things turned out, the evening's affairs did not finish until very late. Along with Pat, my wife, I left before the evening drew to a conclusion, this being so that we could catch our train back to Bedford. The COM and his wife remained behind, as did a number of other people. Unbeknown to me, during the evening, the pub's landlady had been tipped off that an audit of the pub stock was going to be carried out the following morning. When the COM was about to leave, the landlady requested that the bill be settled there and then, but did not go into the reason why. Fortunately, the COM's wife had her personal cheque book to hand and the bill was taken care of by the writing of a cheque. Naturally the COM was on the phone to me the following morning, demanding to know what was going on! When I had established the correct course of events for myself, I called him straight back and told him the full story. Arrangements were quickly made for the local railway cash office to reimburse his wife, and all was forgiven. Incidentally, I reminded him of this during a recent conversation that we had, and we had a good laugh about it together!

The second unexpected bonus which came my way occurred in January 1991, when I received a letter from the Inter-City Manager Mr Peter Strachen, inviting me to a luncheon at Watford, at which I was presented with a small silver 'Swallow' lapel badge (the 'Swallow' in question being the insignia of the Inter-City sector at the time) for my part in the South West Scheme. Apparently, I had been nominated for the Inter-City 'Service Excellence Award' by my area manager for all the work that I had put into the scheme. I also received a personal letter of thanks from no less a person than Sir Bob Reid, chairman of the British Railways Board. Later, in June that same year, I was invited, together with Pat, to join other railway staff, who for various reasons had also won the same award. This prestigious event consisted of a special luncheon aboard a floating five-star restaurant, the 'Silver Barracuda', the backdrop being the River Thames. During the event, we were all individually thanked by Dr John Prideaux, who was then the director of Inter-City.

The conclusion of the South West Sidings remodelling scheme was by no means the end of the major upgrading projects in the Willesden area. During the remainder of 1992, as part of a further programme of infrastructure changes, a series of new junctions were laid in the area, along with new interlocking being brought into use in a relay room based at Sudbury. In October 1992 this scheme was brought to a conclusion with some repositioning of a clutch of signals, this being in connection with the North Circular Road bridge alterations mentioned in the previous chapter, and also in readiness for the new freight yard. As part of the scheme, a further week of ticket working was initiated, but only on the fast lines between Willesden North Junction and South Kenton. Once again, I had to arrange to get staff to cover the work required, sort out temporary accommodation and give them a couple of day's training in the classroom.

One upgrade scheme followed another. Major work in the Willesden area did not come to an end when the bridge-related work came to a conclusion. As I mentioned in the previous chapter, Willesden Brent was going to be

British Railways Board

Sir Bob Reid
Chairman

23rd October 1990

J. Turner, Esq,
Chief Movements Inspector,
A.M.O.
EUSTON.

Dear Jack.

The work at Willesden South West sidings went very smoothly indeed, our customers must have wondered what all the fuss was about !

Clearly the detail planning and execution of the signalling alterations and operating arrangements was to a very high standard - please pass on my congratulations to all concerned.

Yours sincerely,

Bob

BOB REID

Euston House, 24 Eversholt Street, PO Box 100, London NW1 1DZ   Telephone 071-922 6301   Telex 299431 BRHQLN G quote HQCH

__Appendix 6__ The personal letter of thanks from Sir Bob Reid (chairman of the British Railways Board) to the author dated October 1990 (Author's collection).

<u>Appendix 7</u> Programme cover and welcome message from Dr John Prideaux for the awards ceremony aboard the 'Silver Barracuda', June 24th 1991 (Author's collection).

I would like to welcome all award winners, their partners and guests, to the first InterCity Excellence Award Lunch on board the Silver Barracuda on Monday 24th June 1991.

John Prideaux
Director, InterCity

Excellence
AWARD LUNCH

Monday 24 June 1991

INTERCITY

__Picture 52__ The author is seen with his wife receiving his award from Dr John Prideaux , director of Inter-City, at the 'Silver Barracuda' event, June 24th 1991 (Author's collection).

the new freight yard for the Channel Tunnel traffic – this would be where goods trains would be re-marshalled for despatching to onward destinations throughout the UK. Prior to the physical work beginning, a series of meetings were held between the different railway departments that had an interest in the proceedings. Willesden Brent freight yard itself had become part of a new management set-up, which had its headquarters at York! The representatives of this team therefore had to attend all the project meetings.

One of the problems that arose during the later stages of the actual scheme itself was getting materials to the site where the work was being carried out. The project manager concerned suggested a method of working whereby a facing connection (or set of points) was to be laid in off the up slow line, this then being clipped, padlocked and a chair (this latter item being what the rail sits in) turned in the normal running position. When access to the yard was required, these items would be removed and the points reversed. The whole operation would be overseen by an Operating Inspector, who would previously have taken possession of this part of the line, and the physical work would be carried out by the permanent way department.

When I heard of this idea I put my foot down straight away. This was completely against all the safety requirements of a ninety mph passenger line. In addition, the time taken to do this operation would have caused considerable delay to both passenger and freight services. In the end, the required materials were transported to site by rescheduling the actual phasing of the work. This then allowed the materials to reach the site via the goods lines.

CHAPTER TWENTY-THREE

WATFORD AND BEYOND

Throughout my career I, like numerous other railway members of staff, was affected in different ways by the many re-organisations that took place over the years. In mid-1992, there was yet another series of changes that were made to the hierarchy of the London Midland Region. These changes were to reduce the number of Area Manager zones to a mere four, these being London, Birmingham, Crewe and Manchester respectively. The new London area was made up of the enlarged Euston zone (which of course included Willesden) and its neighbour at Watford. At the same time that Euston had taken over Willesden, Watford had absorbed both Bletchley and Rugby. On paper I had once again been made redundant, but as the Senior Operating Inspector for the London area, I was automatically appointed the Chief Operating Inspector for the new, enlarged area. Whilst I was fairly familiar with both the Watford and Bletchley areas, having previously been involved in engineering possessions that had taken place within these two sections, I had scant knowledge of either the Rugby or Northampton areas. The little that I knew of these sections of the railway had been gained from my days working in the operating engineering department – however, even this was during the late 1960s since when, of course, much had changed. My overall responsibility now extended from Euston to a point two miles south of Nuneaton on the Trent Valley line, and two miles south of Coventry on the Birmingham route, including the Northampton loop. The total distance was just over a staggering ninety miles in length!

It was imperative that I widened my current knowledge of the northern-most parts of my new 'beat' at the earliest opportunity. On taking over, the first thing that I did was to contact the Area Signalling Inspector at Rugby in order to meet up with him. The purpose of our meeting would be so that he could introduce me to the staff who worked in the Rugby power box, who also covered train movements in the Northampton area. When I arrived at Rugby for our meeting, I made my way up a flight of stone stairs to his office, which was situated on the station itself. Whilst climbing them, I had a strange feeling of having been there before, especially when I entered his office. It came to me then that, yes, I had climbed those same steps before – forty-six years previously to be precise, this being on the occasion when I was interviewed for my first job after leaving school and joining the railway. This was for my junior goods clerk position at Aylesbury High Street. In those far-off days, the office in which I was now standing had been the District Goods Managers Office of the-then London Midland and Scottish Railway. Apart from my meeting at Rugby, I also boosted my knowledge of my new surroundings by spending a couple of Sundays going round the area with one of the Bletchley Area Inspectors; one benefit of my doing this was that I was shown different access points to the running railway line north of Bletchley.

During my time covering the Rugby area, I was fortunate inasmuch as there was only one major signalling failure. This took place just north of Northampton and was one that I was called out to cover early one morning. There were also two more minor occasions, one being when the automatic level crossing barriers at Banbury Lane failed (Banbury Lane being located between Blisworth and Roade, on what is known to railwaymen as the 'Old Line' – the original direct route between Rugby and London Euston). I found myself having to work them manually until a technician from the Signal & Telegraph (S & T) Department arrived to repair the fault that had arisen. Unhappily, and in stark contrast, this was not always the case in the Watford and Bletchley areas. I recall that the most serious incident that I had to deal with around this time took place at Castlethorpe station, just north of Wolverton. A night of continuous torrential rain resulted in all four lines (up and down fast, up and down slow) being flooded up to the level of the platforms. Just south of the station, where a set of water troughs had been located in steam days, the lines were also flooded up to a depth of no less than two feet, the situation being worsened by water coming down off the hillside adjacent to the up slow side of the line. I got a phone call from the Inter-City director himself at the unearthly hour of 05.00, asking me to go straight to Bletchley, get on board an available diesel locomotive and travel to the site of this incident, my aim being to assess the gravity of the situation and decide when it would be safe to run trains through the area again.

Utilising the diesel, I was able to get no nearer than two hundred yards from the site of the old troughs. It was impossible to proceed any further because of the depth of the water, which in addition was still strongly flowing with nowhere to go. I phoned the Inter-City director and gave him an update on the situation. He then advised me to remain on site and to keep him up-to-date with what was going on. After about two hours the local permanent way ganger and his team arrived, having unblocked the drains and dug a new channel out within the boundaries of the station itself. The result of their endeavours was that the water was able to clear sufficiently for trains to start running again. In addition, the flooding problem in the area south of Castlethorpe was resolved utilising the local knowledge of the gangers. They uncovered two old drains on the down fast side of the line and unblocked them which, as with the drains at the station, resulted in the water level dropping to a point where I was able to give the go-ahead for trains to start running through the affected area, but at a reduced speed. I then had a Permanent Way Inspector look at the track more closely, this being to check that no damage had been caused by the flooding. Happily, there were no ill-effects, and the scheduled train services were soon able to re-commence running at normal speeds. Incidentally, whilst wading through the water to get to the site, the inspector was bowled over by the force of it and became soaked through!

During this period of time there was a second occasion when I was contacted personally by the Inter-City director to resolve another difficult situation, this coming about as the result of a points failure at Harrow & Wealdstone, just before the morning rush hour. Before I made my way to site, one of my inspectors had already been called out and, after clipping the points concerned, was hand signalling trains on the up slow line, which fortunately was the only line affected. At the time, I was already on my way to work and my instructions were to ring the director once I had got to Harrow. When I arrived and spoke with him, he asked me to ascertain from the resident S & T technicians how long they thought it might take to resolve the problem. I re-directed the question to my S & T colleagues, who estimated that they would need a good fifteen minutes blockage to fully restore the fault and then test it. They then went onto say that the Headquarters Control at Crewe would not agree to this, saying that the technicians should work between trains whenever a gap in the service allowed. I double-checked this with Control, who reconfirmed their stance, re-stating that they were not prepared to 'block' the line for the required length of time. I then spoke once again to the Inter-City director and advised him of what Control had said. He replied, "Jack, if you are confident that the S & T technicians can complete their work in fifteen minutes, then they can be given the blockage." Having got the go-ahead, I am pleased to say that my track-based colleagues did not let me down and fully rectified the fault in that time, thus avoiding major problems on a very busy section of railway.

A far more gruesome incident, which I can still recall clearly after all these years, was a fatality that was blocking the slow lines that were situated opposite an industrial site at North Wembley. It would appear that the person involved had been disturbed breaking into one of the factories located on the industrial estate and was crossing the railway in order to make a getaway, when he was struck by a train. I was called out in the early hours of the morning in question and when I arrived on site, the police were already present. I started to try and resolve the situation by requesting that they move the dead body clear of all the running lines, so as to get the train service (in particular the overnight freight services) running again, and out of the way, before the start of the morning peak passenger service. However, they refused to do this until a police doctor, who was attending another fatality, arrived and confirmed that the person in question was deceased. I was caught between the wishes of the police and the request of our Headquarters Control, who were pushing for the body to be moved and the lines to be re-opened. I argued with the police stating that, like me, they could quite clearly see that the unfortunate individual was very much deceased. The police agreed with me, however they were still obliged to wait for the police doctor. I was lucky that the doctor arrived soon after and was able to give permission for the body to be moved, which in turn enabled me to advise Control that I was re-opening the line – just in time for the morning peak to begin.

The majority of my work involved duties of a more routine nature than those related above. During this period of time I was still heavily involved in various projects, as well as more normal duties. With no fewer than three extra power boxes to visit, and the greater numbers of staff involved, it meant finding additional time to carry out their annual rules exams, as well as passing out new signalmen, who were destined to work not only in the power boxes, but the manual boxes that still existed on the Bletchley to Bedford route. Earlier in this story I related how, in the late 1960s, I had spent time as a Relief Station Master on the branch, and it seemed funny to be responsible for the branch once again, almost thirty years later!

Another duty which I found myself involved in was signal sighting. In railway terms, the definition of signal sighting is to ensure that the driver of a train can see the relevant signal in sufficient time to act upon its aspect. One such occasion that especially comes to mind took place at Bushey, just south of Watford Junction, on the down slow line. Complaints had been received from train crews about the restricted view approaching the signal in question, this being due to the curvature of the line, and the overhead line gantry spanning all the tracks at this point. As a result of these complaints from the drivers involved, a Signal Sighting meeting was called, and after viewing the sighting of the signal in question, both from the ground and from the cab of a train, it was agreed that as there was no other position where the signal concerned could be re-sited, the only solution would be for the line speed (which at that point was ninety mph) to be reduced to seventy-five mph. The reason for doing this would be that when the train approached the signal at the new, lower speed, it would be able to stop in the remaining distance before the signal if this became necessary.

Thinking back, the first problem that I had concerning the Watford area took place even before I had taken up my new position! It will be recalled that in the previous chapter I described a method of signal substitution known as ticket working. In May 1992, there was a major re-signalling project in the Watford area, which involved the use of ticket working in order to keep the scheduled train service running. As before, I became involved in arranging the ticket working system and organising the additional staff that were required, but things unfortunately did not go to plan. Due to problems incurred by the S & T Department, the work overran its original time slot by no less than three days and caused a number of headaches, due to the fact that the temporary timetable for both passenger and freight traffic had to be kept in operation whilst the work required was completed.

Alterations and changes in the layout of the railway track itself are, of course, visible to everyone. However, one of the tasks that is not seen by the railway's customers, but which has to be carried out whenever a track alteration is made, is that corresponding alterations have to be made to the diagram that is located in the signal box which controls the section of line in question. At the same time, changes are also made to the instructions that are issued regarding isolation of the appropriate electrical sections. In addition, those diagrams that detail the overhead line equipment (OLE) are also changed to show the alterations made. When amendments such as these were undertaken, one of my duties was to go to Birmingham and, together with one of the draughtsmen based in the drawing office there, make the necessary alterations to what were known as the master diagrams. When we had completed this part of the task, the draughtsmen would make new overlays and I would then deliver them personally to the relevant signal box, at the same time destroying those no longer in use. An overlay was a plastic strip which was shaped to fit over the exact area as shown on the relevant signal panel.

When physical alterations of this kind are being made it is, of course, vitally important that the very high amount of electric passing through the OLE is switched off and isolated from the section of line that is being worked on. Let me explain what happens when, for any reason, the power to a section of the OLE has to be turned off. The Overhead Line Controller will contact the signal box in question, his dedicated contact being the supervisor in the case of a power box, whilst in the smaller and old-fashioned manual signal box, the signalman present will be the contact. Both the power box supervisor and the signalman will complete what is known as an 'isolation form', this showing all the required details. Such details will include things such as the date, the time, the location and details of the isolation involved. In addition, the name of the person giving over this information has to be included. In a similar way to the Royal Mail postcode system, each isolation section has a unique reference number. Each signalman will then put a special reminder collar over the levers controlling entry into the isolated section of track – once this is done, the signalman in question will sign the isolation form to confirm that this procedure has been carried out, noting the time that this was done. The details on the form are then phoned over to the Electric Controller, who will then give permission to the Overhead Linesmen to physically isolate and earth the section of railway track in question. In each power box, because of the complexity of the overhead line sections under their control, overlays are placed on their diagrams, over the area of the isolation, this being in addition to the reminder collars. This is a necessary additional safety precaution.

CHAPTER TWENTY-FOUR

RETIREMENT BECKONS

When I first became a District Signalman's Inspector, one of the major tasks that I became involved with were the operating audits that were carried out every six months by members of the Operating Manager's staff, who were normally based at Crewe. During these audits, all of the records that I had previously collated during my visits to the signal boxes that were under my command were checked by the Operating Manager's team, one of the reasons for doing this being to make sure that the requisite number of boxes had been attended in the time since the previous audit, these visits having to include at least one 'out of hours' attendance. These regular visits were not only carried out by myself, but also by my area manager (AM), the AM's operating assistant or, in later days, by other colleagues of mine. Another part of the audit was the cross-checking of the entries in each signal box train register, with a small sample of them being looked at in depth. Records of the annual rules and regulations examinations would also be covered as part of the audit, as would the certificates of competency in the working of a signal box. The latter were completed for staff that had moved into the box in question, either as a first posting, or those who had become a member of a signal box's staff as the result of a promotion. Other parts of the audit included a close examination of a number of the overhead line isolation forms. The records of incidents, delays and how they were dealt with (these being normally kept in the custody of the Operating Office) were also checked, as were train crew records.

In later years, when I became the Chief Operating Inspector, the whole system of taking and protecting of line blockages for both engineering work and in connection with incidents had been updated. Members of the management staff now had to pay a visit to one of the work sites each weekend, this being to check that the protection for the staff working within the affected area was as laid down in the rulebook and also to confirm that all relevant paperwork was correctly completed. In addition, the managers made sure that the right entries were made in the train registers of the signal boxes in the areas covered by the work being carried out and also that the reminder appliances were in place. These visits, I hasten to add, were shared by the various operating managers who were based at Euston. Whilst the audit requirement for these visits was once per month, our Senior Operating Manager at Euston insisted that the audits be undertaken each and every weekend, therefore I found myself carrying out these visits every third week.

The audit process became more and more refined as time went on. In early 1990 a new format of auditing was brought into use by the British Railways Board (BRB) with independent auditors being utilised. These people would award points for each part of the area that passed the audit. Each section was divided up into main and supplementary parts. The only drawback with this method of marking was that if the main part of the section in question was not up to the required standard, then no marks were given for the supplementary parts, even if they were all in order. On the first occasion that the new format was introduced, not one of the London Midland Region Inter-City areas received above average marks! I myself fell foul of the new 'points scoring' system during the course of a later audit. On the occasion in question, an auditor was present in Willesden power box whilst I was engaged in passing out a new signalman – this being so that he could work the main signal box panel. This exercise involved my watching him working the box during a busy period of time, being followed by examining him in the special instructions that applied only to this particular box, this being in addition to the more normal rules and regulations. Having watched what I was doing for a short period of time, the auditor asked me where I was recording the movements that the signalman was making. I replied rather sarcastically, "In my head," which of course was exactly what I was doing. I went onto say that having worked and passed signalmen out for Willesden power box for some twenty years, I could instinctively tell whether the signalman being tested could satisfactorily work the box. To reinforce my point, I mentioned to the auditor that since all the scheduled trains were running through the area controlled by the box with no delays whatsoever, this in itself showed that the signalman knew exactly what he was doing. My sound reasoning cut no ice whatsoever with the auditor – the result being not a single mark for that part of the audit!

In the meantime, work was still going on with the remodelling of what became the Channel Tunnel Freight Yard (CTFY) at Willesden. Although the new yard was overseen by the freight manager who was based at York, I was still very much involved with the setting up of this new installation. The CTFY had its own Yard Operations Manager, who was a young lady that had recently been appointed to her new position after completing her management training course, an awesome responsibility for one very inexperienced in matters of a railway operations nature. The inspectors that were working directly for me were in charge of the engineering possessions organised as part of the remodelling project which, amongst other things, included the construction of a brand new power box. When completed, this new installation would require releases from the existing box at Willesden so that goods traffic could enter and exit the new yard, on and off the West Coast main line (WCML). (In a railway operating context, the term 'release' refers to an electrical release button which, when operated, allows a person at a separate location to carry out a particular function, for example release a ground frame or operate a signal). Because of this arising situation, I had to attend the project meetings associated with the new scheme, as did the female Yard Operations Manager. She was very inexperienced as regards signalling plans and signal box panel layouts, therefore I had the job of checking what was proposed and making any necessary alterations.

My involvement in the CTFY project even extended to a visit to the Darlington premises of the company that was actually making the panel for the new signal box. I recall that there were one or two positions of release buttons and indicators which had been situated on the panel for reasons of convenience, rather than where they actually related to the corresponding signal 'on the ground'. Having explained to the company representatives that, for safety reasons, it was essential that the fittings on the panel matched exactly to the location of the relevant signal, the necessary alterations were agreed and carried out before the final installation of the completed panel.

This period of time during the early 1990s was a quiet one, lacking in drama and incidents, apart from a derailment that took place at Euston station itself. This came about as the result of a passenger train leaving the tracks as it was being routed into platform sixteen. The train in question was a push-pull set, being of a fixed formation, with an AC electric locomotive at one end and a driver vehicle trailer (DVT) at the other. The derailment occurred when the train was passing slowly over a set of points and the leading set of wheels left the track. The cause (which was immediately accepted by the permanent way department) was a broken rail. The train was carrying a full load of passengers, but what worked in our favour was that it was travelling so slowly at the time of the incident that nobody noticed! The leading vehicle was detached and the remainder of the train soon re-platformed.

In chapter twenty I wrote about a series of table-top emergency exercises which were held at various locations. During late 1992 a request was received from Northampton County Council for a full-scale emergency exercise to be carried out in Northampton itself. To begin with, a number of meetings were held to decide the actual form that it should take. These meetings were held either at Northampton General Hospital or the regional Police Headquarters. The people who were present represented various parts of the different emergency services, these being the police force, fire service, hospital and ambulance units, together with the Northampton Emergency Organisation. This last-named unit was of a type that each council was required to have, the idea being to have plans to deal with all kinds of emergencies that might have arisen and to have a person (or persons) responsible for the overseeing of the plan. Obviously, I attended on behalf of British Rail together with a member of the Chief Operating Manager's office at Crewe. During the course of our various meetings, it was decided to hold the exercise at Brackmills, which had been situated on the former Bedford to Northampton cross-country route, a line which had seen its last passenger train as long as ago as March 1962, although freight services had survived on different parts of the old railway into the 1980s.

The scenario for the 'accident' would be that a train which had been charted by a fishing club (the train formation being made up of two carriages) had collided with a car that was trying to access a level crossing. This car had been used as part of a robbery and was looking to make a quick getaway. We were able to obtain two condemned carriages from nearby Wolverton Works and these were worked to site under special arrangements in the week leading up to the day of the exercise. Once this had been done, and on the night before the exercise was due to take place, the Bletchley breakdown crew placed one of the two carriages on its side. For their part, the fire brigade provided a badly damaged car with two dummies inside it. The local ambulance service arranged for a casualty organisation to supply volunteers, who would act as the injured passengers. The Northampton Emergency Organisation (NEO) undertook to open up a nearby school, which would receive those individuals who were suffering from shock – in addition the NEO arranged for a bus service to transfer people between the accident site and the school. Would-be staff from Northampton General Hospital were called out to the emergency, as well as provide extra personnel for the hospital itself to receive the serious casualties. In addition, for any overflow of casualties, Kettering General Hospital would also have been put on standby.

It was agreed by all parties that the exercise would be held on a Sunday morning, commencing at 10.00, and those of us who had attended the planning meetings would act as observers. So, on the Sunday in question, just a few minutes before the designated starting time, I made my way to Bridge Street signal box (this being just along the line from Brackmills) in order to make a phone call to both the emergency services and to the railway Control at Euston, to report the 'accident' using a pre-arranged code word. Whilst I was doing this, the fire service representative started a small fire in the guards compartment of one of our two requisitioned carriages. Following this, it was not too many minutes before sirens could be heard and the emergency services arrived. A casualty station was set up in a nearby car park, the fire brigade soon put the fire out and then the firemen assisted the ambulance crews in releasing those people trapped in the carriages. These casualty 'actors' (for want of a better term) played their respective parts really well, even to the extent of individuals breaking away from the emergency crews who were trying to lead them to safety and shouting out, "My mate's still in there – I'm going to get him out."

During the time that this rescue work was being carried out, the fire brigade quickly set up their own command post within the vicinity, this being in the form of a large inflatable tent. The police's role in the scenario was to find the bodies in the stolen vehicle, call out their plain-clothes detectives and then place a cordon around the vehicle, so that any evidence would not be disturbed. I happened to be inside the police cordon when the CID arrived and was threatened with arrest until I showed them my observer's armlet, following which I received an apology. When, as far as could be ascertained, everybody had been removed from the carriage which was on its side, the Bletchley breakdown crew (which had now been called out to attend the incident) used a special inflatable type of balloon to raise it upright, which was very different from the usual packing and jacks that were normally utilised to sort out situations of this kind. During the course of the exercise, we had a visit from the MP for South Northamptonshire who was most impressed with what he saw. The whole event went off without any major problems and, at a special de-briefing, it was agreed by all parties that it had been very successful.

The period of time over the Christmas and New Year holiday of 1992/93 was a quiet one for me in my official capacity, with only the occasional points failure, some minor derailments and various cases of staff shortages to disturb the day-to-day running of the railway. However, prior to the holiday period in November 1992, along with all other members of the senior operating staff, I had received a letter from the Inter-City Director which stated that the British Railways Board needed to make cost savings, and to do this a reduction in staff was necessary. We were all invited to consider taking voluntary redundancy which would take effect from March 1993. In addition (and once again), the number of area manager organisations were to be reduced, with Euston and Birmingham joining together, the main headquarters being situated at the latter location, whilst Manchester and Crewe were to combine, Crewe being the new HQ of the larger set-up. It was obvious that such changes would lead to duplication of staff in many roles. Having considered my options I, along with my Operations Manager, the Safety Manager and two colleagues from other departments at Euston, all decided to take voluntary redundancy.

Early in 1993 those of us who had applied for redundancy were advised that our applications had been successful and that our actual finishing dates would be Friday March 19th 1993. In my particular case however, I finished a week earlier, having previously booked one week's leave. After Christmas 1992 was over, I spent the last few weeks of my service ensuring that all my paperwork and records were up to date. I also travelled round my 'parish', saying farewell to many old colleagues, some of which I had known from my days as a relief station master. There were even one or two individuals who I had come across in my younger days working on the footplate!

On my final day of service, March 12th 1993, it was arranged that I would travel home to Bedford from London St Pancras in the cab of a High Speed Train (HST). As Bedford was the first stop for this particular working, the train crew and the footplate inspector decided that they would see how quickly they could get there, whilst observing all the line speed restrictions. Any thoughts of record-breaking were quickly scuppered however! On approaching Harpenden, we were brought to a stand at the adjacent junction signal. I climbed down from the footplate to contact the power box at West Hampstead, in order to see what had caused the delay. Apparently one of the signalmen had forgotten to reset this signal after crossing a preceding train through the junction! I never did find out if the signalman in question received a 'please explain' for the resulting delay.

On arrival at Bedford, I was not only greeted by a tannoy announcement wishing me a long and happy retirement, but I was also met by Pat, my wife, and my six-year old grandson Scott. I can truthfully admit that I did not know that any of this was going to happen!

CHAPTER TWENTY-FIVE

NOW AND THEN
(or A Different Railway From When I First Started)

As I mentioned at the end of the previous chapter, I retired from the railway in 1993, after no less than forty-six years spent on an interesting and varied career. I had witnessed many changes during this time and since then there have, of course, been many more. At the end of the day, railways have to be run as a business, and have to try and utilise the most up-to-date technology that they can. The domestic transport market is a very competitive one, and the railways must keep up with the challenges presented not only by road and aerial methods of transport, but also challenges from the wider areas of society in general. In this final chapter of my memoirs, I will try briefly to remind readers of some of the more significant changes.

When I first entered the railway industry in 1947, working as a junior clerk in the goods department at Aylesbury High Street, virtually every station up and down the country had a goods and coal yard, and there were also many large marshalling yards, these dealing with thousands of wagons between them. In the country areas, a farmer could hire sacks for his grain, which would then be sent by rail to many destinations. In addition to those freight train services which traversed the main lines, local pick-up goods trains called daily at country stations, where all kinds of material would be either dropped off for onward conveyance to their final destinations or picked up, for sending onto locations such as shops and markets. It seems unbelievable looking back from a modern day viewpoint, but many gas works received up to thirty or forty wagons of coal daily. More long-distance coal trains, along with others carrying produce such as brick traffic, beer, fish, milk and cattle, were to be regularly seen sharing the tracks with the passenger services. It should be remembered that, although passenger services have always been seen as more glamorous and, as a result, attract much publicity, railways were originally designed and built for the conveyance of freight traffic, and much revenue has come from this source. Nowadays, despite heavy congestion on our roads, the only freight traffic carried is a mixture of what are known as 'block trains', company trains (these being vehicles that are dedicated to carrying loads for a single company), 'Freightliner' container workings and, in the case of coal, by 'Merry-Go-Round' trains, taking the coal from the original source of supply to the power stations.

During my time working on British Railways (BR), the change which was more visual than any other which occurred during those years was the final abandonment of steam locomotives during the late 1960s, and their replacement by (in the main) diesel locomotives, which in due course were superseded in a number of areas by the spread of electrification, the main examples of this policy being the West Coast and East Coast main lines, heading to the north of England and to Scotland from their respective London termini at Euston and Kings Cross. In addition to those steamers on the main line turns that were replaced, the old-fashioned commuter trains fell victim to an invasion of shiny new diesel multiple units (DMUs). The Midland Region main line from London St Pancras received a fleet of these trains in the late 1950s and these put in many years of sterling service until the early 1980s, when they in turn were replaced by electric multiple units (EMUs). Now many of the main line services are operated by a variety of multiple units, both diesel and electric, many of which are capable of running at speeds up to 125 mph. We in Britain also have the High Speed One (HS1) line running from London St Pancras to the Channel Tunnel and Western Europe, the 'Eurostar' trains deployed being capable of achieving no less than 186 mph in daily service!

Over the last sixty years or so, locomotive-hauled coaching stock has evolved out of all recognition. In the 1950s, the ubiquitous Mk 1 carriage was everywhere and was used on BR for many years. Coach design under BR then progressed through Mk 2 and Mk 3 to the Mk 4, which is used on the East Coast main line services in a push-pull formation with Class 91 electric locomotives and driver vehicle trailers (DVTs). Gone are the separate compartments, which have been replaced by open carriages with aircraft type seating. Dining car and sleeper car services, both features of the railway scene for so many years, have all but disappeared. These days, carriage doors throughout a train are centrally locked and, on local services, the old fashioned 'slam-door' stock (which was most common on the former Southern Region) has long since been withdrawn, air-operated sliding doors becoming the norm.

All of these technical changes have also meant many alterations to the working lives of the railway staff themselves. For example, with the demise of steam and, in a lot of cases, the introduction of single manning agreements for footplate crews, unfortunately many train crew staff and guards have been made redundant. We now have train managers and revenue protection staff with no operating responsibilities in place of the former guards.

Signalling is another part of the railway scene that has had many changes, most notably during my service within the industry. From the late 1950s onwards, many of the old-fashioned semaphore signals were replaced by modern installations in colour light form, and most manual signal boxes (and even a few power boxes) have been closed, and their work transferred to new power boxes which control a much wider area. Points which had been manually operated by levers located in a traditional signal box were gradually being motorised, and level crossing gates which had for many years been operated by a large wheel in the adjacent signal box were gradually converted to power operation. I can recall that many crossing keepers situated along secondary routes (a good example of this being one of my old stamping grounds from Bedford to Bletchley), who operated level crossing gates by hand, lost their jobs as automatic barriers were gradually introduced.

Power boxes began to appear during the 1950s as part of the railway modernisation plans, controlling large areas of the system and replacing many older manual boxes. This in turn brought multi-aspect colour light signalling with full track circuiting and automatic track warning systems into being. Telephone communication between train drivers in their cabs and signalmen in their boxes were introduced at the same time. In the power box itself, visual display units (VDUs) were brought in to monitor remote level crossings. In addition, opportunities were also taken in many areas to rationalise the track layouts as part of these schemes.

The railway station is, of course, the place where the customer (or 'passenger' in old railway-speak) makes contact with the railway. This is another area where many changes have taken place. For example, main line terminal stations have become more like airports, with much of their respective concourses taken up by retail outlets. Whereas before, one could walk leisurely down to the train that you were catching and find a seat, now you have to hang around on a crowded concourse, often until only a few minutes before your train's departure time, to see which platform that the train is leaving from. Then you have to join a mad rush to get aboard and if you have not already reserved a seat, to try and find one that is unoccupied! Many stations now have automatic ticket barriers, although staff still have to be employed to let people with heavy luggage, push chairs, or even certain types of tickets, pass through.

The buying of humble railway tickets has also changed out of all recognition. You now have facilities to purchase your ticket 'on line' and, at the stations themselves, there are always automatic ticket machines, encouraging passengers to use these, rather than the ticket office. Train fares and times, which are many and varied (depending on when you intend travelling), can also be obtained via the internet – that is, of course, if you have access to a computer. In addition, apart from on major stations, there are now no longer separate enquiry offices.

What of the railway infrastructure itself? I suppose the most significant change has been the replacement of the old 'clickity-clack' of the former sixty foot length rails with longer welded rails up to a mile in length. Many junctions have been repositioned so as to allow much higher speeds through them, which can entail trains travelling part of the way through them in the wrong direction. Even a casual observer has no doubt noticed that a considerable amount of track has been re-laid on concrete sleepers, as opposed to the old wooden type. As mentioned before in this chapter, overhead electric wires have appeared in many parts of the country, and the former Southern Region has now finally completed its extensive third rail electrification programme, a scheme which first commenced in the early twentieth century. Track relaying methods have also been modernised, with many new on line machines replacing ordinary manpower. Unfortunately, because of what in my opinion are 'over the top' safety regulations (whereas in my day every effort was made to keep services running during engineering work – not always one hundred per cent possible, I admit!), today whole routes are completely closed and blocked, and the travelling public has to suffer the inconvenience of putting up with substitute buses!

During my time working on BR, the most significant changes took place as a result of the 'Beeching Report', which was published in March 1963, and which still causes bitter controversy to this very day. Whole swathes of lines up and down the length of Britain were closed and many stations on other routes were either taken out of service or turned into unstaffed halts. It should be remembered that more than 70,000 jobs were lost as a result of the Report. All sorts of groups were set up to oppose line closures and were successful in a few cases. Probably the most famous counter-proposal of this type came in the fight to save the Leeds-Settle-Carlisle line. Although this battle took place many years after the Beeching Report, between 1983 and 1989, the campaign forced the Government of the day to refuse BR permission to close this well-known route. Today local passenger trains, a miscellany of freight, diverted main line passenger workings and specials of many types, ensure that the former Midland Railway's main line to Scotland has become a vital piece of the modern network. On another positive note, with the growth of passenger numbers on the railways, we are now seeing some lines being re-opened with the backing of their respective local authorities – something almost unheard of during the 1950s and 1960s. For us steam enthusiasts, we have a strong and flourishing heritage railway network (bringing many redundant lines back into operation), and it is getting more common to see steam-hauled special trains running on many parts of the national network.

What of the future? After many years of neglect and even open hostility by the powers-that-be, environmental concerns have forced a more pro-railway stance onto the political agenda. Many schemes are planned or in progress at the present moment in time. A start has been made on the Cross-London Line, and the upgrading of the Thameslink route is well under way. Work too is progressing on the remodelling of the track layout in the Reading area, as well as Reading station itself. At the time of writing, the Coalition Government has announced plans for the electrification of the Midland main line northwards from Bedford to Sheffield, the former Great Western main line to Cardiff and Swansea, the route from Manchester to Liverpool via Chat Moss, and a link from Southampton to North Yorkshire, which will include the Oxford to Bedford line. So far no date for the commencement of the work required has been given. In a bold new development, it is planned to concentrate the whole of the signalling system in no more than five or six giant power boxes – contrast that with the large miscellany of old manual signal boxes that used to dot the railway landscape! However, depending on one's personal point of view, the most controversial project is High Speed Two (HS2). Plans for both the first stage to Birmingham (which as expected has caused widespread opposition) and the second stage onwards to Manchester and Leeds have also been announced by the government: this too will no doubt invite much opposition. Not wishing to be morbid in any way, shape or form, but I doubt if, at my time of life, whether I shall see any of these schemes completed.

Map of Euston area layout, circa 1970s and 1980s (Author's collection).

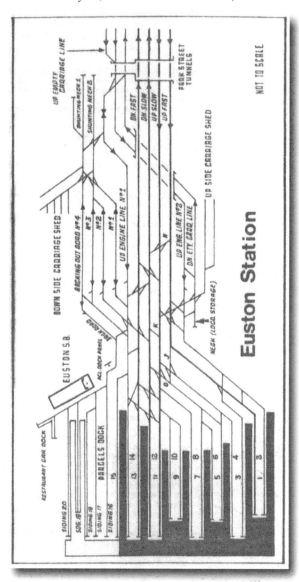

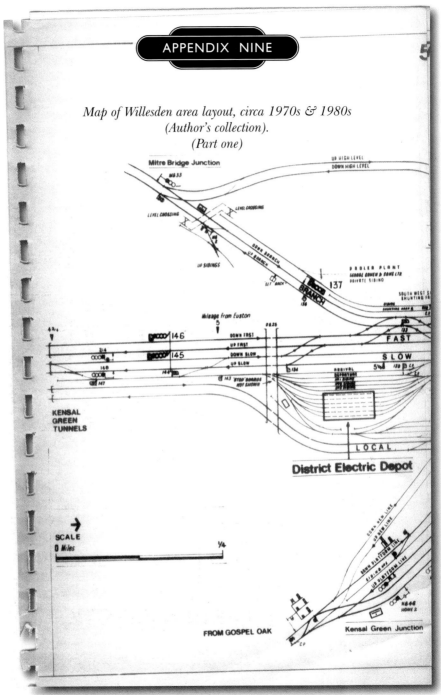

APPENDIX NINE

Map of Willesden area layout, circa 1970s & 1980s
(Author's collection).
(Part one)

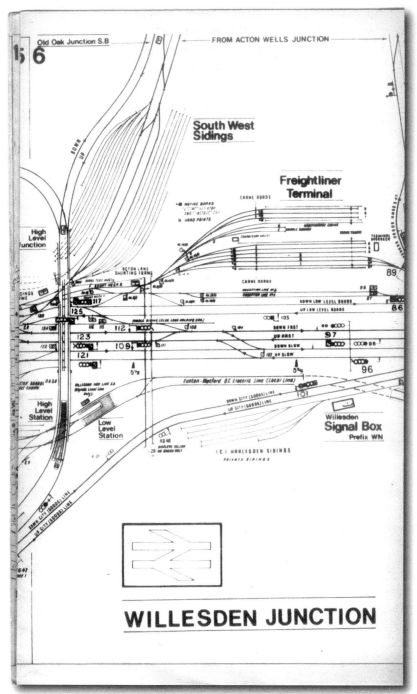

WILLESDEN JUNCTION

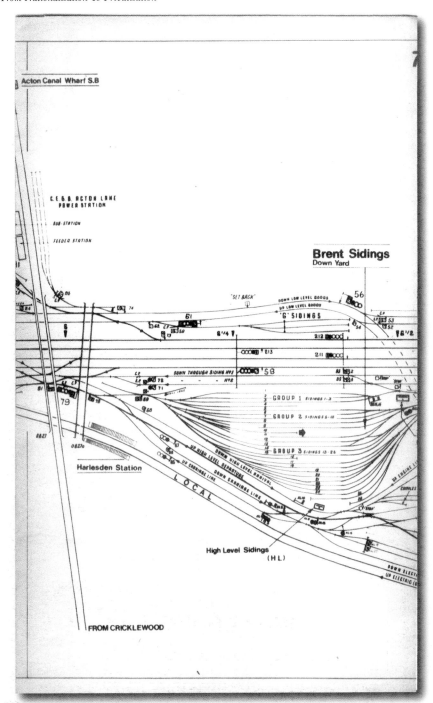

Acton Canal Wharf S.B

C.E.G.B. ACTON LANE
POWER STATION

SUB-STATION

FEEDER STATION

Brent Sidings
Down Yard

"SET BACK"

DOWN LOW LEVEL GOODS
UP LOW LEVEL GOODS

'G' SIDINGS

DOWN THROUGH SIDING Nº1

GROUP 1 SIDINGS 1-3

GROUP 2 SIDINGS 6-18

GROUP 3 SIDINGS 13-26

Harlesden Station

UP HIGH LEVEL DEPARTURE
DOWN HIGH LEVEL ARRIVAL
UP CARRIAGE LINE
DOWN CARRIAGE LINE

L O C A L

High Level Sidings
(H L)

UP ENGINE LINE

DOWN ELECTRIC
UP ELECTRIC

FROM CRICKLEWOOD

8

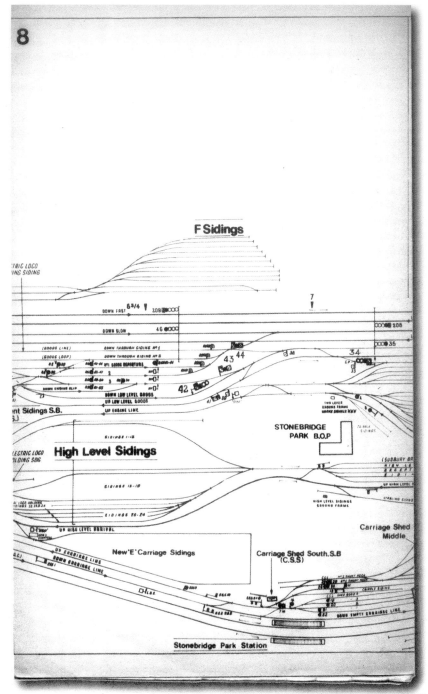

F Sidings

STONEBRIDGE
PARK B.O.P

High Level Sidings

Carriage Shed
Middle

New 'E' Carriage Sidings

Carriage Shed South.S.B
(C.S.S)

Stonebridge Park Station

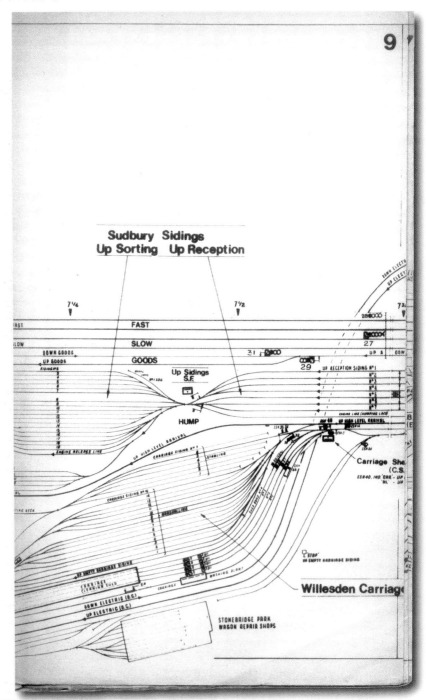

10

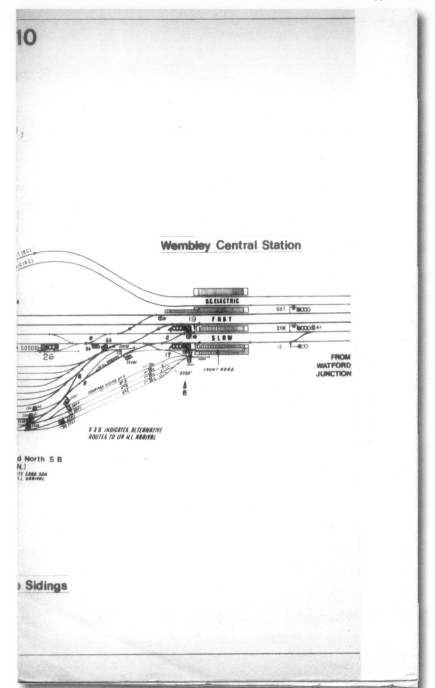

Wembley Central Station

D.C. ELECTRIC

19   F A S T   207

S L O W   206

GOODS   12

28

FROM
WATFORD
JUNCTION

'A' & 'B' INDICATES ALTERNATIVE
ROUTES TO UP W.L. ARRIVAL

d North S B
N.)

Sidings

LCGB

THE LOCOMOTIVE CLUB
OF GREAT BRITAIN

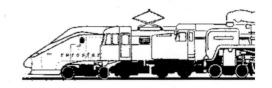

INTERESTED IN RAILWAYS?

**The Locomotive Club of Great Britain would like to invite
you to become a member of our organisation.
Benefits of membership include:**

The opportunity to participate in overseas rail study tours.

House magazine issued ten times per year.

Meetings held at eight countrywide branches.

Annual Christmas and overseas study tour reunions.

Club sales and publications.

Photographic competitions.

**For details on how to join the LCGB,
please visit the Club website on http://www.lcgb.org.uk
or write to the Club Membership Secretary at
4A Northbrook Road, Ilford, Essex. IG1 3BS.**